Shame
& Enaurance

Shame & Endurance

THE UNTOLD STORY OF THE CHIRICAHUA APACHE PRISONERS OF WAR

H. HENRIETTA STOCKEL

THE UNIVERSITY OF ARIZONA PRESS
TUCSON

The University of Arizona Press
© 2004 Arizona Board of Regents
All rights reserved

Library of Congress Cataloging-In-Publication Data

Stockel, H. Henrietta, 1938–
Shame and endurance : the untold story of the Chiricahua Apache
prisoners of war / H. Henrietta Stockel.
p. cm.
Includes bibliographical references and index.
ISBN-13: 978-0-8165-2414-3 (cloth : alk. paper)—
ISBN-10: 0-8165-2414-9
ISBN-13: 978-0-8165-2614-7 (pbk. : alk. paper)—
ISBN-10: 0-8165-2614-1
1. Chiricahua Indians—Wars. 2. Chiricahua Indians—Relocation. 3.
Chiricahua Indians—Government policy. 4. Chiricahua children—
Relocation. 5. Ft. Sill Boarding School (Fort Sill, Okla.)—History. 6.
Indians, Treatment of—Oklahoma—Fort Sill. 7. Indians, Treatment
of—Florida—Fort Pickens. 8. United States—Politics and government—
19th century. 9. United States—Race relations. I. Title.
E99.C68S765 2004
323.1197'256073'09034—dc22
2004001860

Publication of this book is made possible in part by the proceeds of a
permanent endowment created with the assistance of a Challenge Grant
from the National Endowment for the Humanities, a federal agency.

Manufactured in the United States of America on acid-free, archival-quality
paper containing a minimum of 50% post-consumer waste and processed
chlorine free.

11   10   09   08   07   06   7 6 5 4 3 2

Contents

Illustrations

Introduction:
A Broad Overview

This book presents an important portion of the written record of the Chiricahua Apaches' twenty-seven years of imprisonment in Florida, Alabama, and Oklahoma, told mainly through dispatches, reports, and news items. Along with disclosing the confusion, contradictions, and other raw emotions expressed by several high government and military officials regarding the Apaches, the documents also occasionally reveal the language of American colonialism, a special vocabulary that victorious compatriots easily comprehended and accepted without question; with it, those in positions of power understood each other completely.

The Chiricahua Apaches' long struggle to retain and preserve their unrestricted way of life in the southwestern United States and northern Mexico almost ended bloodlessly with a surrender to General George Crook[1] in March 1886, but then it continued unabated until September 4, 1886. On that date Geronimo and his small group of followers met with General Nelson Miles[2] at Skeleton Canyon,[3] lowered their weapons, and voluntarily put themselves in the hands of their enemy. For all practical purposes, the Apache wars were over.[4]

The United States was a proud, Protestant nation at the end of the Apache wars, emerging gradually from the plantation society of its past, but it had been terribly embarrassed, humiliated, and frustrated by its obvious inability to capture the obstreperous Geronimo Apaches. Pragmatists above all else, this holdout band of more than thirty men, women, and children finally admitted to themselves that surrender was the only way to avoid certain annihilation, as Crook had previously declared that the U.S. or Mexican armies would hunt them down until the last Chiricahua Apache was dead.[5]

With the Chiricahuas in government hands and their land relinquished, the Southwest was thought to be safe for settlement. In 1886 the popu-

Geronimo at Fort Sill, ca. 1906. FROM THE AUTHOR'S PRIVATE COLLECTION.

lar political concept of Manifest Destiny had taken on a life of its own in North America.[6] Under the metaphorical banner of this political slogan, the eastern populace had already begun to bulge westward, out of the germ-infected cities and into the healthier high deserts and mountainous regions. Adventurers from all walks of life turned their thoughts and their steps toward Apacheria in search of riches, a new start, relief from health problems, or the fulfillment of long-held dreams.[7]

The Chiricahuas were not alone in losing their ancestral homelands. Indian tribes all across the West had been overwhelmed by colonial American persuasion or force and were relegated to recently created reservations that encompassed only a portion of their former territories; the remaining land was then opened for railroad rights of way and pioneer settlement. However, despite similarities with other western tribes, the Chiricahuas were unique in that they were the only American Indians imprisoned for so long a time in environments that continually exposed them to deadly contagious diseases against which they had no immunity.

Tuberculosis and other ailments devastated families and sapped the people's essence, creating a situation that not even the multiple tragedies of long-standing warfare equaled. Fostering the medical catastrophes were the differences in the eastern climate and an unfamiliar diet, rich in carbohydrates and starches, both of which created physical weakness and vulnerability. In addition, forced idleness eroded the physical and emotional stamina of a warrior people whose existence had previously depended on strenuous activity, endurance, and resiliency.

After reading and analyzing, rationalizing, excusing or accusing, damning or understanding the historical materials presented here, one can assemble and interpret the pieces only from outside the event, but not really inhabit the captors and captives' bodies and minds or fully comprehend the times in which they lived. What results when everything is pieced together is a picture of a nation often divided in its actions for or against the Chiricahua Apaches. No matter what the government and military officials proposed or actually did, a public outcry in favor of better treatment for the prisoners continued; the Indian advocacy organizations of the day acted as watchdogs and, with the help of interested citizens, goaded the government into what was often a minimal response to the prisoners' needs.

Conferring names on indigenous peoples was one of the methods that "conquerors" used ostensibly to "civilize" members of Indian tribes and to assimilate them into the dominant culture. Seldom was any thought given to the meaning or the importance of the individuals' names within their culture, and that was a mistake. Nonetheless, for example, among the Chiricahua Apaches, Go-yah-kla became Geronimo and the child Tsi-ta-da became Rachel Morgan.

Even when various military and civilian officials who were charged with recording information about the individuals did not change ancestral names, they often spelled those names differently. Particularly difficult names, such as Ka-e-tennay, have been reproduced in so many ways that it becomes a task for readers to identify properly the people who bore those names.

One way of besting this problem would be for an author to standardize the spelling—to reproduce the name consistently rather than to allow the various spellings to remain. To do that in this book, however, would require me to participate in one of the most offensive colonizing acts committed against the Apache people, the obliteration of an important cultural custom—naming—by changing or modifying a name to suit another's wishes. I choose not to do so, and the spelling of names remains varied in both my text and historical documents. Readers familiar with American Indian cultures will acknowledge the significance of my choice; those who do not recognize my reasons will be introduced to it in the pages that follow.

Readers will note my bias in favor of the Chiricahua Apaches. After decades of close association with multiple generations of the Apache people I have come to understand and appreciate deeply the personal tragedy their ancestors experienced at the hands of the governments of Spain, Mexico, and the United States.

To appeal to as many readers as possible, I wrote this book in a manner that I hope satisfies both professionals and the public. Thus, it is neither an academic treatise nor an Old West novel, but rather something in the middle range. One caveat: I may not include certain records because of my purposes in selection or the documents' lack of availability. If this work can be enhanced, or if it may serve as a foundation or inspiration for a more detailed look at the Chiricahua Apaches' years of imprisonment, I will be glad. Until then this portrayal of the U.S. government's incarceration of the Chiricahua Apaches, written for the most part by its own political officeholders and military personnel, must suffice.

H. Henrietta Stockel
Hereford, Arizona

Shame
& Endurance

1.
Fort Marion

IN MARCH 1886 CHIHUAHUA,[1] a respected leader of a band of about seventy-seven Chiricahua Apaches, surrendered quietly with his followers at Cañon de los Embudos, a Mexican site just south of the Arizona border. The idea of capitulating had loomed over the group for months, so when General George Crook gave Chihuahua an opportunity to yield without bloodshed, Chihuahua took it without hesitation, preferring to be an American prisoner of war rather than a dead Apache.

Geronimo and his group, also at the surrender site with Chihuahua and Crook, turned their backs on the offer after a night of drinking and fled back to their familiar way of life, willing to fight it out. The standoff lasted six months, until September 4, 1886, with Geronimo's last surrender to General Nelson Miles, which high Washington officials believed to be an end to the Apache wars for all times.

Although the fighting, bloodletting, and killing in the Southwest had indeed stopped, another battle had begun—a war of words at the highest level of the U.S. government in Washington, D.C. The tribe's ongoing notoriety and celebrity while prisoners of war would embarrass and humiliate successive political and military administrations and create a bureaucratic paper blitz that would record for all times the officials' concerns about managing these Apache prisoners of war. No matter how sincere an effort the government mounted to help the Chiricahuas adjust to the terms of their confinement, it often failed. The administration's actions on behalf of the prisoners were not based on altruism, however, but rather on its apprehension regarding both the public's careful scrutiny of its actions and the endless rising tide of negative publicity.

The dispatches, reports, and news items presented here span nearly three decades and are a rich mother lode of material. In many cases the documents, including those that contain the language of colonialism, uncover the raw humanity of the political and military personnel involved in seeking a satisfactory outcome to the problems that continued to swirl about this tribe of American Indians. Hindsight reveals that incarceration was, in the long run, not a satisfactory solution; the terrible results still haunt U.S. history and the Chiricahua Apaches today, more than one hundred years later. Angry and exasperated political officials of the late 1880s, eager to demonstrate their superiority over a tribe of Indians who had successfully challenged the U.S. military for years, had very little, if any, regard for the consequences of confinement, whatever they might be.

Prior to leaving Cañon de los Embudos with the Chiricahua Apache prisoners (still including the Naiche/Geronimo group at this point) on March 29, 1886, Crook composed a handwritten telegram to be carried by a soldier on horseback to Fort Bowie,[2] Arizona Territory, and from there transmitted to Lieutenant General Philip H. Sheridan in Washington, D.C.[3]

> In conference with Geronimo and other Chiricahuas, I told them that they must decide at once upon unconditional surrender or fight it out. That in the latter event hostilities should be commenced at once and the last one killed if it took fifty years. I told them to reflect on what they were to do before giving me their answer. The only propositions they would entertain were these three. That they should be sent east for not exceeding two years, taking with them such of their families as so desired, leaving at Apache, Nana, who is seventy years old and superannuated; or that they should all return to the reservation on their old status; or else return to the warpath with all its attendant horrors. As I had to act at once, I have today accepted their surrender upon the first proposition.
>
> Ka-ya-ten-nae, the young chief who less than two years ago was the worst Chiricahua of the whole lot, is now perfectly subdued.[4] He is thoroughly reconstructed, has rendered me valuable assistance, and will be of great service in helping to control these Indians in the future. . . .
>
> Mangus, with thirteen Chiricahuas, six of whom are bucks, is not with the other Chiricahuas. He separated from them in August last and has since held no communication with them. He has committed no depredations. As it would be likely to take a year to find him in the immense range of mountains to the south, I think it inadvisable to attempt any search at this time, especially as he will

undoubtedly give himself up as soon as he hears what the others have done.

I start for Bowie tomorrow morning, to reach there next night. I respectfully request to be informed whether or not my action has been approved and also that full instructions meet me at that point. The Chiricahuas start for Bowie tomorrow with the Apache scouts.[5]

All appeared to be well in this March surrender. But Crook, ever wary of duplicity, asked two interpreters to listen in as a check on Geronimo's chosen translator, a Mexican named Concepción:

Two or three words are enough. I have little to say. I surrender myself to you (shaking Crook's hand). We are all companions, all one family, all one band. What the others say, I say also. Now I give myself up to you. Do with me what you please. I surrender. Once I moved about like the wind. Now I surrender to you and that is all. I surrender to you, and want to be the same as if I was in your pocket. Now I feel like your brother. . . . I was very far from here. Almost nobody could get to that place. But I sent you word. I wanted to come in here, and here I am. Whatever you tell us is true. We are all sure of that. I hope the day will come when my word will be as strong with you as yours is with me. What is the matter that you don't speak to me? It would be better if you would speak to me and look with a pleasant face. It would make better feeling. . . . I'd be better satisfied if you would talk to me once in a while. Why don't you look at me and smile at me? I am the same man; I have the same feet, legs, and hands, and the sun looks down on me a complete man. I want you to look and smile at me. . . .

I never do wrong without a cause. . . . There is one God looking down on us all. We are all children of one God. God is listening to me. The sun, the darkness, the winds, are all listening to what we now say. . . . Now I can eat well, drink well, sleep well, and be glad. I can go everywhere with good feeling. Now, what I want is peace in good faith.[6]

Crook broke off the negotiations at that point and scheduled resumption for the next day, March 27, 1886. Meeting again with the general after a night's rest, Chihuahua and Geronimo deferred to Naiche, who, as the leader of the group, spoke first:[7]

I surrender just the same as he [Chihuahua] did. . . . I give you my word, I give you my body. I surrender; I have nothing more to say than that. When I was free I gave orders but now I surrender to you. What you tell me to do I do. Now that I have surrendered I am glad. I'll not have to hide behind rocks and mountains; I'll go across the open plain. I'll now sleep well, eat contentedly, and be satisfied, and so will my people. . . . I will go wherever you may see fit to send us, where no bad talk will be spoken of us.[8]

Crook's confident assumption that the Apaches would be on their way to Fort Bowie was premature. Whereas Chihuahua and his followers kept faith with their agreement, Naiche and Geronimo—drunk on whiskey supplied by a Tombstone, Arizona, whiskey peddler—along with about thirty-five followers, silently left the canyon overnight, leaving nothing of value behind. In a March 30 telegram an unhappy Crook informed Sheridan of the group's disappearance from the surrender site: "during the night Geronimo and Naiche, with twenty men and thirteen women, left his camp, taking no stock. . . . [T]here was no apparent cause for their leaving. Two dispatches . . . reported everything going on well and the Chiricahuas in good spirits."[9]

To move the emphasis away from Geronimo's getaway, Crook's next telegram on March 31 described the circumstances of Chihuahua's surrender.

We found them in camp on a rocky hill . . . in such a position that a thousand men could not have surrounded them with any possibility of capturing them. They were able, upon the approach of any enemy being signalled, to scatter and escape through dozens of ravines and canons which would shelter them from pursuit until they reached the higher ranges in the vicinity. They were armed to the teeth, having the most improved guns and all the ammunition they could carry. The clothing and other supplies lost in the [previous] fight had been replaced by new blankets and shirts obtained in Mexico. Even had I been disposed to betray the confidence they placed in me, it would have been simply an impossibility to get to that point either by day or by night without their knowledge, and had I attempted to do this the whole band would have stampeded back to the mountains. So suspicious were they that never more than from five to eight of the men came into our camp at one time and to have attempted the arrest of those would have stampeded the others to the mountains. Even after the march to Bowie began, we were compelled to allow them to scatter. They would not march in a body and had any efforts been made to keep them together, they would have broken for the mountains. My only hope was to get their confidence on the march through Ka-e-tena and other confidential Indians and finally put them on the cars, and until this was done it was impossible even to disarm them.[10]

Two thousand miles away Washington officials were at a loss to understand or appreciate the army's inability to contain or capture the Chiricahua Apaches, especially Geronimo. Outsized political egos were insulted, and each evasive action or defeat by the Apaches became a personal affront to many members of the military high command, to the bureaucrats, and even to the president himself. In addition, the settlers and business people in southeastern Arizona and southwestern New Mexico—Apache country— were outraged by the continuing warfare; boisterous groups of indignant citizens demanded that the government take decisive action.

Squeezed by public criticism, government officials pointed to Crook's success in convincing Chihuahua to surrender as a measure of the government's firm intentions to force the Apaches out of their homelands and to punish them severely. But Chihuahua was not Geronimo, whose slippery band continued to thwart even the most intensive and concentrated military campaigns.

In his communications Crook continued to focus on Chihuahua. Another telegram, bylined Fort Bowie, A. T., and dated April 2, 1886, reported on Chihuahua's group:

The hostiles . . . arrived today. About eighty. I haven't ascertained the exact number. Some of the worst of the band are among them. In my judgment they should be sent away at once, as the effect on those still out would be much better than to confine them. After they get to their destination, if they can be shown that their future will be better by remaining than to return, I think there will be but little difficulty in obtaining their consent to remain indefinitely. When sent off a guard should accompany them.[11]

Charles Fletcher Lummis, a reporter for the *Los Angeles Times* in the spring of 1886, was sent to Fort Bowie to report on the army's pursuit of the Apaches.[12] After Chihuahua and his followers arrived at the fort, Lummis was invited to sit in on a conference between Chihuahua and Crook. The offer was most unusual, but then the government needed good publicity, and Lummis was in the right place at the right time. He sent a dispatch to the *Los Angeles Times* on April 2 in which he described certain aspects of the meeting.

This afternoon Chihuahua had a conference with the General, lasting an hour. Chihuahua said . . . he knew he had committed many depredations, but Geronimo was to blame for all. Geronimo had dragged them off the reservation by lies. He thought that Geronimo would never come in now. He said "I've thrown away my arms. I'm not afraid; got to die sometime. If you punish me very hard, it's all right, but I think much of my family. You and almost all your officers have families, and think much of them, so I hope you will pity me and will not punish too hard."[13]

In a lengthy follow-up news story dated April 5 Lummis explained Geronimo's change of heart about surrendering, attributing it to

more of Triboulett's[14] whisky despite all possible precautions to keep them from it. Some of [Lieutenant Marion] Maus's[15] Indian scouts had smashed this white scoundrel's whisky barrels and destroyed all the liquor in sight. . . . Triboulett and his emissaries played also upon the fears of the prisoners, telling them they were putting their necks inside the halter. . . . Lieut. Maus's eighty-four men were entirely inadequate to surround, bind, or disarm the . . . prisoners. . . . It would have taken 1000 men to make even a stagger at doing it, and even then, many a life would have been lost in the operation. At the faintest hint of either proposition, the Apaches would have been off like a flock of quail; and from the first cover their rifles would have sent back their defiance.

The conspirators succeeded; and that night, during a rainstorm, Geronimo and Nachita [Naiche], accompanied by twenty other bucks and fourteen squaws—one an immature girl—SLUNK OUT OF CAMP noiselessly, and vamosed. They took their weapons, but only one horse. The prisoners had camped only a short distance from Maus, and no one knew of their departure until morning. If any martial reader of the TIMES thinks he could have held these drink-crazed demons there is a good chance for him now to come out here, drop a little salt on the fugitives, and end the war.[16]

On April 6, 1886, Lummis reported from Fort Bowie about the sending of Chihuahua's group to Fort Marion, writing that

The Chiricahua Apaches who surrendered to General Crook . . . arrived here April 3 [and] will be sent to Fort Marion, St. Augustine, Florida, as prisoners of war. The squaws and children go too. . . . The prisoners know that they are going away, but don't know where. They take it very philosophically. . . . Chihuahua . . . hoped he would not suffer imprisonment too long, because he would lose a wagon he had. . . . All this morning the bronco camp was a scene of confusion. The bucks were greasing up their hair, and gathering their cartridges. The squaws were . . . catching and saddling the mules and horses, and packing cleverly upon them the blankets, muslin "tents," pots and cups, canteens, baskets, and hunks of jerked meat. . . . A queer procession it was that wound down Apache Pass and out upon the dusty plain.

Here was a gaily painted scout wearing the army blouse, and with his rifle or carbine across his saddle. . . . Next you might have seen a burro so hidden by big bundles that only his slender legs and comical head were visible, while on top and bestride the whole aggregation would be a squaw, with the peculiar Apache cradle under one arm and across her lap, while the other hand was occupied with whip and bridle. . . . One little pony carried a big buck, a solid squaw and a cradled baby. General Crook and Major Roberts's little sons accompanied the procession with a buckboard. . . . [T]he strange passengers were loaded into the emigrant sleepers, and now are trundling eastward. . . .

They could have escaped en route to the train. But they didn't make the slightest offer of it, though they had a good many forebodings as to what will be done with them. So far as this honesty was concerned, they could safely have been sent to Florida without a single guard. The soldiers were necessary to protect these poor savages from the "civilized" whites along the way. . . . There are plenty of alleged white men who would jump at the chance to signalize their bravery by shooting a captive squaw through a car window, if they had received sufficient notices to brace themselves with brag and whisky.[17]

It is curious that Lummis remarked on the Chiricahuas' "honesty" but then described the guards as having to protect the Apaches from "civilized" whites. Given the general tenor of those times, his dispatch must have caused a few raised eyebrows in California.

His editors at the *Los Angeles Times* no doubt wanted more detailed information about Chihuahua's capitulation and Geronimo's failed surrender; Lummis obliged on April 13.

In answer to questions about Geronimo's stampede after the surrender, Keowtennay[18] said that the first unpleasantness began the night before the surrender. They had got hold of Tribolet's whisky, and were filling up. Some one flirted with one of Nachita's squaws, Natchita grew jealous, quarreled, and shot the woman through the knee with his six-shooter. On the night of the stampede, Chihuahua, Keowtennay and Alchesay [a White Mountain Apache scout] camped close to Lieut. Maus; while Geronimo, Nachita and their immediate followers settled upon a hill a short distance off. None of them knew of the escape till next morning. The fugitives took so few women, because more would burden their flight. Nachita would undoubtedly get lonely, as he is fond of a good many fat young squaws. Chihuahua said he thought it very likely that NACHITA WILL RETURN, though it is a quien sabe [who knows?] case. He didn't believe, however, that Geronimo would ever be seen again. He said the one fat young squaw Natchita took along was very good looking.

Chihuahua Holds Forth

"When a man thinks well, he shows it by his talk. I have thought well since I saw you. Every since you were so kind to me in the mountains [at the surrender] my heart has quieted down. My heart is very quiet now. Geronimo has deceived me as much as he did you. I was very glad when I saw my sons and wife. I think well of my family, and want to stay with them. Those who ran off did not think well of their families, nor show love. I am a man that whenever I say a thing, I comply with it. I have surrendered to you and I am not afraid of anything. I have to die sometime. If you punish me very hard, it is all right. I am very much ashamed that the others ran off, and hope you don't think I had anything to do with it. I am much obliged to you for your kindness. I surrendered to you, and have thrown away my arms. I didn't care any more for my gun nor any weapon. . . . I surrender to you and ask you to have pity on me. You and nearly all your officers have families, and think very much of them as I do mine, and I want you to remember your families. I hope you will not punish me very hard, but pity me. I am very grateful to you. . . . I was sleeping very quiet and happy with my family at Camp Apache but Geronimo came and deceived me, played me a trick and made me leave.

Wherever you put me, keep me away from Geronimo and his band. I want nothing to do with them. People will talk bad about me and get me into trouble. I don't want anything to do with him.

I was very quiet and happy at Camp Apache, looking after the little crop which I had in the ground, and my horses and wagons, but Geronimo came along and told me so many lies that I had to go. It is true we have stolen many cattle and horses, and done many depredations, but Geronimo is to blame for all we did. Now I have surrendered to you, I am quiet and happy. It is very good to see my children, and I want to live happy and quiet all the time. That is all."[19]

Lummis's report was partially incorrect in that he wrote about "so few women" going off into the night with Naiche and Geronimo. It is probable that all of the women in the Geronimo band were included in the escape, according to custom; ordinarily no one would ever have been left behind unless it was necessary owing to injuries or pending death. Realizing the importance of his communications, Lummis may have begun to embellish his reports somewhat in response to editors' pressures that were, in turn, either a consequence of a business decision—sell more newspapers now that interest was high—or a reflection of readers' demands for information. If so, the Angelenos of the time were typical of Americans all across the country who were gripped by the dramatic events occurring in southern Arizona, and newspapers were the best means of keeping them informed.

In Washington President Grover Cleveland made the decision to confine the Apache prisoners to Fort Marion during a private meeting with Sheridan and the secretaries of war and interior.[20] Fort Marion was on the president's mind because it had been the subject of a two-year debate in the Senate, where an appropriation of ten thousand dollars for repairs was mired down in the Committee on Military Affairs.[21] It is not unreasonable to conclude that the president's selection of Fort Marion was political, made with an eye toward forcing the legislation out of committee and onto the Senate floor for a vote. However, the urgent need to relocate Chihuahua's group to Florida superseded congressional inaction, so arrangements proceeded apace.

An unnamed staff reporter from the *Florida Times-Union* chronicled the prisoners' arrival in St. Augustine on April 14, 1886. He described a pathetic scene, writing that when the doors of the train were opened, the Apaches emerged

dirty, ragged, half-clad, and with long unkempt locks of coarse black hair flying loose about their heads. In their eyes they were typical savages. First came the men, each with shoulders and head wrapped

Courtyard at Fort Marion, Florida, 1991. PHOTO COURTESY OF THE AUTHOR.

in a blanket and all marching with expressionless faces and stately gait; then came the young bucks with less dignity and fewer blankets, as well as fewer clothes of any kind; then straggling along one by one, came the young women, girls, and children. . . . [L]astly came the old women, each hugging a baby or bundles, and a wounded squaw in a truck, her head shrouded in a blanket, brought up the rear.[22]

The Chiricahuas had traveled across country in an airless train with no sanitary facilities, and it is to their credit that they were able to exit the train as they did. The reporter had no way of knowing that the train's windows had been nailed shut to prevent escape.

Waiting for them at the fort was Lieutenant Colonel Loomis L. Langdon, the commander of the post.[23] A naturally compassionate man, Langdon was in charge of both Fort Marion and Fort Pickens, three hundred miles west, where Geronimo and his warriors would eventually be confined. On August 20, 1886, Langdon noted that Chihuahua's people

have the run of the place [and are] allowed full liberty within the walls. They sleep in comfortable tents on the terrepleins of the bastions. I am having substantial tent floors constructed for such of the tents as have not been already provided for in this respect. In the day-time the Indians are allowed to pass in and out unrestrained, not going further, however, than the crest of the covered way. There and in the dry ditch of the fort they have their games of ball. Occasionally small parties of them, under charge of Lieut. S. A. Mills, Twelfth Infantry, are permitted to visit the stores in town for the purpose of making little purchases of articles not supplied by the government. On these as well as on other occasions a watchful care is exercised to prevent any friction between evil-disposed people and the Indians.

The general health of these prisoners is good. There have been, however, two deaths among them, one a female child about four years old, the daughter of Indian woman No. 22, one of the wives of the fugitive Chief Geronimo. The child died July 31. A male infant about fifteen months old, No. 25, died on the 17th of August.

Both of these children were very feeble when they were brought here and have required constant and particular care to keep them alive. It is hardly necessary to say that everything was done for them that could be done. They had the best of medical attendance in the person of Dr. DeWitt Webb, a humane, skillful, and conscientious surgeon.

They were supplied with all the medicines needed, and from the first, milk and other food suitable for children, but not included in the regular rations, has been procured for them. . . .

The Indians appear contented and cheerful, and they thoroughly understand that they are being well treated. They are orderly and docile, and improving in their habits as regards cleanliness.[24]

It is interesting to note that once again mention is made of "evil-disposed people," most likely the white residents of St. Augustine. Like Lummis, Langdon seems protective of the Apaches, disregarding their bad reputation.

Two examples of the language of colonialism appear in Langdon's report, the first one in the use of the word *comfortable*. Comfortable according to whom? Certainly not the Chiricahuas, who were at first confined to empty, dark, and damp rooms off the fort's courtyard until Sibley tents could be erected on the terreplein atop the fort. The army initially provided no privacy or individual shelter from the elements on the walkway bordering the parapet. When the tents were erected, sheets of rain furi-

13

ously pounded the wet canvas, and the brick-and-mortar floor upon which the Apaches ate and slept was always damp. Although Langdon wrote in August, later in the winter of 1886–87 the cold winds blew unobstructed off the sea and through the canvas shelters.

Despite good intentions and well-meaning actions regarding milk and medicines, the government did not consider the adverse effects these items could have on the prisoners' bodies. The Apache had never taken Western medicines previously, so no doubt physiological reactions, some fatal, ensued. Also, cow's milk for the children was too severe a change for young bodies that had always been nourished with breast milk. The consequences of such an assault were, at best, gastrointestinal distress, but, at worst, death from irreversible disorders.

It is true that state-of-the-art medicine of 1886 was not very sophisticated, but a little thought about the potential unknown effects of Western medicines and cow's milk on this population would have saved lives.

Langdon arrived at his conclusion that the Chiricahuas were "contented" through the dominant society's intellectual framework: that as long as the prisoners were not raising hell or trying to escape, they could be viewed as being "contented." Had Langdon asked the Apaches if they were comfortable or contented, the fearless truth tellers among them would have responded with a resounding "No." Those more wary of their captors would have held their tongues. Regardless of their possible response, Langdon's choice of words is understandable. Despite his knowledge of the Apaches' situation and his sincere sympathy for his newly arrived charges, he was a product of his education, military training, and upbringing as a white male in white America in the late years of the nineteenth century.

After closely watching the prisoners for a short time, Langdon passed on his recommendations in a special report to the Headquarters Division of the Atlantic, Governor's Island, New York City.

> So far as the imprisonment of these Indians may have been designed to impress upon them, for the rest of their lives, the power of the Government, that object has certainly been attained.
>
> If it were originally intended to confine them here until arrangements could be perfected to place them amid more suitable surroundings, the adults could be taught how to earn a living, and the children brought up to do the same thing at a proper age, then they have all been kept here quite long enough for their own good; and this because they have far less to do here than they had when

roaming in freedom over the plains. Consequently they are rapidly acquiring habits of laziness and dependence on the white man. . . .

This is as good a time as any to make a permanent disposition of them; or if not a permanent one, then at least one having a more definite purpose in view than their mere confinement here as prisoners. Nor can they very well always remain at Fort Marion without necessitating the constant retention at this post of a battalion of troops, not so much to guard them from escaping as to prevent bad white men's introducing liquor amongst them or bringing them into collision with the disorderly and provoking elements of the contiguous population.

Therefore I respectfully recommend that the whole party of prisoners be sent as soon as possible to Carlisle, Pa. There are in the party . . . twenty-seven children and youths. The proper place for most of them is the Indian school at Carlisle, and even the youngest will, in a few years, be old enough to attend the school.

I have been told often that when the Indians surrendered they were promised by the Government officers that they should not be separated from their children. At all events, these people assert that such a promise was made. A breach of faith in this respect—a separation—is what they constantly dread. Even a present of clothing to their more than half-naked children excites their mistrust and makes them very restless, because it looks to them like preparing them for a journey, a separation from their parents.

I have not consulted Captain Pratt[25] in regard to the practicability of removing the whole party to Carlisle, but if the objection is made that there is no means of guarding them there, I will say that the fourteen adult Indians of the party will be enough guard under the command of Chihuahua, the chief, as the only object of having a guard is to keep the white people away from the Indians, and if there is a reserve of any size at Carlisle, that will be more easily accomplished there than it can be here.

But in conclusion I desire to say that if the whole party cannot go, or at least all of those whose children are with them here, I would not recommend the transfer.[26]

Langdon expressed two important opinions, formed after personal observations: first, unscrupulous white people should not have access to the Apaches, and, second, families should be kept together and transferred to a larger facility. The origin of his first conclusion is self-evident:

he was aware that unprincipled citizens of St. Augustine would attempt to provide the Apaches with liquor. And although he had not had much exposure to a major tribal characteristic that had sustained the Chiricahua people for generations—their reliance on the family as the tribe's bedrock—he identified it. However, if Langdon believed that his recommendations would be given credence in Washington, he was mistaken; government officials ignored his correspondence.

The next communication made regarding this situation, a telegram sent to Langdon by Acting Secretary of War R. C. Drum, asked, "What number of Indians—men, women, and children—can, in addition to the number now at St. Augustine, be accommodated there? Should it be determined to increase the number by some four or five hundred, what preparation would be necessary and what probable expenditure required?"[27]

Langdon's response contained no hint of his feelings about having his advice disregarded, but his response to Drum left nothing in doubt. "Can accommodate seventy-five men, women, and children in addition to those now here. Fort Marion is a small place. Would recommend no more Indians sent here."[28]

Dismissing Langdon's advice once again soon after receiving his terse communiqué, the government relocated to Fort Marion nearly four hundred Chiricahua Apaches from the Fort Apache and San Carlos Reservations, where they had been living peacefully and working industriously as farmers. One of the prisoners' descendants, the late Warm Springs Chiricahua Apache Ruey Darrow, recalled in 1991, "Papa [Sam Haozous] was a boy when they left for Florida, and he told me that he remembered roll call that day. The soldiers called everyone to a central point and then split them up."[29]

Two former army scouts, Kuni and Toclanny, also remembered the day. Said Kuni,

> One day near noon they [the soldiers] told me they wanted to count the Chiricahuas. They surrounded us with scouts and soldiers. Five scouts were mounted. . . . They told us that where we were going it was the same as it was there. We were scouts in one place and would be in the other. When they had surrounded us, the White Mountain Indians [Fort Apache] drove off our horses and cattle; they went to our farms and took what they wanted while we were surrounded. . . . They told us that we were going to be taken off, but not very far away, about a day's travel by railway.

Added Toclanny, a Warm Springs Apache married to a Chiricahua woman:

> The White Mountain Indians said that the Chiricahuas were bad. Their chiefs had been talking against us. . . . The officers told us we would be sent to a good country and we would have more houses and farms than we had at Camp Apache. . . . We did just as they told us. The day they rounded us up at the post all the men, women, widows, and poor of the tribe that had stock had it driven off by the White Mountain Indians, who stole it.[30]

Another example of the government's high-handed treatment of the Apaches is especially revealing. Chatto, formerly one of the most brutal Chiricahuas, renounced his former lifeways on July 1, 1884, when he became employed as an army scout.[31] He served loyally, and during the course of his duty he earned the respect of American officers and enlisted men. In the summer of 1886, after his former colleague Chihuahua had surrendered, Chatto was singled out and, with a delegation of a dozen of his peers, was summoned from Fort Apache, his home, to the nation's capital. The thirteen Chiricahuas met with the secretary of war, William C. Endicott, who extolled the virtues of leaving Arizona and moving to a reservation in Indian Territory. Political officials trusted that the faithful Chatto would agree and would influence his relatives and friends to follow suit, but they grossly underestimated him. At a meeting with the secretary of interior, L. Q. C. Lamar, Chatto politely and firmly insisted that he did not want to leave the place where he and his tribe were happy and productive. Disappointed, Lamar nonetheless presented Chatto with a "certificate of good character" and a silver medal.

While the delegation was returning by train to Arizona, a flurry of telegrams among military and civilian officials across the country discussed their fate. At Fort Leavenworth, Kansas,[32] Chatto and the other Apaches were ordered off the train and held as prisoners for nearly two confusing and worrisome months. They finally were informed that they would not be able to go back to their Arizona homes, but instead would be incarcerated at Fort Marion.

On August 26, 1886, Lamar sent a confidential telegram to Drum ordering the imprisonment of Chatto and his group. The message read, "I think it is the wish of the President that the Indians who came to Washington should, none of them, return to Arizona within reach of communication with those at Fort Apache until transfer to Fort Marion has been consummated."[33]

The vagueness and uncertainty of the phrase "I think" cleverly and deliberately protected Lamar, the sender, and put the onus on Drum for the "correct" interpretation. Drum apparently got the message: Chatto and the small delegation left Fort Leavenworth under guard on September 12, 1886, on a special train headed for Florida, where they were to be confined right next to the people whom some of them had betrayed earlier, an action that caused at least one Indian advocacy group, the Indian Rights Association,[34] to object in writing.[35] Chatto's own words and thoughts about the government's actions against him, spoken several years later to Crook, were still full of hurt:

When I left Washington, I expected to go back to Camp [Fort] Apache. A letter came from General Miles stating that it was a bad place for Indians at Camp Apache. All the white people were down on us and the other Indians also. He told us one part of the country belonged to Washington, the other part on the other side was Arizona, so he would put us on the Washington side where there were good people. . . . From Fort Leavenworth we were taken to a place where Chihuahua was. . . . The letter also said that we could raise lots of horses, cattle . . . that there would be plenty of room on it for all [our] stock.

Chatto then took from his chest the medal that had been presented to him and asked Crook, "Why did they give me that? To wear in the guardhouse? I thought something good would have come to me when they gave me that, but I have been in confinement ever since I have had it."[36]

Next to arrive at Fort Marion were the approximately 383 men, women, and children who had left Fort Apache under guard on September 7, 1886, and detrained almost a week later at Fort Marion.[37] Herbert Welsh,[38] the founder and secretary of the Indian Rights Association, continually monitored the conditions under which the Chiricahuas were imprisoned. After personally examining the circumstances at Fort Marion, he sent his unsolicited findings on to the War Department:

A Brief Statement Regarding the Chiricahua Apache Indians Held as Prisoners of War in Fort Marion, St. Augustine, Florida.
    Number of Indians confined in Fort Marion, 447 (at this date [no date included]).

Men—82

Women—206

Children under 12 years of age—159

77 of the total number were on the war path in Arizona and surrendered to General Crook. . . . This particular party were under Chihuahua. Only 14 of them were men, the rest being women and children. Although they were wild Indians, and had just been on the war path, the commanding officer at St. Augustine found them so tractable that, having no proper work for them at Fort Marion, he recommended (August 23, 1886), that the whole party should be taken to the Carlisle, Pa. Training School and be placed under Capt. Pratt's care. This was not done.

The number of Chiricahua Apache prisoners was increased last autumn to about 500. The additional number included all the women and children who had remained quietly on the San Carlos Reservation during the outbreak of Geronimo; Chatto and 13 men, who were sent under a safe conduct to Washington last July, to visit the authorities there with a view to their possible transference to another reservation; also those Indians who had remained on the reservation during the outbreak or had served as scouts in our Army against the hostiles. But a minority of the 82 men now in captivity at Fort Marion (less than 30), have been engaged in any recent hostilities against the Government. . . . It is General Crook's testimony that Chatto, who was a wild Indian and committed in former days many bloody deeds, surrendered to Gen. Crook. Since then he has faithfully served the Government as a scout. . . .

The promise of safe return [to Arizona] which had been given them [Chatto and his group] was not observed, for . . . they were sent directly to Fort Marion where they have remained ever since in confinement, and without useful work of any kind. . . . Fort Marion is not large enough to hold, with safety to health, the prisoners now within its walls. They should all be removed before summer to some suitable reservation where, under the care of an experienced military officer, they can be instructed in the ways of civilized living.

Executive Document No. 117, 49th Congress 2nd session Senate, contains the dispatches of the authorities in Washington to Gen. Miles, and from Gen. Miles to them, wherein the history of this affair is to be found in full. . . . The President told Prof. Painter [agent of the Indian Rights Association in Washington] that no discrimination had been made between the guilty and the innocent among these Indians because of the necessary haste in their removal. Five months have elapsed since their imprisonment.

The President also said he did not believe that they were so crowded as to endanger health.

I make the above statements after a recent visit to these Indians and a full examination of the official documents bearing on the matter in question.[39]

The potential for health problems was becoming a concern owing to the overcrowding at the fort and to the prisoners' exposure to contagion through contact with soldiers and civilians. By October 1, 1886, Langdon was openly worried about his charges' health, as the growing number of illnesses among them demanded attention. In a monthly report he wrote,

There are at present confined in Fort Marion four hundred and sixty-nine Indians, including adults and children, also including fourteen paid Indian scouts.

Much improvement has been made by the Indians in habits of cleanliness, and the two bath-tubs provided for them are in constant use.[40] The rations issued to the Indians are of good quality. While the attending surgeon reports the quantity sufficient, I desire to express the opinion the ration should be larger. Seventy-six cases of sickness were treated during the month, sixty of which were of intermittent fever, contracted by the patients before leaving Arizona. One birth occurred on the 13th of September. The child is a female, and the daughter of Geronimo. One death occurred on the 25th ultimo, that of an aged female said to be over ninety years old. . . .

I have permitted these Indians to take exercise daily outside the fort, and to stroll in parties of fifteen or twenty through the town; one party being out at a time, and always attended by one of the guards. This last is a precaution against any accidental collision between evilly disposed whites and the Indians.

The Indians seem indisposed even to come in contact with the whites unless an officer or soldier is present to take care of them, being apparently more afraid of the whites than the whites are afraid of them.[41]

DeWitt Webb was the acting assistant surgeon at Fort Marion when the Chiricahua prisoners arrived. One year later, in September 1887, he gave a speech before the Dutchess County Medical Society, New York, about his experiences.

After the arrival of the main body in September, there were 130 tents—each family occupying its own. Their rations were furnished by the Government and were full rations for each person above 12 years of age, and half that amount for the younger ones. The bread was furnished every day. . . . [A]ll else was cooked by themselves. The meat was mostly cooked in a kind of stew with a gravy of flour and fat. . . . They were fond of coffee, browning and grinding it in their own peculiar manner in mortars. . . . They were fond of a cake made only of flour and water and made thin, not by rolling, but by a peculiar tossing from one hand to the other. Of sugar they were very fond, but seemed to have no taste for milk. . . . Potatoes and onion were furnished them occasionally . . . and they appeared to be very fond of them. After all, however, their principal diet was meat. This furnished every day was either cooked first or else cut into thin slices and hung up in the sun to dry.

Their beds consisted of blankets or skins. . . . [They] made good use of the large bath tub provided. The great change in elevation from 9,000 or 10,000 feet to the level of the sea produced in some great disturbance of the circulation, especially in cases of illness, even if the illness were ever so slight. . . .

The outbreak of malarial fever came on at once on the arrival of the main body in September.[42] They had been camped, before leaving Arizona, on the banks of some river, and had suffered there to some extent, but the fatigue of the long journey and the change to the sea shore seemed to have brought it all to the surface at once, and the second day of their arrival, there were 28 cases of malarial fever, almost all intermittent and controlled by the use of quinine in solution.

During October and November [1886], there occurred a number of acute bronchitis among the nursing children. Of these, 6 died. I think the outbreak was largely due to the condition of the mothers who had not yet become accustomed to the change of locality . . . and for that reason their milk was of poor quality. All of the children out of arms did well enough, but these little ones ran down and died very soon. . . .

Under the head of contused wounds, I may mention the little son of Chihuahua, who was pushed by some playmate from the top of the wall and fell to the bottom of the moat, striking his head on the step at the bottom of the stairs that goes down into the moat. He lay in convulsions for fully thirty minutes, and then recovered and had no symptoms of trouble afterward except the bump on his head.

Among the incised wounds, there was nothing remarkable except the tendency to rapid recovery. From old age there were two deaths, both women. Except Nana, there are no very old men in the tribe. The fortunes of war has prevented the men from attaining great age. The women however, grow old and live on until they look like centenarians. . . .

Of the 2 cases of epilepsy, one was that of a child of Dutchy. This child had already cost Dutchy four ponies given to a medicine man of the tribe [prior to imprisonment] as the condition of cure. The child, a boy of four years, soon died. The other appeared to be hysteroepilepsy, and occurred in the wife of Hosea [probably José First or José Second], one of the principal men, and was first observed at the death of her baby, one of the victims of bronchitis. She had had these convulsions for some time previously on occasions of excitement or grief. . . .

Of the deaths from tuberculosis, all but the child, a little girl, showed symptoms soon after their arrival and ran down very slowly. The treatment of these cases was more difficult than that of almost any other, as finding little relief from medicine, they were averse to taking any, and the appetite failing, they could scarcely be induced to take food, and they ran down, making no sign for weeks, until they died. . . .

Many of the Indians show some remarkable recovery from gunshot wounds, even where the joints have been implicated. One of the knee joints in particular, the bullet having entered above the patella and passing beneath it, coming out below the head of the tibia, and yet the man has as good use of the joint as ever.[43]

Indian Rights Association vigilant watchdog Welsh visited Fort Marion in March 1887, six months after all the prisoners had arrived. His observations led him to conclude that

Fort Marion is entirely inadequate to contain with safety and convenience the 447 prisoners now within its walls. The ramparts are closely crowded with tents, so that but a narrow space is left for passage way. Most of the tents are crowded with occupants. . . . I noticed scraps of bread or meat lying about. . . . The rations are insufficient. . . .

. . . [A] copious stream of water was introduced [into a large sandy-floored room used as a toilet] by which drainage was secured directly to the sea. But even this precaution, and the free and constant use of carbolic acid as a disinfectant, is not sufficient to prevent an unhealthful condition of affairs if the present large number of prisoners be continued in the fort during the approaching summer. . . . [F]ilth cannot be prevented from being absorbed by the sandy soil and highly porous coquina stone of which the fort is composed. The danger of contagious disease attacking these Indians . . . is, in my judgment, a matter worthy of prompt and serious consideration.[44]

Welsh's report created a sensation. As a consequence of the public outcry, government officials wondered about the value of moving the prisoners to a more hospitable climate. As elected and appointed officials in Washington debated the feasibility of a relocation, the citizens of St. Augustine continued to observe and interact with the Chiricahuas. A few townspeople gave oral accounts of their experiences to Josephine Burgess Jacobs, a woman about whom nothing is known other than that she documented these reminiscences.

On March 8, 1949, J. D. Edwards Sr., a longtime resident of St. Augustine, recalled his family's employment as baggage haulers for the railroad:

On the night of September 20, 1886, my father, my brother, and myself met the Jacksonville, St. Augustine, and Halifax train. We were to haul the baggage for the Indian prisoners who were arriving from the West. They were to be stationed at Ft. Marion until further arrangements could be made. We waited for hours for the train to arrive as did crowds of local people but the prisoners never appeared that night.

· The next night we drove our two horse wagon to the station again. The government was going to pay us 3 [cents] a bundle and we were anxious to make the delivery. The train finally arrived with about 18 men, squaws and papooses.[45] They were in the custody of Capt. Darst and were not in chains. They were tired, dirty, and many were sad because they had left their homeland and their tribes.

The Indian men were . . . fine and healthy looking people. They were fond of games and shooting matches. Many of the local people gathered at the fort green on Sundays to watch the Indians. People would set up dimes for the Indians to shoot. It was not unusual for them to hit the dimes at 30 and 40 feet away. They kept the dimes which they shot down. This added to the amusement.

The Indian women upon arriving at the fort went immediately to the well, drew up water and began to wash clothes and blankets. They did all the work and one of the most difficult tasks was drawing the water. One Sunday while the visitors were at the fort an Indian maid was drawing water, an impudent negro made advances and offered to draw the water for her. This angered the maid and she threw the bucket of water on the negro as she yelled "Negro no good." She ran away but was caught and punished by Sgt. Brown. The Indian women paid no attention to anyone except members of their own tribe. The Indian children played games all day long on the fort green. One of their games was similar to checkers.

On Oct. 26, 1886 another band of Indians arrived. Chihuahua was their leader.[46] They marched with their scouts from the depot, across the bridge and up Orange Street to the fort. Geronimo wasn't with these Indians. He was imprisoned at Fort Pickens, Pensacola. His wife was imprisoned at Fort Marion, and soon after her arrival at the fort she gave birth to a girl, which she named "Marion" after Fort Marion. Her name, Marion Geronimo, was on a silver tag dangling from the baby's cradle. Another baby was named "Coquina" and she was the child of Chihuahua, the head chief of the Indians at the fort. The Indian men were always playing games and exercising. They smoked long Indian pipes and relaxed while the children played on the green and the women worked. They took long walks with their guards. One favorite walk was to the North Beach. When some of the Indians died they were buried with their possessions on the North Beach. They wished to be buried with the greatest secrecy as they did not wish the "pale faces" to discover their last resting place. The local people seemed to enjoy having the Indian prisoners at the fort. Many people came to see them, and they learned about their habits and skills, many of which were similar to the white man.[47]

On March 8, 1949, R. F. Sabate, another resident of St. Augustine, Florida, remembered that

These Indians were younger men and quite intelligent. They learned rapidly and were helped by the Carlisle School Industrial Education project.[48] With these men and women was a darkey named "Indian Dick." The Indians left him in St. Augustine and people here gave him work. He changed his name to Dick Hicks, and some of his descendants are still living here.[49]

My people owned a store and sold a lot of bandanna handker-chiefs to the Indian men and women. We often sold as high as 4 or 5 gross per week. The women wore several at one time. They also liked beads. They showed a fondness for good shoes, which we often exchanged for moccasins.

There were some very handsome squaws with this group. They cared for their families and did the cooking and washing for the men.

The men strolled on the streets usually in groups of 15 or so without guards. Those men could ride horses back with the great-est ease and swiftness; it was a beautiful sight. They rode like the wind. . . . Their rations consisted of smoked meat and the Indians craved fresh meat. They didn't need a bow with their arrows because they could throw the arrows 300 yards. Those Indians were no one's fools and don't you believe they couldn't take care of themselves.[50]

On March 16, 1949, Ernest Johnston, then of Syracuse, New York, recalled his contact with the Apaches at Fort Marion.

In 1886 I was 10 years old and I learned a great deal from the Indi-ans. Our store was on Charlotte Street (back of the Monson Hotel). They came there to shop. They were dressed in blankets and went through the store looking and talking. I recall we regarded them rather suspiciously as they could easily conceal articles under their blankets. The town's people considered the Indians prisoners and criminals. There was very little association with them, as far as adults were concerned. However, the youths of that day were wild about them and their bows and arrows.

The Indians were great gamblers. We often saw large groups of men behind the first retaining wall of the fort gambling. One game was played by rolling the hoop and the player attempting to throw a bamboo spear through the rolling hoop as it sped forward. This was a betting game but sometimes their stakes were nickels, a nick-el a throw.

A most vivid recollection was of an Indian singing at sunset. He would go to the Watch Tower and sing every evening. The song started with high pitched notes, then gradually getting lower and lower until it sounded like a lament. The Indian song expressed a loneliness and a desire to go back to his people.[51]

The *Florida Times-Union* occasionally printed news items about the Chiricahuas, including:

[April 15, 1887] It is unofficially announced the Indians will be transferred to a reservation near Mt. Vernon, Ala.

[April 19, 1887] The War Department has issued orders transferring the Apache Indians now at Fort Marion to Mt. Vernon, Ala. And they will leave in a few days for that place.

[April 21, 1887] Apaches number 450. Removal is made on account of the crowded condition of the quarters at Fort Marion[;] although the health of the Indians has been good, it is thought advisable to send them to a healthier location where they will have plenty of room and be free from the gaze of hundreds of curious people who flock about them every time they appear in public.[52]

Approximately 469 Apaches, including adults, children, and 14 scouts were confined to Fort Marion by October 1, 1886. Along with worrying about the consequences of overcrowding, Langdon fretted about what would become of the Chiricahua children, and his various communiqués with the Department of Interior conveyed his apprehension. After receiving Langdon's telegrams and monthly reports, Secretary of Interior Lamar brought the situation to the attention of the secretary of war:

in order to relieve the crowded condition of the fort and for other reasons, I now have the honor to inform you that it has been ascertained that Captain [Richard Henry] Pratt, superintendent of the Indian Industrial Training School at Carlisle, Pa. can provide for about one hundred and twenty-five more pupils than are now at that school.

This Department has no definite information as to the ages of the children and youths among those Apaches, but from general information it is believed that not less than seventy-five will be found of suitable age, &c. to be sent to the Carlisle School.

It is therefore suggested that the War Department cause all of the Apache youths now at Fort Marion, Florida, that shall be found, after proper examination by the post surgeon, to be of proper age and physical condition, to be sent to Carlisle, Pa., there to be turned over to this Department for education and training in the school at that place.[53]

No one in authority in Washington apparently remembered or cared that the Chiricahuas had been promised when they surrendered that they would not be separated from their children, even though Langdon had reminded headquarters of this promise in his earlier report of August 23, 1886.

Government officials met and decided to educate the very youngest of the prisoners right there at Fort Marion. After a long bid process, contract negotiations with the sisters of the Convent of St. Joseph in St. Augustine began with the mother superior's request for payments of twenty to forty dollars per child each month, depending on the appropriate grade.[54]

On December 9, 1886, J. D. C. Atkins, the commissioner of Indian Affairs, wrote to the mother superior at the Convent of St. Joseph, stating that there were

> twenty-six girls and forty-two boys over five years of age that you are willing to take for the purpose of educating them at your school as day scholars.
>
> This office is willing to enter into contract with you at the same rates given to other day schools, i.e., $7.50 per capita, per quarter. If you wish to enter such a contract, please inform me, stating what number you can accommodate.[55]

The nuns accepted the offer and began teaching, but before long they recognized that they had an unexpected audience. The children's fathers, uncles, brothers, and other male relatives stood in the doorways, overseeing the entire process and absorbing the lessons as well. Bolstered by the men's apparent interest in learning, three women of St. Augustine—the Misses Mather, Caruthers, and Clark—volunteered to teach twenty-five Chiricahua men for two hours each morning, using primers and a blackboard. After a brief difficult period of adjustment to a routine the men forged ahead quickly in acquiring basic arithmetic and spelling skills, and in learning how to pronounce English words. Welsh and a friend, Bishop Whipple, observed the lessons, and Whipple remarked that "in his long experience of half a lifetime with Indians he had seen none who in so short a time had made so great progress." Welsh commented on "the quickness with which they followed the words of their teachers and caught their pronunciation."[56]

The older children—twenty-four boys and fifteen girls between the ages of twelve and twenty-two, and forty boys and sixteen girls below the age of twelve in good physical condition—were to be removed from their families and sent to the Carlisle School.

2.
Fort
Pickens

FROM THE MOMENT GENERAL GEORGE CROOK reported that Geronimo and his followers had slipped away from Cañon de los Embudos, a furious U.S. government rededicated itself to hunting the Chiricahuas. On April 3, 1886, Acting Secretary of War R. C. Drum sent a telegram to General Nelson Miles, then at Fort Leavenworth; Miles would replace Crook, who resigned. "The Lieutenant General directs that on assuming command . . . the most vigorous operations looking to the destruction or capture of the hostiles be ceaselessly carried on."[1]

The order of the wording indicates that killing the thirty-five or thirty-six men, women, and children would have been preferable to capturing them. By annihilating the small band, the political administration and the army would rid themselves of the humiliation and ridicule they must have felt. In mid-April Captain William A. Thompson, Fourth Cavalry, issued General Field Orders No. 7 from the Headquarters Department of Arizona in the Field at Fort Bowie. In part the instructions for information and guidance of the five thousand troops read, "The chief object . . . will be to capture or destroy any band of hostile Apache Indians found in this section of country, and to this end the most vigorous and persistent efforts will be required of all officers and soldiers until the object is accomplished. By command of Brigadier General Miles."[2]

Here again, the words *destroy* and *capture* indicated the government's intentions and permitted the soldiers and officers in the field a wide latitude of interpretation.

On July 22, 1886, Miles telegraphed the Headquarters Division of the Pacific at the Presidio of San Francisco: "Captain [Henry] Lawton reports through . . . Fort Huachuca[3] that his camp surprised Geronimo's camp on the Yongi River, about 130 miles south and east of Campas, Sonora,

2 9

or nearly 300 miles south of Mexican boundary, capturing all the Indian property, including hundreds of pounds of dried meat and nineteen riding animals. This is the fifth time within three months in which the Indians have been surprised by the troops."[4]

There is no doubt that the Apaches were feeling intensified pressure from the U.S. army; adding to their troubles was the pursuing, regular Mexican army, spreading out in the Sierra Madre mountains of northern Mexico. This ever-tightening vise was calamitous because it affected the Chiricahuas' supply of food, water, and plant medicines; they were unable to hunt or gather in safety. Given the people's splendid physical condition, however, several days without food was not debilitating, but lack of water was another matter. Because the desert water holes were guarded by U.S. or Mexican troops, the Chiricahuas' lack of access to water became a serious problem.

Less than a month after Lawton disrupted the Apaches' camp, on August 19, 1886, Miles sent another telegram to the Headquarters Division of the Pacific.

> Dispatches today from Governor Torres [of Sonora, Mexico] . . . confirms the following: Geronimo with forty Indians is endeavoring to make terms of peace with Mexican authorities of Fronteraz district. One of our scouts, in returning to Fort Huachuca from Lawton's command, met him, Natchez [Naiche], and thirteen other Indians on their way to Fronteraz; had a long conversation with them; they said they wanted to make peace, looked worn and hungry. Geronimo carried his right arm in a sling, bandaged. The splendid work of the troops is evidently having good effect. . . .
> The Mexican officials are acting in concert with ours.[5]

After receiving a copy of the telegram, President Cleveland responded by sending instructions to Drum on August 23, 1886, going on record with a statement that, in a few words, revealed his anger and frustration. "I hope nothing will be done with Geronimo which will prevent our treating him as a prisoner of war, if we cannot hang him which I would much prefer."[6]

Miles received a copy of Cleveland's telegram and contacted Major-General Oliver Otis Howard[7] with this reply:

> The hostiles are in the mountains some distance from Fronteras; the Mexican authorities were to answer Geronimo's overtures yesterday; the Indians [are] apprehensive of trickery on part of the Mexicans. I am informed by Governor Torres that he had directed his officials

to offer only terms of unconditional surrender, the same as our officers require.[8] All report that the Indians are much worn down
and tired. Captain Lawton's command is in good condition, and
he believes he can kill, capture, or force the Indians to surrender,
and I have every confidence in his ability and untiring energy.
Should he force them near our lines our troops will assist him.[9]

In the field at the same time as Lawton, Chiricahua Apache army scouts
Martine and Kayitah, under the leadership of Lieutenant Charles Gatewood,[10] located Geronimo's camp in Mexico and subsequently convinced
Naiche, Geronimo, and their followers to surrender.[11] According to a
mid-1950s oral history recorded by Ruey Darrow and told by her father,
Warm Springs Chiricahua Apache Sam Haozous, Geronimo asked the
scouts during one part of the conversation, "Who sent you here?" They
replied,

"General Miles, the officer's name is General Miles. He sent us
down here to find you and he try to save your life for you, that's
why he come down here. And we been out here with you when we
was boys. We was raised out here with you. And been fighting for
you. Then we don't—you know it pretty well, we been fighting for
you."

Geronimo said, "You go back to that army, go back to General Miles and tell General Miles I be there in two weeks to see him."

In two weeks time he came to General Miles. And he took everything and put it down. That's all. No gun, no knife, just put it away.
"I'm not going to bother anybody again. All right. Then if you
want to do anything to me, if you want to kill me, well that's all
right. If you want to hang me, that's all right. I just give myself to
you. Whatever you want to do, do it." General Miles said, "No, I
don't want to do nothing."

Then, before General Miles say anymore, Geronimo say, "If you
not going to kill me, get people good food, good water, good grass,
good milk."

Miles said, "Well, we can't move you to the western states. That's
the reason why I'm going to send you out east where nobody
knows you. You live a long life that way. But you can't do nothing
wrong, or you can't live down here. All right."[12]

Haozous's account relates his perspective, but more details are revealed
in Miles's memoir. Of particular interest is Miles's admission that he was
worried about his troops, who, waiting for him in the canyon, were going

back and forth between their own camp and the Apaches' camp. "The state of affairs gave me much uneasiness," Miles acknowledged. As was to be shown, there was no need for worry. Geronimo and his followers were ready to accept the terms of surrender and entrust their lives to the enemy. No doubt Geronimo was as jittery as Miles, but his task at the time was to avoid any sign of weakness and to live up to his warrior reputation. Miles, however, detected a soft spot in Geronimo's armor and described it: "His greatest anxiety seems to be to know whether we would treat him fairly and without treachery or . . . order them shot to death, as had been the fate of some of his people."[13]

Unfortunately, the exact terms of the surrender agreed upon by Miles and the Chiricahua leadership will never be known because the army recorded nothing formally.[14] However, after long talks, Miles placed a large stone on a blanket, saying that the stone symbolized the written word, and the agreement between them would last until the stone crumbled to dust. According to historian Woodward Skinner, "Miles smoothed out a bit of sandy soil and said, 'Your past deeds shall be wiped out like this and you will start a new life.'"[15]

On September 3, 1886, the day before the surrender, General Oliver Howard had sent a telegram to the secretary of war. "General Miles telegraphs that he will commence moving the Warm Springs Indians [Apaches who joined the Naiche/Geronimo group after their chief, Victorio, was killed on October 15, 1880] and Chiricahua Indians tomorrow or the next day. Shall they, in accordance with the President's orders, go straight to Fort Marion, Fla? Please instruct me."[16]

The next correspondence, dated September 7, from Howard to the secretary of war, was to the point:

> General Miles has returned to Fort Bowie with Natchez the son of Cochise, Geronimo, and his brother, with three other Apaches, all as prisoners of war; surrender unconditional. Captain Lawton is following with the remainder of the hostiles, thirty-six adults and three children in all. After congratulating General Miles and his command on the successful issue, I have instructed him that the Apaches and Warm Spring Indians must be sent on straight to Fort Marion, Fla., as the President, through the War Department, directed. What shall be done with Geronimo and the hostiles now prisoners of war?[17]

President Cleveland, still vacationing in New York State, received a copy of the telegram and replied on the same day. "All the hostiles should be very safely kept as prisoners until they can be tried for their crimes or otherwise disposed of, and those to be sent to Florida should be started immediately."[18]

The president's words, "otherwise disposed of," are chilling. Had Geronimo been "accidentally" shot and killed, it appears that the president would have had no objections. Nonetheless, it did not happen, and on September 7, 1886, General Philip Sheridan telegraphed instructions to Miles, who was still at Fort Bowie. "As the disposition of Geronimo and his hostile band is yet to be decided by the President, and as they are prisoners without conditions, you are hereby directed to hold them in close confinement at Fort Bowie until the decision of the President is communicated to you."[19]

Here was a second chance for Miles to "dispose of" Geronimo and his group, but, irritated and impatient, he replied to Sheridan from Fort Bowie in the evening of the same day.

> There is not accommodation here for holding these Indians and should one escape in these mountains he would cause trouble and the labor of the troops be lost. Everything is arranged for moving them and I earnestly request permission to move them out of this mountain country, at least as far as Fort Bliss, Union, or Fort Marion, Fla. for safety. Any disposition can be made of them hereafter as the Government may direct. I ask this in behalf of the troops and myself. There may be a few still out and should they hear of the detention here of these they will remain out. If I am permitted, I will clear this country in a few days.[20]

Again, Cleveland received a copy of this reply and on September 8, 1886, sent a telegram to the acting secretary of war, but not to Miles, who was waiting at Fort Bowie for instructions. "I think Geronimo and the rest of the hostiles should immediately be sent to the nearest fort or prison where they can be securely confined. The most important thing now is to guard against all chances of escape."[21]

Frustrated and arrogant, Miles disobeyed Sheridan, his superior officer, and immediately put the Apache prisoners on a train at Bowie Station, Arizona, bound for incarceration in Florida. Miles's actions distressed high military officials, especially Howard, who sent a telegram from his office at the Presidio of San Francisco to the adjutant general of the army in Washington, D.C., the next day, September 9, 1886.

> I sent yesterday morning to General Miles the orders of the President and Lieutenant-General to hold Indian prisoners at Fort Bowie under guard until further orders. Today I got the order of the Pres-

ident, sent direct to General Miles from the War Department, to send Indian prisoners to nearest fort or military prison. Meanwhile General Miles has sent Geronimo and his band to San Antonio, Tex., en route to Fort Marion, Fla. which is certainly not a compliance with the President's orders to send them to the nearest fort or military prison. Will you not arrange so that orders may come to me, and that I may thus be able to enforce obedience? Three times General Miles has asked to be relieved from the President's orders; he postponed obedience to the instructions of the Lieutenant-General, and whether he is to blame for all this I cannot tell on account of the constant departure from the prescribed mode of transmitting orders. I request that this dispatch be laid before the President.[22]

Secretary Drum forwarded Miles's response to Howard's concerns, dated September 10, 1886, to the president.

Your telegram containing the President's dispatch received. His desire is being carried out. There is not a post in my department where that number and kind of Indians could be confined without the chance of escape, and, if one was out he would be immediately in familiar mountains. They are now en route between El Paso and San Antonio, Tex., under Captain Lawton and the men who hunted them down. If not stopped they will be taken to Florida in accordance with your order. They could be safely confined within the high walls surrounding quartermaster's department at San Antonio, or at Leavenworth prison, if it is desired to stop them short of Florida.[23]

Drum telegraphed General D. S. Stanley, Commanding, Department of Texas at San Antonio, on September 10, 1886, with these instructions: "Captain Lawton, Fourth Cavalry, will arrive at San Antonio today in charge of Geronimo, Natchez, and other hostile Indians who recently surrendered. You will take charge of these Indians and securely confine them at San Antonio barracks and hold them until further orders. Take all possible precautions against the escape of these Indians. Acknowledge receipt and report action."[24]

Stanley replied quickly on the same day: "Your dispatch received. Geronimo and party have arrived and are quartered in quartermaster's depot under guard. There is no permanent or safe guard-house and no place of security at the post proper, which is only now in course of construction. As the force for duty here is already very small, I shall order one company infantry in from Concho."[25]

And so the band of Chiricahua Apache prisoners of war were stopped for a period of approximately six weeks in Texas until a decision about their fate could be reached in Washington. During the many discussions no one in the administration reminded the decision makers that Miles had promised the Apaches that if they surrendered "in five days [they would] see [their] families now in Florida with Chihuahua, and no harm [would] be done to [them]."[26] That promise was ignored, and Crook's assurance of only two years' incarceration was consigned to oblivion in the excitement of the moment. Forgotten, that is, by everyone but the Apaches.

In her work on Geronimo, Angie Debo points out that through a variety of unsolicited comments Washington officials realized that the "surrender, instead of being unconditional, was, contrary to expectations, accompanied with conditions and promises."[27] When asked about these conditions, Miles evaded a direct answer, but Stanley questioned the captives at San Antonio to get to the truth as the Apaches perceived it. They told him about Miles's promise to sweep away the past, his assurance that within five days they would see their families, and his promise of a reservation. However, their impressions were meaningless to the authorities. Until some conclusions could be reached in Washington and the situation thus resolved, the Chiricahua Apaches remained in Fort Sam Houston.

Frank Leslie's Illustrated Newspaper was an eastern publication that attempted to look at and report the Apache problems objectively. On September 25, 1886, an item appeared about the Chiricahuas in Texas:

> The captives are held at Government headquarters in San Antonio to await the decision of their fate. They are a hard-looking company, and have attracted crowds of curious visitors ever since their arrival. While refusing to talk of their exploits, they do not appear to be depressed. Geronimo and Natchez passed their first Sunday in captivity playing cards in their tent. Captain Lawton, of the Fourth Cavalry, left San Antonio last week. . . . Geronimo was very sullen after hearing that Captain Lawton, in whom he had great faith, was going away.[28]

Interpreter George Wratten[29] traveled with the prisoners from Arizona, stayed at the Texas fort with them, and shared their confidences. He recognized that they were fearful of being murdered and promised to help should their fears be confirmed beforehand.[30] "In my tent," he told the nervous group, "I have guns and ammunition about which the soldiers do not know. I cannot see unarmed men butchered. There are not enough guns for all to have arms, but what I have you are to use. If you are attacked, you know where to find them." Wratten knew the consequences of his action if a rebellion occurred, but he valued his friendships with the Chiricahuas so highly that he was willing to risk the penalties. When he learned that their lives would be spared, Wratten said to Geronimo, "At last, word has come from Washington that you are not to be killed but are to be sent to Florida." Historian Eve Ball reports that "Geronimo received the news calmly. He nodded and said, 'Ussen [God] has spoken.'"[31]

On October 20, 1886, Sheridan ordered the fifteen warriors to leave San Antonio by train for Fort Pickens, across the bay from Pensacola, Florida. Part of the instruction was that the eleven women, six children, a baby several weeks old—probably Geronimo's grandchild through his son Chappo—and two enlisted scouts were to be sent to Fort Marion. If Miles had indeed promised the men that they would see their families in St. Augustine, his statement either was a deliberate deception designed to facilitate capitulation or was made in all honesty but later rejected by the political administration.

The selection of Fort Pickens as the site to confine the Apache men was likely made as a result of political lobbying by a group of influential citizens of Pensacola. In a letter to their congressman, P. H. M. Davidson, these activists of the time listed the advantages of their idea:

- the Santa Rosa Island fort was a superior location from a sanitary point of view because it was on a remote island;
- it was twice as large as the St. Augustine facility;
- the Fort Barrancas troops would be able to guard the prisoners; and
- because the Pensacola forts were subordinate to the commander at Fort Marion, Colonel Loomis Langdon, the prisoners would be as much under his jurisdiction as if they were at Fort Marion three hundred miles east in St. Augustine.

The congressman wisely agreed with his constituents and ultimately convinced the War Department. Soon afterward, the move was underway, confirmed by a telegram sent by William C. Endicott, the secretary of war, to Sheridan.

By direction of the President, it is ordered that the hostile Apache adult Indians, fifteen in number, recently captured in Mexico and now at San Antonio, Texas . . . be sent under proper guard to Fort Pickens, Florida, there to be kept in close custody until further orders. These Indians have been guilty of the worst crimes known to the law, committed under circumstances of great atrocity, and the public safety requires that they should be removed far from the scene of their depredations and guarded with the strictest vigilance. The remainder of the band captured at the same time . . . you are to send to Fort Marion, Florida, and place with the other Apache Indians recently conveyed to and now under custody at that post.

You will see that all details and arrangements are made for the prompt and efficient execution of this order.[32]

An unanswered question arises as to the secretary's purpose in writing that the Apaches had been captured in Mexico when he must have known that they had surrendered in Arizona.

On Friday, October 22, 1886, at four o'clock in the afternoon, a special train carrying men, women, and children left San Antonio and arrived on schedule at Pensacola early Sunday morning. The railroad cars separated there, with the one containing the women and children continuing on to St. Augustine without an explanation to the husbands and fathers. The coach containing the fifteen warriors and thirty soldiers from the Sixteenth Infantry was switched off onto a side track. Tired and confused Apache men left the train and were marched single file between double rows of soldiers toward a steamer that was to ferry them across Pensacola Bay to Fort Pickens. Contrary to the purported assurances made by Miles at the time of surrender and to the Chiricahua warriors' expectations, they would not see their wives and children for another year, nor would they be incarcerated beside them until then. There is no detailed written description of the warriors' response when their wives and children were taken away, but a notation in a Senate document reveals that Naiche and Geronimo regarded "the separation of themselves from their families as a violation of the terms of their treaty of surrender."[33] Although Wratten, when asked, confirmed the warriors' version of the agreements made in Skeleton Canyon, it appears that no action was taken to change the situation.

At least one member of the local press recorded the arrival of the Chiricahua men at Fort Pickens:

The powers that be in Washington have . . . selected Fort Pickens as the most suitable place to incarcerate the greatest living American general and his principle officers. Fort Pickens is well suited as an abiding place for Geronimo's genius, for there he can, like his great prototype Napoleon at Saint Helena, live over again his conquests without being disturbed by the outside world. Fort Pickens is large and solid and can hold Geronimo and his band very well, and a few hundred more if the government sees fit to send them. We welcome the nation's distinguished guests and promise to keep them so safely under lock and key that they will forget their hair raising proclivities and become good Indians.[34]

Soon to be joining the warriors would be the male members of the last Chiricahua Apaches to surrender: a small group headed by Mangus, the son of one of the greatest Apache warriors, Mangas Coloradas, and two warriors named Fit-A-Hat[35] and Goso. Five children and a few women, including Mangus's wife Dilth-cley-hen, who was Victorio's daughter, were sent on to Fort Marion. During transport from Arizona eastward Mangus changed his mind about surrendering and tried to escape by slipping out of his handcuffs and jumping through an open window. The train stopped while soldiers found and returned the slightly injured man.

Mangus and Goso joined Geronimo and his warriors at Fort Pickens, bringing the total of the men incarcerated at the fort to seventeen: Naiche, Mangus, Geronimo, Perico, Fun, Ah-nan-dia, Na-pi, Motsos, Chappo, Ya-nozha, Tis-nol-thos, La-zi-yah, Kilth-de-ga-ah, Zhonne, Be-she, Hun-lo-nah, and Goso. The warriors likely talked among themselves about being separated from their families but, being pragmatists, would have recognized and accepted that there was nothing they could do. Ever practical, they simply lived out each day.

A letter written on March 24, 1887, from Langdon to the assistant adjutant general, provided information about Go-so, whom he called José.

> This . . . is a boy of the right age to teach. Without taking the liberty to discuss the propriety of increasing his capacity for suffering by giving him an education without placing him in a position in which he can earn his living, I desire to say that he is just of the age to fit him for Carlisle School and if the government is still sending Indian youths there, I respectfully recommend that he be sent as soon as possible.
>
> I have another recommendation which I desire respectfully to submit for the action of higher authority. I would recommend that the wives and children of the Indian prisoners confined in Ft. Pickens be sent to join them. This will have to be done sooner or later in response to public opinion and the War Department cannot do a more popular act than to initiate the movement. Besides, these Indians, however bad they may have been, have, since they have been here, earned the praise of every one cognizant of their behavior for their exceedingly good conduct. It has never been necessary to punish one of them nor to correct one. Their cheerful obedience

and zeal in the work is something very commendatory. They deserve
the favor recommended.[36]

This letter provides a look at Langdon and offers insight into his understanding of the situation. Unlike the bureaucrats and elected Washington
officials, Langdon interacted with the prisoners and was able to evaluate
them—favorably—from his firsthand experience. Many of his recommendations were carefully considered by the high military command, who still
had scores to settle, and then rejected; several were so appropriate that they
were accepted.

Geronimo was eager to contact his family at Fort Marion and asked
Wratten to write a letter to his wives and children. As Geronimo dictated,
Wratten simultaneously translated and wrote,

My dear Wives, Faith-si-la and Tede, and My Son and Daughter:

How are you at Fort Marion? If so, how do you like it there?
Have you plenty to eat, and you sleep and drink well? Send me a letter and tell me all the news. I am very satisfied here, but if I only
had you with me again I would be more so. I work every day,
excepting Sundays. It is very healthy to work. My work is not hard.
It consists of hoeing and raking in and around the fort. It seems to
me that the Great Father and God are very closely united. I do hope
he will let us see one another soon. As sure as the trees bud and
bloom in the spring, so sure is my hope of seeing you again. Talking by paper is very good, but when you see one's lips move, and
hear their voice, it is much better. I saw Gen. Miles, heard him
speak, and looked into his eyes, and believed what he told me, and
I still think he will keep his word. He told that I would see you
soon; also see a fine country and lots of people. The people and the
country I have seen, but not you. The sun rises and sets here just the
same as in our country, but the water here is salty. The government
is good, and does not like to see the Indian imposed upon. It has
given us pants, and coats with pockets on, and shoes, and enough
to eat. I think of God, the President, and you in the same light. I
like you so well. When I get your letter I will think well over it. I
hope you think the same of me as I do you. I think you have influence with the sun, moon and stars. If the government would only
give us a reservation, so we could support ourselves—Oh! would-
n't it be fine? We are at peace now, and by God's help will remain
so. There are seventeen of us here, and not one of us thinks or acts

bad. Everybody is well and contented. Chatto is a bad man, and has caused us lots of trouble. His tongue is like a rattlesnake's—forked. Do not let him read a word of this letter. Do what is right, no matter how you may suffer. Write me soon a lovely letter.
Your husband,
Geronimo.[37]

The long, empty years at Fort Pickens prior to the Apaches' arrival had given free rein to varmints and vegetation, and the Apache men were in the right place at the right time to rid the area of these unwelcome elements. Geronimo's reference to "hoeing and raking" was actually an understatement of the men's duties. On June 28, 1887, a letter written by Langdon to the assistant adjutant general elaborated on the men's efforts and work habits.

> They scrape, paint and pile shot and shell; they clean the grounds of weeds and dirt that has accumulated in a quarter of a century; they root out from the chinks of the walls the plants and young trees that are constantly getting a foothold there, and they are also engaged in setting out Bermuda grass in the parade ground. . . .
>
> Their light and continually varied employments keep them in good health, not only by the exercise they thus secure, but by preventing their brooding over fancied wrongs or chafing under a confinement, which, even under mildest rule, must be radically different in its surroundings from the free life to which they have been accustomed since childhood. . . .
>
> There has been no occasion to reprimand, much less to punish a single one of the Indians since their arrival here. Of course, no credit is due them for behaving well when it is clearly understood that an offender will be promptly put in irons. But they deserve commendation for their cheerfulness of demeanor, for their prompt alacrity in obeying orders and for the zeal and interest they show in the duties assigned to them.[38]

Despite the extremes of Florida's winter and summer weather, the constant humidity on the island, and the severe disruption in their customary lifestyle, none of the warriors confined to Fort Pickens became ill with a life-threatening ailment, which in and of itself was extraordinary, but even more incredible given their exposure to the citizens of Pensacola. In early February 1887 Langdon began allowing tourists to cross the bay on a ferry, visit the fort, and mingle with the prisoners. Admission was fifty cents for an adult's ticket or twenty-five cents for a child's ticket, payable to the boat captain. The weekly trips were so popular that on one Sunday there were 459 visitors; the count never fell below 20, and the positive publicity this occasion generated was a welcome change.

Always alert to recognizing a good opportunity, Geronimo promoted himself to the visitors and sold souvenirs—trinkets he had carved from driftwood, buttons from his clothing, even his mark on a piece of paper. Most guests came away quite favorably impressed with him and the other men. Popular opinion in the Pensacola area supported the army, as reported in news items such as the one written by a staff member of a local newspaper:

> As the visitors stroll around the fort the idiosyncrasies of the prisoners are freely ascertained. It is learned that they gamble, and that Mangus is the great monte player of the lot; that more than one of them manifested great grief when the squaws and papooses were recently removed to St. Augustine; that they have been allowed to bathe on the sandy beach closely guarded, and that they have greatly enjoyed the exercise. As regards the inner man, they have two messes, headed by Natchez and Geronimo respectively. The food is clean and wholesome, but they decidedly prefer a "ragout" of intestines to a dish of boiled army salt beef. They will not eat before strangers. All have excellent memories, and Geronimo recalls the names of several ladies who have paid more than one visit. One of them takes great delight in sketching in Indian style. All have readily helped to clean up the fort, beside their own apartment, and which, when night comes, they are securely locked up.[39]

A close reading of this news item reveals an example of the language of colonialism: the men "were allowed to bathe on the sandy beach." Presumably the salty water Geronimo mentioned in his letter to his family was the bath water, but some newspaper readers would not have made the connection and been satisfied that the prisoners were being handled with sensitivity and thus permitted to take a cleansing and cooling bath.

Possibly in response to Langdon's recommendation of March 24, 1887, and in the endless search for good publicity, Washington officials agreed to permit the wives and children at Fort Marion to join the men at Fort Pickens. After the required bureaucratic procedures were followed, twenty women and eleven children left St. Augustine in one railroad car on April 27, 1887; they arrived at Fort Pickens on the same day. Housing the larger group was easily accomplished. Families occupied the cavernous casemates that were formerly officers' quarters, while the men who lived alone stayed where they had been assigned initially. Visitors from across Pensacola Bay were now limited, and without the presence of sightseers the entire situation became closer to normal insofar as family life was concerned. Women assumed their wifely and motherly duties, and the men continued their chores under military supervision.

Oddly, not all the wives opted to join their husbands. A letter from Langdon to Herbert Welsh of the Indian Rights Association, dated June 23, 1887, reveals the circumstances of their refusal.

> My dear Mr. Welsh,
>
> You will surely excuse my troubling you . . . about my Indians. I will state the case and then if you can help me any in the matter I earnestly ask your assistance.
>
> At the time the wives and children of the prisoners Apaches now in Fort Pickens were sent over here from Ft. Marion, I have no doubt that the authorities believed all were sent. But such was not

Living quarters of the Chiricahua Apache prisoners of war, Fort Pickens, Florida, 2000. PHOTO COURTESY WESLEY BILLINGSLEA.

the case.

There is 1st, An Indian in Ft. Pickens, one of the prisoners by the name of Mo-tsos (the interpreter spells it) whose wife did not come. She has three children by him with her—Presumably gone to Mt. Vernon Barracks.[40] His case is particularly hard because he is remarkably attached to his family. There may have been some intriguing to effect this separation, on the part of the chiefs, who only had to keep silence to prevent her coming here.

2nd

There is another Indian in Fort Pickens by the name "Tis-nolth-tos" whose wife did not come. The other squaws believe, that at the time of the transfer to this place this woman, being rather young, was sent away to the Indian school at Carlisle, Pa. Her name is "Ge-in-ka."

3rd

One of the Indian prisoners in Fort Pickens is named Chappo. He is the most intelligent Indian in the lot. His wife did not come. She too is supposed to have gone to Carlisle. Her name is "Na-clon."

4th

Another Indian is named "Ah-nan-dia." His wife is here. But the man has a boy four years old who was not sent here. As I understand the case, the boy's own mother, when living on the Reservation in the West, used to get drunk and when in that condition beat the child. The grandmother of the child has been taking care of it and at the time the separation of the prisoners at Ft. Marion was made, and preparations were in progress for transferring the squaws and the children that belong to Ft. Pickens to that fort, this old grandmother when questioned about the child said it belonged to "no one." The grandmother's name is "Ta-clo-then." She and the child have gone to Mount Vernon Barracks.

Now, if there is any influence that can be brought to bear on the government to send the above described Indians to Ft. Pickens, I earnestly request that it may be done.

Of course, my name had better be kept out of all the correspondence. The government can commend my services but it is always glad to treat with consideration the wishes of influential citizens and encourage their efforts to aid it.

If you can get this thing accomplished, I shall be very glad. . . . You must be glad to know that not one Indian, squaw, or child has died since these people have been under my charge at Ft. Pickens.[41]

Now that most of the families were together, it seemed natural to hold the celebratory Dance of the Mountain Spirits. Langdon invited approximately three hundred Pensacolans to attend the dance. A local newspaper's staff reporter was among those who witnessed the event, and he filed the following dispatch.

A large fire had been built in the center of the parade [grounds]. Near the east front, a buffalo hide had been placed on the ground, its hairless side up. Squatting around it, holding long switches, were Natchez, Geronimo, and about eight other men. A crude drum was positioned before one of the Indians forming the circle.

Suddenly, the spectators were startled by a cry which seemed to come from all parts of the fort. It was a peculiar cry, "commencing very low and rising until it became very shrill, then dying away with a low wailing sound." It originated with the women and was the signal for the beginning of the dance. The group around the hide commenced a wild chant, and beat the hide with switches, while the drummer pounded the drum. The dancers, three in number, now appeared. Two were dressed in fancy garb, having on skirts which reached to the knees, and long streamers of colored cloth attached to their arms. They were bare to the waists, and their heads surmounted by pieces of wood resembling horns. The third dancer, with the exception of having his face covered and a breech clout, was naked. Each held in his right hand a long wooden sword and in his left a wooden cross. In perfect rhythm to the chant, they danced around the fire, doing "some doughty deeds in a mimic warfare with evil spirits." Occasionally, they seemed in need of assistance and retreated. Then brandishing crosses, they rushed forward and demolished the foe. This kept up until time for the Pensacolans to return to their vessels at 10 o'clock. The dance, however, continued till dawn.[42]

This news item allows insight into what the men carried with them from Arizona in the way of sacred material goods: a hide, probably from a cow rather than a buffalo; the sacred dance attire; and accompanying accouterments and drums—hollowed out tree trunks with cow hides stretched across an open end and held in place by rawhide ties. The drumsticks were likely thin willow branches with one end formed into a circle.

While still a free people in Arizona, the Chiricahuas had performed this dance to rid the group of evil, to celebrate special occasions, and to mark private family occasions. Contagious illnesses, which had taken eighteen to twenty-four lives at Fort Marion, were less of a problem at Fort Pickens, although ailing women and children brought contagion with them from Fort Marion. Based on the description given, the dance this time was probably performed socially.

During that same month Langdon wrote to the assistant adjutant general. Although formatted as a letter, this document was actually a formal report.

I have the honor to submit the following report for the month of June 1887, of the condition of the Apache Indian prisoners confined in Fort Pickens, Florida, under my charge.

These Indians number, all told, 48 (forty eight) including men, women and children. Of this number 17 (seventeen) are adult males (or "bucks"), 20 (twenty) are adult females (squaws), and 11 (eleven) are children. Among the men are the following: the Chief Natchez, son of Cochise; Mangus, another chief, and Geronimo (Jerome), the medicine man. The ages of the children range from two months to seven or eight years; and two or three of the adults must be over sixty years of age and hence incapacitated for hard work or exposure.

How Quartered

The Indians are living in the otherwise unused and dilapidated casemates, which were formerly occupied by the troops that garrisoned the fort. The married Indians occupy the casemates known as the "Officers' Quarters," on the southern front of the work; while the bachelors, and the two or three married Indians whose wives and children have not joined them, are living in the casemates called the "Company Quarters," the "Old Hospital" on the northern front of the fort. The doors, windows, floors, and fireplaces of all these casemates rooms are in very bad repair, nothing having been done to them since the rebellion [Civil War]. Indeed, in some instances, the doors that opened onto the parade are entirely gone, exposing the inmates to the "northers" which are sometimes very severe here between November and April.

Considerable repairs should be made before winter, to make these casemates habitable. I do not know whether the quarters (all casemates) in this fort were ever formally transferred by the Engineer Department to the Quartermaster's Department. If not, the Engineers might be, I suppose, called upon to make these much needed repairs. But, on the other hand, the fort is under my command, and looking at the matter from that point of view, it would seem the Quartermaster's Department should make the necessary expenditures. If the latter view is adopted by superior authority, the work would be done under my supervision, which would be in harmony with all the circumstances of the case.

The Indians are well supplied, for the present, with clothing, including canvas suits, cotton socks, shoes, and good under clothing.

Their bedding is composed of blankets and bedsacks filled once a month with fresh straw. Their supply of fuel is ample, for, in addition to their allowance, they are permitted to gather from the sea-beach all the driftwood they desire.

Health of the Prisoners

I attribute the maintenance of their good health partly to the splendid climate of this locality, but [it] is mainly due to the finding of constant occupation for them. . . . Indeed, no Indian has the endurance and the will power of the white man required for a long continued task. Besides, these Indians have lived all their lives in elevated, mountainous regions and they would break down in this lower country if kept continuously at tasks expected of white men more accustomed to labor in this region. Their light and continually varied employments keep them in good health, not only by the exercise they thus secure, but by preventing their brooding over fancied wrongs or chafing under a confinement which, even under the mildest rule, must be radically different in its surroundings from the free life to which they have been accustomed from childhood.

I have recently sent over to Fort Pickens four (4) worn but serviceable wall tents complete. These will be kept there for the purpose of promptly isolating any cases of sickness among the Indian prisoners or the guard, which develop symptoms that warrant suspicions of the presence of yellow fever.

There was no rain here from the 9th of March to the 25th of June, and the cisterns were nearly exhausted of their water, but a supply of tolerably good water was obtained from the wells dug among the sand hills two or three months ago, in view of this very contingency. By boiling that water it is good enough for drinking in an emergency. . . .

Conduct of the Prisoners

Their interpreter, George Wratton has a good influence over them and is of great assistance to me. The Chief, Natchez, who is a much younger man than Geronimo, has a great deal more influence than he over his fellow prisoners. Natchez is very manly, respectful and patient. He not only never asks for anything, nor complains of anything himself but he discourages others who may be inclined to a different course. He sets a good example to the other Indians who are not slow to imitate it, as they have been quick to see that Natchez has, apparently, won a certain degree of confidence and a friendly consideration by his behavior.

About a month ago the interpreter told me that two or three of the Indians had asked him to tell me they were very desirous of going into permanent homes on the lands they could cultivate as their own. I told him to say, in reply, that they had had that chance given them before and they had acted badly and lost it deservedly, that they came here with their lives spared by a strong but merciful government and they should be thankful if they were only allowed to let the government forget them for a while, and that the worst thing they could do was to remind the people of their existence as it might be remembered they had not as yet been punished for their crimes. Since then nothing more has been said about farms.

Recommendation

I have not been called upon to make any recommendation, but I hope it will not be considered out of place if I recommend the granting by the Department of the Interior of about $50.00 with which to buy seeds to enable these Indians to make a garden and I would respectfully request through military channels that this sum be sent me for that purpose by the Commissioner of Indian Affairs.[43]

Despite Langdon's concern and equitable treatment of the prisoners, the language of colonialism appears in his report: for example, "no Indian has the endurance and the will power of the white man required for a long continued task"—an incorrect and surprising conclusion given Langdon's understanding of the people. Prior military reports issued while the

Geronimo campaign was under way, a military activity with which Langdon must have been familiar, described the Chiricahuas' superb physical condition, their unique ability to travel sixty miles a day on foot, and their finely honed adaptive skills, so well developed that they were able to live richly off a land that could barely support others.

The prisoners' declining health had become a sore spot among government officials because of the Indian Rights Association's persistent public comments and criticisms. Aware of Washington's public vulnerability, Langdon addressed the medical situation of the forty-eight prisoners at Fort Pickens in an August 9, 1887, report, confirming that although several Apaches had been ailing, no deaths had occurred. "Among these cases was that of one women who was ill a long time . . . and there was another woman who was dangerously ill. . . . It seems remarkable that there has not been a single death among these Indians since [the] first of them landed at Fort Pickens over a month ago. . . . [T]hese Indians seem, somehow, to thrive. What a second year will do for them remains to be seen, but at present they are remarkably healthy."[44]

Still, the national outcry in support of the Apaches grew, thanks to the tenacity of the publicity-minded advocacy groups. Becoming increasingly frustrated, the War Department asked Captain John G. Bourke, an old foe and friend of the Apaches, to investigate the circumstances of confinement at Fort Marion and to make recommendations for a future course. After a quick visit Bourke strongly supported moving the prisoners totally out of St. Augustine. Mount Vernon Barracks, an area of 2,100 acres about thirty miles north of Mobile, Alabama, was being considered as a transfer site, and Bourke was again called upon to evaluate the location. He left Washington, D.C., on Sunday, April 10, 1887, and returned about a week later, full of praise for the Alabama site that was situated on a sand ridge 224 feet above sea level and surrounded by a dense pine forest; the air was fresh and sweet. Bourke noted that a rail line linked Mount Vernon with larger cities in Alabama, in particular Mobile. He submitted his recommendation to the army's adjutant general on April 19, 1887. The president and his cabinet met immediately after receiving Bourke's report and approved the relocation without a further look into the area's potential for causing even more health problems. A formal announcement appeared in a Mobile newspaper on April 23, 1887: "It is stated that the War Department has ordered the removal to Mt. Vernon of the Apaches now confined at Fort Marion, St. Augustine, Fla. The placing of the Indians at Mt. Vernon will add greatly to the attractiveness of that place as a Sunday school picnic resort."[45]

The last sentence is puzzling, considering the Chiricahuas' former war-like reputation and the general knowledge that many were ailing with contagious diseases. Nonetheless, at 1:00 a.m. on April 27, 1887, the prisoners were put on trains under guard. At 8:30 the wheels slowly ground to a halt at the bottom of an incline. Prodded by the accompanying soldiers, the healthy, ailing, and dying men, women, and children shuffled up the hill, lugging their meager possessions. They had reached the next prison camp—Mount Vernon, Alabama.

The men and their families at Fort Pickens temporarily remained where they were. On August 9, 1887, Langdon sent a routine report to the assistant adjutant general. One section of the document compared the Apaches men's cultural attitude toward work and their wives with their current situation.

> When it is considered that in their own country the women do the work while the men hunt, smoke, and loaf, and that here, the men are marched out to work in the presence of the very women who but recently were their slaves, it might be thought natural if now and then an Indian would object. But there has never been a word of remonstrance on the subject. The men seem to recognize that nothing more is asked of them than what is for their own good—that is proper, healthful exercise. . . . Their bearing towards the officers and the guard and to the interpreter is that of gentle, dependent children and it cannot fail to interest everyone who is thrown into contact with them to observe how completely they trust those placed over them. . . . [However] I do not relax any vigilance nor run any risk of "spoiling" them by indulgence or expression of sympathy. In this, as well as in my efforts at discipline and constant watchfulness, I am ably seconded by my officers and the men of the command, and last but not least by the interpreter George Wratton.[46]

Langdon's description of the Apaches as "gentle, dependent children" would definitely come as a surprise to Arizonans who at that time were still cognizant of the Apaches' depredations; time had not diminished the pain over loss of loved ones. However, others familiar with the pragmatism that characterized the Chiricahuas' existence in the desert and mountain regions of the Southwest would quickly attribute their exemplary behavior in prison to their survival instincts.

All the Apache prisoners at Fort Pickens were eventually transferred to Mount Vernon. About one year after their friends and relatives were incarcerated in Alabama, on May 13, 1888, forty-seven men, women, and children detrained without fanfare and walked the one-half mile up the hill. There they sat on their bags and stared at the Apache village until a girl, said to be Geronimo's daughter Lenna, came to greet them.

3.
Educating the Children

APPROXIMATELY 160 APACHE CHILDREN at Fort Marion and 5 more at Fort Pickens were U.S. prisoners of war. These youngsters were the true innocents in the deadly drama that had been played out between their parents and the U.S. military. Their fate and the responsibility for it fell upon official Washington.

As part of his August 20, 1886, report to the assistant adjutant general, Colonel Loomis Langdon addressed one issue—educating the children:

> Since my last report I have been enabled, with the kindly offered services of the sisters of the Roman Catholic Church here, to establish a school for the Indian children. The exercises are held every day from 9 to 10:30 A.M. in the fort. At that hour no visitors are allowed in the fort, and the children's attention is not diverted. The older Indians have not been asked to join the class. I feared they would soon become disgusted, and when the novelty wore off they would absent themselves, and their example would be followed by the children. The older ones look on, however, and it is hoped as their curiosity and pride are aroused they will be attracted sufficiently to ask instruction as a favor.[1]

The nuns had already been teaching the children for four months when the agreement between them and Indian Affairs commissioner J. D. C. Atkins was issued (quoted in chapter 1), but, it seems, they had not been paid. There is no way of knowing if the sisters donated their time or if they were paid through private contributions from the townspeople or from other sympathetic sources.

On January 10, 1887, Atkins sent a letter to the secretary of interior stating "a contract has been entered into with the bureau of Catholic Indian Missions to educate sixty pupils at a day school for six months commencing January 1, 1887."[2]

Until the nuns could make ready a day school for the students, one of the casemates was used as a classroom. The children initially received instructions in reading, writing, drawing, and singing, but they were not entrusted totally to their teachers. Wary of unfamiliar white people, the Apache fathers stood in the doorway and watched over the lessons. The ages-old tribal regard for learning was evident even in captivity, but singing patriotic songs, as the warriors did, was a new addition to the culture.

Allowed to walk to the convent under the supervision of the younger nuns, the children skipped and fussed and behaved like any other group of boys and girls. They used a bathhouse on the convent's premises to change their clothes before playing in the ocean, carefully watched over by the nuns. The youngsters were lined up afterward and led into the church for religious lessons, which they certainly did not understand. But the nuns' full-hearted intent and benevolent shepherding were not lost on the children. James Kaywaykla was one of those youngsters. In his later years, referring to the sisters, he said, "I will never forget the kindness of those good women, nor the respect in which we held them. For the first time in my life I saw the interior of a church and . . . realized more fully that not all White Eyes were cruel and ruthless, but that there were some among them who were gentle and kind."[3]

Herbert Welsh, the ever-vigilant watchdog from the Indian Rights Association, observed the nuns with the youngsters and included in an 1887 written report a few sentences about what he saw.

> I visited the commodious school-room where the children are taken every morning and are taught by the sisters. I heard the children singing and in their recitations, and I was entirely pleased with all that I heard and saw. The sisters are ladies of cultivation and refinement, and, from all that I could learn during my brief visit, are well fitted to perform the task assigned them.[4]

The solution of what to do with the youngest Apaches (eight were eligible neither for the lessons nor for payment, according to Atkins) had been found, but what about the older boys and girls? Educator Richard Henry Pratt had either heard or read about the wishes of the government to instruct the Chiricahua children at Fort Marion. Because the Carlisle School was already populated with Indian students from many tribes, Pratt convincingly claimed in private conversations and public statements that he had much experience in managing the education of diverse Indian children. He was proud of his abilities and prouder still of his many personal dealings with bureaucrats interested in Indian education, which made his face familiar in Washington. Still, the government was careful in not showing any favoritism as it solicited proposals for educating the Chiricahua Apache children. Secretary of Interior L. Q. C. Lamar sent a letter to the superintendent of the Hampton Institute, with a copy to Pratt, on October 13, 1886.

> There are among the Apache Indians now held by the military at Fort Marion, Florida, a number of children of school age. It is desired that these children should be placed in some industrial training school as soon as practicable.
>
> I will thank you to inform me at once how many of them can be accommodated in your school. There are among them also some young Indians who are past the school age, but who are young enough to be educated and trained to useful employment.
>
> I will be glad to have from you any suggestions as to the best disposition to be made of them, and whether any of them, and, if any, how many, can be properly trained and cared for at the Carlisle School?
>
> An early reply is requested.[5]

Two days later Lamar wrote to Secretary of War W. C. Endicott, describing the efforts made to place the older Apache children in educational facilities:

> in order to relieve the crowded condition of the fort and for other reasons . . . I now have the honor to inform you that it has been ascertained that Captain Pratt . . . can provide for about one hundred and twenty-five more pupils . . . and suggests that only those Apaches between the ages of twelve and twenty-two be sent there. While this limit of age should be observed as a general guide, it should not be too rigidly followed. The general condition and fitness of the pupil should also be considered. . . . It is believed that not less than seventy-five will be found of suitable age, &c. to be sent to the Carlisle school.
>
> It is therefore suggested that the War Department cause all of the Apache youths now at Fort Marion, Florida, that shall be found, after proper examination by the post surgeon, to be of proper age and physical condition, to be sent to Carlisle, Pa., there to be turned over to this Department for education and training in the school at that place.[6]

Lamar corresponded again with Endicott on October 23, informing him that

> there are thirty-nine Indian youths . . . between the ages of twelve and twenty-two years, and fifty-six below the age of twelve years, all physically and otherwise suitable to be sent to the Indian schools, and . . . instructions have been given to Captain Pratt, superintendent of the Carlisle Indian School, to receive at that school such of these Apache youths, between the ages of twelve and twenty-two years, as may be delivered there by the War Department and he is ready to receive them as soon as the War Department will deliver them there.[7]

The Apache parents were heartsick at losing their children, to say nothing of the terror in the children's hearts and minds. But not all the boys and girls were taken away. Oral history reveals that at least one child was kept in hiding: the mother of a young boy named Sam Haozous put him in a rain barrel so he wouldn't be discovered.[8]

Jason Betzinez,[9] who was twenty-seven years old and unmarried at the time of imprisonment, was one of the older "boys" whom Pratt personally selected to attend the Carlisle School. In his autobiography, cowritten many years later, Betzinez recalled, "I well remember that when Captain Pratt came to me he stopped, looked me up and down, and smiled. Then he seized my hand, held it up to show that I volunteered. I only scowled; I didn't want to go at all. I was . . . too old to be a school boy. I had never been to any school, didn't know a word of English. This made no difference to Captain Pratt. He must have seen something in my face, sensed some future possibility in me, that I didn't know was there."[10]

Betzinez was always a model student and, whenever he could, praised the white man's system and the good-citizenship principles that formed its foundation. In the latter years of the nineteenth century, when Betzinez was in school, the government and Protestant churches endorsed four widely recognized and accepted truths of education for Indians:

- Teaching Indian students the rudiments of "American" education—for example, the ABCs and the English language—was the first step toward civilizing the children;

- Individualization—the certain result of education—was expected to change the Indian's traditional role as a consumer to the more significant role of producer;

- Christianization of all American Indians was absolutely necessary in a society anchored in Christian ideals and morality; and

> Citizenship training included learning the basic principles of American democracy, the rights of Americans, and the rule of law in a democratic society.[11]

Taken together, these educational aims ensured that Indian children would be totally transformed into "Americans"—more specifically, Protestant Americans—who would join the mainstream, work, pay taxes, and respect and support the nation's policies, including those that went against their own people. These goals were similar to the policies that had been in effect on the Spanish colonial frontier but had failed insofar as the Chiricahua Apaches were concerned. When assimilation, acculturation, Christianity, and civilization finally changed all native children's behavior, the goals of Indian education would be reached. Hidden behind all this, of course, were the officials' political, economic, religious, and sometimes personal aims that could not be accomplished if Indians stood in the way.

The Protestant churches' role in Indian education, especially at Carlisle, is important. Lawrie Tatum, a churchman appointed by President Ulysses S. Grant to be a reservation agent, noted that at the Carlisle School there was a pervasive "religious influence":

Religious service is held in the institution each Sabbath afternoon, usually conducted by a minister of one of the congregations in the city of Carlisle. The students all attend this service; also a prayer meeting in the evening and they can attend the church services in town in the morning. A large percentage of the students have been converted. . . . Nearly two hundred are members of the Young Men's Christian Association, and a larger number of the young ladies are members of "The King's Daughters' Circles." Some of the students belong to the Christian Endeavor Societies in town. It seems very evident that Carlisle School is largely blessed of the Lord, to whom be the praise.[12]

Although a few Indian students still observed their traditional religions, others had been exposed earlier to Christianity back home, creating a mix of religious thought and belief among the pupils.[13] For example, the Jesuits had been active among Great Plains tribes for long years, and many of Carlisle's Sioux students had been baptized and were practicing Catholics. Other students' tribes had historically observed one of the Protestant denominations. Members of the more isolated Indian groups or those few tribes that had successfully repelled outside religious influences were often unfamiliar or only superficially conversant with Christian doctrine.

Despite their past experiences or religious preferences, however, all of Carlisle's students were without exception routinely indoctrinated into Protestant Christianity. This demand was especially difficult for pupils who had worshiped traditionally, for no longer were they allowed to practice their ancestors' religion openly; no longer were they permitted to assume there was spirit in everything alive in nature; no longer could they participate in or even re-create ancient rituals that they believed the deities had given to their people; and no longer were they able to share their sacred stories or dance the old steps of their heritage. As Carlisle students, they now had to follow Pratt's prescribed ways of worship and had to become familiar with Protestant tenets.[14]

Moral training for all children shared equal footing at Carlisle with academic and religious instruction in classrooms. Teachers were obligated to instill in the children's minds the ideals of chastity, pure thought, respect for the Sabbath, honesty, and temperance. In particular, the Christian concept of sin and all its manifestations were carefully explained again and again until it was clear. When the instructors were certain that the youngsters comprehended, they discussed at great length the notion of guilt from having sinned. As a natural progression, they raised ideas of heaven and hell in the classroom.[15]

These new concepts and others awaited sixty-two mostly healthy Chiricahua Apache students who in October 1886 traveled by train from Fort Marion to Charleston, South Carolina. They sailed to New York and then traveled by horse-drawn cabs to the tip of Manhattan, where a ferry took them across the Hudson River to Jersey City. The last segment of the trip was by train from New Jersey through Philadelphia to Carlisle, where they arrived on November 4, 1886, without any immunity whatsoever to rampant contagious diseases.

Tuberculosis was already present at the school, so infection was immediate among the new students. Within one year more than fifteen died.[16] Nonetheless, on April 27, 1887, disregarding the medical danger, Pratt recruited forty-four or fifty (numbers vary) more students from among the Apache prisoners of war in Florida, who also were vulnerable to contagious diseases. Two years later the obviously catastrophic medical conditions of the children could be ignored no longer, and on May 24, 1889, Pratt wrote a long letter to the commissioner of Indian Affairs.

Chiricahua Apache children prisoners of war arriving at the Carlisle School, Pennsylvania, November 4, 1886. PHOTO COURTESY U.S. ARMY MILITARY HISTORY INSTITUTE.

Chiricahua Apache children prisoners of war arriving at Carlisle School, ca. 1890.
PHOTO COURTESY OF FRISCO NATIVE AMERICAN MUSEUM AND NATURAL HISTORY CENTER.

Of the 106 Apaches brought to this school . . . in the winter and spring of 1886–87, twenty seven have died and two others will die within two or three days. Others are drooping and will take their places soon. The school ought not to bear this affliction any longer.

Quite a number of those who remain are drifting downward. We should either be relieved at once of the care of the whole party or they should be thoroughly sifted, and those in precarious health sent to their people.

The cause of death, so far, has been, without exception, inherited consumption from venereal taint. While climate may to some extent have an influence in aggravating and bringing a speedier termination, I think the deplorable and almost hopeless conditions surrounding them have a greater influence. They have no home, no country, no future, and life has become hardly worth living. I hope that at the earliest practicable date something may be arranged covering the disposition of the whole party. If thoroughly sifted and the unhealthy disposed of, there is no possible objection to the others.

It is important that we make immediately a change for seven of the girls. Two, or it may be three, will take [to] their beds next week and we may be compelled to bury them here.[17]

The language of colonialism is apparent here in Pratt's reference to "inherited consumption from venereal taint," implying that Apache parents practiced a wanton lifestyle that resulted in the children's acquiring tuberculosis. Regardless of his capabilities as an educator, Pratt was clearly ignorant of the principles and moral codes of many of the Indian tribes, including the Chiricahua Apaches, who in particular eschewed promiscuity. Or perhaps he was aware but deliberately chose to point a finger at the Apache tribe rather than take responsibility for the death of these children. In either case he could have been casting about for a scapegoat because growing concerns among the public about the Apache children's health were evident through that old bugaboo adverse publicity. Indian advocacy organizations began publicly commenting that the life-threatening illnesses afflicting the children were the consequences of their separation from their parents. The resultant publicity caught the attention of a powerful military officer, General Oliver O. Howard, who was still involved, albeit peripherally, in Chiricahua affairs, and he added his voice to the opinions. Possibly as a result of Howard's concerns, Pratt felt it necessary to correspond again with the commissioner of Indian Affairs on June 18, 1889.

Referring to the remark of Gen. Howard that these children are liable to "disease principally caused by their separation from their parents," I have respectfully to inform you that Gen. Howard is quite mistaken in that. The disease rests where I placed it in my former letter. They came here under its influence. It was chronic and, in our judgment, heritary [*sic*]. But there is another reason why Gen. Howard is mistaken in his statement that the disease is caused by separation from parents and in suggesting as a remedy the returning of all the children . . . and that is, of the one hundred and twelve who came to us from the Chiricahua prisoner Apaches, fifty-nine had no parents living, and a good portion of the others had only one parent living, so that if absence from their parents causes their disease and death, they are doomed under any circumstances.

My suggestion now would be to let them remain as they are at present. . . . There will be no objection to, and good might come from a thorough examination of the whole party here by a competent army physician, who has had some Indian experience. The students are, in my judgment, entirely free from homesickness.[18]

Pratt's specious logic—that fifty-nine orphans had no parents from whom they had been separated and thus were doomed anyway—is a revealing example of his personality. He seems defensive, trapped perhaps, and angry that his conclusion about the children's "inherited consumption from venereal taint" was challenged. It is likely that he worried about losing his income, his reputation, and ultimately his control of the school itself. He apparently was not a very patient man; taking time to think over the situation, he might have asked Howard and the many other critics to join him in finding an acceptable solution to prevent more Apaches' deaths in the future. Possibly worried that the answer would be to send the children back to their parents and thus surely decrease his income, Pratt continued to resist this solution, a resistance that lowered his status in the eyes of politicians, military personnel, and members of the general public whom he had impressed previously.

To quiet the growing public and governmental concerns, Pratt nonetheless agreed to have a doctor examine the Apache children. John J. Cochran spent three days at Carlisle, from June 22 to June 25, 1889. His report included the following conclusion:

I am of the opinion that the causes of death have been mainly due to (1) removal of Indians from the dry climate and elevated lands of

Arizona to damper climate, and lower lands of Florida, Alabama, and Pennsylvania; (2) to captivity; (3) to more intimate contact with civilization; and (4) to lessened power of the savage races to resist just such diseases as the Apaches have suffered and died from. I consider the children that I saw and examined . . . to be in as good a condition of health as it is possible for them to be in any part of this country away from New Mexico and Arizona, and their mode of living so radically changed as it must necessarily be, if they are to be educated and taught self dependence.[19]

It is fair to assume that all the Chiricahua children, regardless of whether they were well or ailing or had living parents, were homesick for their families, but so too were their parents and relatives yearning for them. Two letters, translated from the Apache language into English by interpreters George Wratten and Sam Bowman, express the parents' aching hearts. One letter was to Jason Betzinez from his mother.

My dear child:

I am thinking about you. I have no friends. I sent my one child to Carlisle. I loved you long ago. It is long since I have seen you. You are my son. You must write to me often. I want you to learn. I have no father or no mother. There are just we two. Perhaps you work. I don't know. I work too. You do not write to me. You must write to me. You must work for I am working too. We are living well here. None of your friends are sick. Do write to me. Good bye. Your mother.

The next letter was from a medicine woman named Chiskio, whose two sons were attending Carlisle.

My dear children.

Are you happy? You must be happy my two boys. I see well yet and I talk kind. When you went away from me I cried every day. I feel better now. We live very well here. I think we shall see each other again. You must not think about me. I don't think about myself. Your mother.[20]

Despite any pain the children felt when they received letters from home, they were expected to continue with their lessons and swallow their feelings. One wonders how many tears were shed into pillows in the darkness before classes started the next day.

Part of Carlisle's curriculum included learning a trade, and one of these occupations was running a printing press. The school's printing shop, staffed in the late 1890s by male students, issued a student newspaper each Friday called *The Indian Helper.* The publication printed poems with Christian lessons and guides, school events, human interest stories and their lessons, and religious activities. Edited by Pratt, *The Indian Helper* was read by the student body and also mailed to alumni and other interested persons who paid ten cents a year to subscribe. Each issue's general circulation was estimated at about ten thousand copies.

Page 1 of the September 16, 1898, issue included a poem entitled "The Helper," written by a James H. West, whose identity cannot be further determined.

> *He who the light to one dark soul shall bring*
> *Among the sons of men is more than king.*
> *No word thou utterest, or good or ill,*
> *But sounds forever—wild or soft or shrill,*
> *Fast held within the vibrant air's embrace,*
> *If words of thine shall brighten one sad face,*
> *Thine accents ease a brother's heavy load*
> *The daily task reveal where truth is stowed.*
> *Then rest content! For there shall come a year*
> *—And soon shall come—when back into thine ear*
> *With ten-fold power the words or ill or good*
> *Shall speed with force that may not be withstood.*
> *Then happy thou if in thine ear shall ring*
> *Words that shall crown thee, servant, helper, king.*[21]

This poem clearly meets two related goals of the four previously stated aims of Indian education. First, it reinforces the rudiments of American education as a tool in civilizing the Indian children by its use of inference and symbolic language. For example, the word *king* refers to and symbolizes Christ, and the overall impression of the poem is Christian in nature. Second, eventual Christianization was being helped along by the use of that symbolic language.

The newspaper also published obituaries, including those submitted from other Indian schools. The death notice that appeared in the September 23, 1898, edition is notable not only because of the detailed description of the way the boy died, but because Pratt had stubbornly insisted publicly and privately that the Apache children were afflicted with inherited venereal disease and that it was this ailment that killed them rather than tuberculosis acquired at Carlisle. Pratt's own words, printed in this obituary, belie his pronouncements, however.

> Bruce Patterson is dead. It is with deep sorrow and regret that we are called upon this week to record the death of Bruce Patterson, who was beloved by a large circle of schoolmates and friends. The following, from a letter from Superintendent Edgar A. Allen of the Albuquerque, N.M. Indian School, tells it all. Bruce, when a small boy was brought to Carlisle from Florida, where the Apache prisoners were held. He was a bright, winning boy, learned rapidly, and was generally healthy, until within a year or two when the seeds of inherited disease came to light. He was nurtured with thoughtful care and finally went to New Mexico to try the effect of a higher and dryer clime. Supt. Allen says: "I regret exceedingly the necessity of informing you of the death of Bruce Patterson last night. He died shortly after I wired you stating that he was beyond aid. We were very hopeful that he would recover and he seemed to be growing stronger. He had a hemorrhage Sunday night, the 4th instant, but made a good recovery and yesterday evening seemed as well as ever: we never thought of his being in any danger. About eight o'clock last night he began to bleed from the lungs and we were utterly unable to check it. He failed rapidly, and by half past nine was dead. We held funeral services today, and he was laid to rest with those of our school who have died before. He has been a good boy while with us, and made many friends who sincerely mourn his death.[22]

In stating that Bruce Patterson went to New Mexico, where the climate was higher and drier, Pratt clearly was describing a popular remedy of the time for tuberculosis. Venereal disease, inherited or acquired, could not be cured by the Southwest's climate.

Publishing obituaries would have been a delicate matter because of the many deaths and their cumulative effect on the student population. One wonders why Pratt permitted this death notice to be printed in such a descriptive format, unless he intended his teachers to use it in the classrooms to reinforce the Christian tenets about heaven: Bruce went to heaven because he was a "good boy."

An item about former president Abraham Lincoln, entitled "When Abraham Lincoln Made a Promise, He Kept It," was published in the October 7, 1898, issue. This example of Christian morality was specifically aimed at the youngsters who read the newspaper and, it was hoped, would understand and appreciate the point of the story.

> While drinking whiskey was the fashion all about him, Abraham Lincoln never forgot his mother's dying request to close his lips against intoxicants.
>
> Once, when he was a member of Congress, a friend criticised him for his seeming rudeness in declining to test the rare wines provided by the host, urging as reason for the reproof:
>
> "There is certainly no danger of a man of your years and habits becoming addicted to its use."
>
> "I meant no disrespect, John," answered Mr. Lincoln, "but I promised my precious mother only a few days before she died that I would never use anything intoxicating as a beverage, and I consider that promise as binding today as it was the day I gave it."
>
> "There is a great difference between a child surrounded by a rough class of drinkers and a man in a home of refinement," insisted the friend.
>
> "But a promise is a promise, forever, John, and when made to a mother it is doubly binding," replied Mr. Lincoln.[23]

The dangers and consequences of drinking alcohol were repeated frequently in print for the children at Carlisle School. The October 14, 1898, issue of *The Indian Helper* contained an item about Geronimo, entitled "A Total Abstinence Indian."

> We have had Geronimo's children and grandchildren as pupils. If what the following clipping from the Indian Journal says is true, some of us may gain a lesson in the life of the famous chief, now on exhibition at Omaha. The Journal says, "Old Geronimo, the famous Apache chief is stationed at Fort Sill, and he spends most of his time playing monte. He is 90 years old, but straight and active with an eye like a Rocky Mountain eagle. Notwithstanding his years, he occasionally gets permission to go hunting and seems to enjoy the sport as much as ever. He has been fighting the whites during most of the time since the war of 1812, but is now reconciled to them and lives peacefully on their bounty, toothless, propitiatory, and composed. He has been a total abstinence Indian all his life and his age and state of preservation show that it has been a good thing for him."[24]

This story is obviously propaganda, designed to impress the Carlisle students, alumni, and financial contributors by holding Geronimo up as a role model and by reporting that he changed his ways purportedly under the good influence of the surrounding white culture. This news item has several errors: Geronimo was not "stationed" at Fort Sill as a soldier would be, but was imprisoned there; in 1898 Geronimo was sixty-nine years old, not ninety; he had not been "fighting the whites . . . since the war of 1812," having been born sometime in 1829; and he had certainly not been "a total abstinence Indian all his life" but had been frequently drunk while still a free man and drank to intoxication at every opportunity while a prisoner of war. Carlisle's Chiricahua Apache students probably got a good laugh out of this piece.

Other than the obituaries, the newspaper made no mention of the terrible illnesses that were devastating the Indian children at all boarding schools, not just Carlisle. On February 21, 1895, a letter from Mary E. Dewey, the corresponding secretary at the Massachusetts Indian Association, an advocacy group, to the secretary of war described the medical condition of three of the Chiricahua Apache children attending boarding school in Virginia.

> Last year, by permission of your Department, our Association sent eight children of the Apache prisoners then at Mt. Vernon Barracks, Alabama, to be educated at the Normal Institute at Hampton, Va.
>
> I am sorry to report that one of the children is dying of consumption, developed by the change of climate, & that two others, Josephine Beshade & Vincent Barzine, are pronounced by Rev. Wm. Frissell, the Principal, & Dr. Waldron, the physician of the school, to be too weak in the lungs to remain in safety so far north.
>
> May it please you to give us permission to send these two to their families . . . & to incur the needful expenditure of the journey?
>
> We regret being obliged to return them upon your hands, as they were making excellent use of their opportunities at Hampton where they have received the best of care. They are about fifteen & we hoped to give them training that would in a few years, have made them independent. . . . [W]e trust that you will place them in good industrial schools near their people.[25]

Some of the children's parents were also ill or growing older, and they longed to have their children with them. In the summer of 1895 a few families asked interpreter George Wratten to write to Pratt and request that their children be returned. Wratten wrote,

I have the honor to address you on behalf of the Parents and relatives of the following named Apache Indian children now at the
Indian Training School, Carlisle, Pa.

Very earnestly and respectfully they beg that these children be
returned to them.

Dexter Loco
Rachel Tsi-ta-da
Mabel Shah-na-ow-tieh
Duncan Balatchu
Oliver Bitchait
Clement Seazilzhay
Naimo Kohten
Dora Cha-en-dee
Lambert Istone
Paul Tee-na-be-kizen
Clay Domieh
Vincent Nah-taileh

They are all old men and women and say that now they are
going to have homes of their own, farms, horses, and cattle, also
good houses to live in, that they want their children with them.

That they are too old to work for themselves and when they get
the farms and cattle, will have no one to work the former and look
after the latter.

It is now more than eight years since these children were sent
to school, having been sent in the spring of 1887. What these old
people (parents and relatives of the heretofore named children) say
is true. They are all unable to work, and if their sons and daughters are not returned to them to help them, they will stand a poor
chance indeed in the battle for life with the younger and consequently stronger men and women of the tribe.

Some of them are very old and have no one but their children
to depend upon for work. In the case of some of the mothers it is
especially so, as they are entirely alone here, all of their children
being at school.

With earnest entreaties and every prayer that an Indian can utter,
they beg of you to do all in your power to have their children
returned to them.[26]

Whether Pratt agreed to release these particular children from school
is unknown, but he would have been smart to do so because the medical

crisis among the Chiricahua children at boarding schools reached flash-point by 1895. At this time Pratt explored his options and decided to send terminally ill youngsters back to their parents to die. The statistics required to continue government funding thus would not show so many deaths and would not raise so many questions in Congress, and the school's continued existence would be assured then, as would Pratt's income. But he had not counted on being outsmarted by government-employed physicians.

For example, on November 1, 1895, Captain J. D. Glennan, an assistant army surgeon, wrote a damning report after examining the Apache children at Carlisle.

> The practice which prevails at the Carlisle School, of retaining students there until in an advanced stage of pulmonary disease, and then sending them back to their people is a bad one. If these cases could be returned to the open air life and dry atmosphere of the western country, in the first stage of this disease, many of them would recover. As it is, they return them when there is no hope of recovery, only to become sources of infection to their people. Some of them are kept so long that they many [do] not reach [home] alive. I have seen a boy from Carlisle, dying from phthisis, compelled to travel in a day coach until unconscious, and then twenty-eight miles in a stage in an effort to get [home] before death, which was accomplished by a few hours. This is bad in every way. If this school cannot be removed to a climate suitable and natural to the Indian, the students who become infected there should, at least, be given a chance for life by a prompt return to the western country.[27]

It should be remembered here that the American Southwest, former home to the Chiricahua Apaches, was ironically being touted in 1895 as having just the right climate to cure tuberculosis. Believing it, thousands of sick white citizens moved westward. However, Chiricahua Apaches of all ages ailing with tuberculosis were not permitted to return to their homelands in the Southwest and were kept incarcerated in an unhealthy climate. Was this policy the government's revenge for the embarrassment and humiliation the Geronimo band had caused? The answer to this question may never be determined.

Politically astute and sufficiently adept to recognize when cooperation was absolutely imperative, Pratt corresponded on December 13, 1895, with Major George W. Davis of the office of the secretary of war in response to a request for a report on the deaths of the Apache children at Carlisle.

Wrote Pratt, "The death rate . . . is excessive. We took practically all the children of proper age without reference to their health, which will in some degree account for this death rate. During the sixteen years of the School we have handled in all 2,969 students, of these 144 have died here. Thus you will see that while the Apache deaths have formed only one-twenty-sixth of the whole, they have contributed nearly one-fourth of the whole number of deaths."[28]

At least three Chiricahua Apache children were still at Carlisle as the decade ended and the century turned. Other students had either graduated by then, dropped out, or perished from contagious diseases. Most of the students had learned how to read and write English and how to do their sums; they also became more than just acquainted with domesticity, trades, and the ways of the dominant society. More significant, insofar as many pupils were concerned, Pratt accomplished his stated goal: "Kill the Indian, save the man."[29] During their years at the Carlisle School most Apache children lost their cultural identity, severed their allegiance to the customs of their ancestors, and dismissed the traditional religious practices of their ancestors. In the near future these educated young people would have a profound and life-altering influence on their families, all of whom, in 1900, were still confined to the Mount Vernon Barracks.

4.
Mount Vernon

EUGENE CHIHUAHUA, SON OF THE CHIEF, described his childhood impression of the Mount Vernon[1] incarceration site. "We had thought that anything would be better than Fort Marion with its rain, mosquitoes, and malaria, but we were to find out that it was good in comparison with Mt. Vernon Barracks. We didn't know what misery was until they dumped us in those swamps. . . . It rained nearly all the time . . . the mosquitoes almost ate us alive. . . . Babies died from their bites . . . our people got the shaking sickness. . . . We burned one minute and froze the next. . . . [N]o pile of blankets would keep us warm. . . . We chilled and shook."[2]

Immediately after the Chiricahuas detrained in Alabama, the military ordered J. H. Patzk, M.D., the post surgeon, to examine them and write a report. In today's parlance the report would have served as a baseline evaluation, or the individuals' medical status at the moment of arrival at a new site. On June 30, 1887, the doctor listed debility (fatigue, weakness, infirmity, frailty) among many prisoners, which, he thought, was "probably the cause of some deaths." He attributed the amorphous medical condition to "previous hardships, privation, and especially insufficient feeding." He urgently recommended increasing the adult rations to the size of the regular army ration and that of the children "in proportion," but there is no indication that the amount of food per person was increased as a result of his report. If this neglect caused Patzk any consternation, he did not put it in writing and carried out his routine work, which included vaccinating the Apaches against smallpox. Although these vaccinations served as preventives, no immediate treatment was available for many Apaches who were suffering from illnesses previously acquired in Florida. During the first month of incarceration at Mount Vernon, three died—one from debility and two from tuberculosis.[3]

Educating the youngest children was again a priority at Mount Vernon, as it had been at Fort Marion, and was now helped along by tutors—students returning from the Carlisle School. The government also hired two teachers—Miss Vincentine Tilson Booth, formerly of the Carlisle School, and Miss Marion E. Stephens, formerly of the Hampton Institute. Not all eligible children participated, however, because many parents were initially wary of the women, believing from prior traumatic experience that they had actually come to remove the children. In time, however, skepticism and distrust disappeared, and then many of the Apache men participated in classroom work, as they had at Fort Marion; the women, many still leery, stayed away.

Because both teachers were also practicing Christian missionaries, they were thrilled with an organ donated by a church in Connecticut. At first the bulky instrument could not find a place for itself. The schoolhouse was the logical site, but it was in the process of being built. The other structures belonged to the army, and the cabins that served as homes for the Apache prisoners were too small. After considerable discussion, the breezeway of Geronimo's house was selected as the organ's resting place.[4] There is no record of Geronimo's reaction, but it is fair to assume that he looked upon this latest opportunity with an eye toward making the best of it, possibly by ingratiating and promoting himself with the teachers and the military supervisors.

Until the school construction was completed, the teachers hung a two-sided blackboard outdoors between two posts. According to historian Woodward Skinner, "Miss Stephens and the adult males gathered on one side of the blackboard while Miss Booth, with some difficulty assembled the tykes . . . on the other side of the blackboard. . . . Geronimo . . . seeing that the men were enjoying themselves, walked over, passed judgment and became a student also. At the close of the class he showed his appreciation while helping put away the materials. He carried a table."[5] These initial efforts at insinuating himself into the good graces of the teachers worked well for Geronimo over the long term. When students occupied the new school, he served as a monitor in the one-room classroom, patrolling the aisles with a willow switch and taking a swat now and then at squirmy children who were not paying attention to the teacher.

On November 17, 1889, the commanding officer at the post, Major W. L. Kellogg, wrote to the adjutant general in Washington,

> it has been most agreeable to me to extend to the teachers of the Apache Indians at this post every courtesy and attention in my power, as I consider them entitled to the utmost consideration.

Two young ladies, Miss Booth and Miss Stephens, came here last February, starting their school with an attendance of one man and two children. When school closed, May 31, 1889, there was an average attendance of 30 men and about the same number of children. . . . It appears that many of them hesitated to send their children, fearing that if they attended the school they would be sent to Carlisle, or some other place away from here; but now as they seem to understand that that will not be done, they are willing, and many of them even anxious, not only to attend themselves but to have the children attend also.

Miss Shepard who has the children more especially under her charge, tells me that Geronimo is of very material help to her as he is always present and takes great interest in maintaining discipline, and in other ways assisting her in her duties. The few that have been returned from Carlisle are also of great assistance.[6]

It is important to point out the dramatic contrast between Geronimo's ferocious activities in defending his people's way of life while a free Apache and his obliging behavior as a prisoner of war. The disparity is remarkable and is an excellent illustration of pragmatism, the characteristic that apparently was the Chiricahua Apaches' major cultural trait. In other words, Geronimo initially did what was necessary to remain free, but as a prisoner he did what then became necessary. Recorded examples of this cultural distinction among the Apaches date back to the Spanish colonial frontier, where the ancestral Chiricahuas accommodated the newcomer European proselytizers—Jesuits and Franciscans—with lip service but kept their traditional religion in their hearts.

It is likely that several military officials at the post believed the Apaches were adjusting so well that members of the general public, at first from the surrounding countryside, were invited to come to the campsite and circulate among the prisoners. The matter of the Apaches' susceptibility to communicable diseases carried by the visitors was of no concern to the authorities. One wonders how the contagious process could have been ignored unless military personnel were ordered to disregard the risks to the prisoners.

In the spring of 1890 an individual identified only as Valliant Julieo visited the Mount Vernon Barracks and subsequently sent a letter to the *New York Times* describing the scene there.

It would be difficult to find anything more picturesque and interesting than the camp of the Chiricahua Apache Indians now held as prisoners of war at Mount Vernon Barracks, Alabama. It consists of a hundred or more cabins and a few wigwams, which the older women have been unable to abandon. Geronimo, who foiled our army again and again, is seated in front of his cabin, beading a whip, and with an overcoat on, the cape of which is lined with the artillery red, nor has he so far neglected artistic effect as to not have perfect harmony exist between the lining of the cape and his complexion. His favorite squaw sits at his feet, almost invariably cooking pumpkins, for which her master has an insatiable appetite.[7]

Julieo's language of colonialism is apparent in words that equate the red lining of the cape—unlikely attire in the warm Alabama weather—with Geronimo's complexion. Geronimo's facial coloring was actually a dark brown, but the prevailing stereotype of Indians at the time was that they were red men and women. Geronimo's face may indeed have been flushed red with the heat and humidity that characterized the Alabama weather.

The Chiricahuas were never able to adjust to the climate; the weather was hotter and wetter than it had been in Florida, and certain non-Apaches who were close to them were worried about their health. A letter from interpreter Sam Bowman to Welsh clearly stated the problem: "There is hardly any improvement in their condition. . . . They will never improve at this place. . . . [T]he inhabitants tell me that no one but the colored race who are born here can stand it being swampy and malarious . . . and they prophesy an early death to the Indians if they are put to work in the bottom lands."[8]

The Apaches' troubles in acclimating themselves to the Alabama climate did not go unnoticed by high army officials. General Oliver Howard, who was worried about the continuing large number of deaths among the Apache prisoners, reported to the adjutant general on December 23, 1889, about their medical problems.

The three hundred and eighty-eight (seventy-nine men, three hundred and nine women and children) at Mount Vernon Barracks are now in a condition which needs prompt action to avoid positive inhumanity.[9]

The normal death rate of civilized people is less than 2 percent per annum. That of these people, including those at school, is more than three times as great, or 6.8 percent.

A number equal to one-quarter of those brought east has died in three and a half years. Consumption has fastened itself among them, and has been rapid and always fatal where it has attacked.

A great death rate must be expected, one-half of the deaths

being of young children whose disease was aggravated by their parents' neglect of the simplest instructions of physicians, and the murderous quackery of old squaws. But the excessive death rate is due to consumption, as have been most of the deaths at Carlisle, where proper sanitary precautions have always been taken.

The condition of health and mind of these Indians other than those at Carlisle precludes the possibility of their improvement and civilization where they now are, for the following reasons:

1st. They are prisoners. Though well fed and well clothed, their labor is prison labor.

2nd. Only the men are required to work, and that, of course, without remuneration. Were they paid it would only give the power of purchasing intoxicants, and add to their degradation. The women have not enough to do, and are without incentive to improvement.

3rd. There has been and is much sickness and many deaths, with resultant depression.

4th. They have been told that good behavior would secure action towards permanent homes of their own, and this promise so long deferred has increased their hopeless feeling. Each year's delay is a greater injury to them.

5th. They are a people who have been bred in mountains and who, as well as the medical officers of the Army who have attended them, believe their rapid dying off is due, in great part, to their location in the moist atmosphere of the sea-coast.

6th. So many of their children have died away at school that not only have those been grief stricken who have lost their absent ones but all are constantly fearful of the taking from them for death at school of others of their children.

To summarize then: We are holding as prisoners, with women in idleness tending to vice, a band of savages till they die, in a place and in a manner that their death is possibly increased by local causes, though we are not now taking their children away from them for school.

The camp at Mount Vernon Barracks is as good as a prison camp can be, but can not be made a home. No military reservation east of the Mississippi River has any better facilities. As there is no arable land for them to cultivate in that vicinity, farming is impossible.[10]

At this time in his long association with the Chiricahuas, Howard was clearly of two minds. Since his earliest contact with Cochise during the peacemaking process in 1872, he understood their situation and must have had some appreciation of their culture. But in this letter he reveals the view of an intolerant colonizer, critical of the Apache parents for, as he wrote, "their neglect of the simplest instructions of physicians and the murderous quackery of old squaws." Based on his past experience among the people, Howard certainly would have recognized the Apaches' language barrier and their loyalty to the ways of traditional medicine—that is, until the white man's contagious diseases presented a catastrophe for which there was no ancestral remedy. Also, he probably should have realized the cultural conflicts that would surely occur when the Apaches were treated with the modern medicine of the time, yet he showed no evidence here of comprehending the tension between the two concepts, nor did he show any tolerance of the Apaches' reluctance to consider the dominant culture's methods of treating illnesses to be better than their ancestors' ways. Surprisingly, in his summary he writes of "women in idleness tending to vice" and calls the Chiricahuas "a band of savages till they die," but he must have known these statements were deceptive. One is at a loss to understand many of Howard's statements, other than as possible evidence of his personal need to ingratiate himself with his superiors. Not to be overlooked in his report, however, is his reiteration that the Apache children's deaths at Carlisle were owing to tuberculosis, not to "venereal taint," as Richard Pratt would have it.

Adding to the Apaches' immediate distress from illnesses and the intolerable climate was the army's insistence that the men discard the ill-fitting cotton and wool uniforms previously issued to them at Fort Marion and instead wear suits made from surplus canvas tents and used mattress covers. Much of the material was so wet from years of exposure to the rain and humidity that the cloth either tore easily or stuck to the men's bodies. No one in authority seemed concerned that the moldy-smelling canvas and dirty covers could have been habitats for disease-producing vectors. Also, the apparel was much too heavy for the climate. After a time it fortunately was "abandoned on the recommendation of the Inspector General. . . . In addition to the misery caused by the uncomfortable clothing, the entire camp fell sick from smallpox inoculations administered as the Apaches arrived from Florida," according to historian and author Bud Shapard.[11]

The climate, the clothing, and the unrelenting sicknesses conspired physically and psychologically against the prisoners, and for the first time in Apache cultural memory two suicides resulted. The first, Geronimo's warrior relative named Fun, fled two miles out of the camp to the river, sat under a tree, and shot himself during a fit of jealousy over his wife's activities. Hearing the news, military personnel acted quickly to calm the excitable (they thought) prisoners by brandishing weapons and dashing around the camp in a state of exaggerated concern. Solemn Apaches stood silently in small groups, watched them, and did nothing. Two years later another self-inflicted death occurred when Seeltoe, assigned to guard duty at the jail, shot his wife and her companion as she tried to escape from the guardhouse and then killed himself; his wife survived. This time the army stood at the ready only, unwilling to be embarrassed once again by its haste. As in the past, the anticipated trouble never came.

The local *Mobile Register* ignored Fun's death but wrote about Seeltoe:

A terrible tragedy occurred yesterday at Mount Vernon, resulting in the fatal shooting of two Indian prisoners, a male and a female, and the instant death of the jealous lover by his own hand.

A special from Mount Vernon to the *Register* says: "This afternoon a female prisoner of war named Belle and Nahtorahghun, a member of the Indian company stationed at Mount Vernon Barracks, were shot and mortally wounded by Hugh Seeltoe, also a member of the Indian company.

"After shooting Belle and Nahtorahghun, Seeltoe turned the weapon on himself and blew his brains out, dying instantly.

"The cause of the shooting was jealousy."[12]

Although periodic explosions of physical violence could be blamed on the heat and humidity, the restrictions of incarceration, resistance to the immediate situation, and personality conflicts with authorities, one other source of serious psychological distress for many Chiricahuas was the loss of their traditional ways of worship. They were unable to perform sacred ancestral religious rituals that had been a mainstay of the culture since the time before time, as they had performed them in the years before imprisonment. Complicating this traumatic condition was the introduction of Christianity, a new religion for most of this generation of Apaches, who had probably listened to their parents' and grandparents' stories about the European Roman Catholics' efforts to impose their ways of worship years earlier.

W. H. Pearson, a Protestant minister and the post chaplain for Mount Vernon, wrote in February 1891, "Each Sabbath morning during the month, Sabbath School was held in the chapel which was largely attended." Pearson did not describe the congregants, many of whom probably were some of the students who returned as Christians from the Carlisle School. Curious Apaches at first sat respectfully in the pews, but the minister, probably exaggerating, reported that there was "a desire on the part of the men to marry in accordance with the customs of the Whites. This involved giving up their custom of polygamy and what is of equal importance, their custom of divorce."[13] Try hard as he did, though, he could not convince even one single Apache to follow the Protestant faith by participating in sacraments such as baptism and communion.

Of all the prisoners, Chihuahua seemed the most friendly toward Christianity and demonstrated his goodwill not to a Protestant minister, but to Father Henry O'Grady, pastor of the new St. Thomas Church, built in the town in early 1890. A formal dedication of the building was planned for the first Sunday in May. Blessing the new church was a local event that stirred public interest as far away as Mobile. Excursion train coaches left Mobile in midmorning and arrived in time for the eleven o'clock ceremonies. Following the mass and lunch, a number of visitors walked up the hill to the site of Apache incarceration, hoping to steal a glimpse of Geronimo and, not incidentally, to buy the Apache-made trinkets that had become popular.

At two o'clock that same afternoon the crowd returned to the church in town to witness the first baptism of an Apache child, Chihuahua's two-month-old son. The baby was named William St. Clair in honor of the former commandant of the prison camp, and his sponsors were two local citizens, a Thomas Rogers and his daughter Maggie. Records show that the child fell ill soon afterward and died.[14]

Other cultural mores from the surrounding society began to drift into the prisoners' community, in particular the concept of money for work. Shapard reports that "From the earliest days at Mount Vernon, one of the most frequently heard complaints among the prisoners concerned the lack of personal income. . . . [I]n St. Augustine they had made substantial profits selling their crafts to the tourists,"[15] and certainly at Fort Pickens Geronimo had been busy creating and selling his handiwork. In late 1890 Lieutenant William W. Wotherspoon, in charge of the prisoners at Mount Vernon, allowed four of the men and their wives to leave the post to work for wages on nearby farms. Three years later all of the healthy men willing and able to work were employed by the army or around the camp for thirty-five cents a day; Chihuahua became the janitor at the school, and Geronimo became the justice of the peace. He was paid ten dollars a month to enforce discipline among men and women.

To his credit, Wotherspoon was concerned about the unstoppable diseases afflicting almost all the Apaches and attributed most of the problem to the living arrangements in the prison camp. He believed that every one of the 362 prisoners was in danger and would become seriously ill if drastic measures to control the deadly infection in their midst were not taken. He decided that their existing log cabins had to be burned to the ground and a new village constructed on a more elevated level, with more exposure to the sun and circulating air. After Wotherspoon contacted Secretary of Interior John W. Noble and discussed the situation with him, Noble agreed and submitted a request to Congress in the amount of $41,500 for the fiscal year ending in June 1892, which included appropriations "for support and civilization of the Apache and other Indians that are now, or may be, located at Mount Vernon, Ala., for pay of necessary employees, including a physician, and for the rent of land for the industrial employment of said Indians, including the building of cabins. . . . For pay of an agent at said agency."[16]

Congress subsequently appropriated the funds, the War Department furnished building materials, and construction of the new settlement was begun. Labor was provided by forty-seven somewhat healthy Apache men whom Wotherspoon had convinced to enlist in Company I (for "Indian"), Twelfth Infantry, a unit he specifically created to provide the warriors with something to do and to put a few dollars in their pockets. More than likely, this was one of the first instances, if not the first, of Indian prisoners of war serving as armed soldiers in their own company while still imprisoned. Publicity about the unprecedented military action focused nationwide attention once again on the prisoners' circumstances, especially with regard to the effects of the unrelenting climate and the terrible sicknesses the Apaches suffered. Unable to manage the resultant adverse public reaction, the army ignored the news items and issued official U.S. Army uniforms and weapons to the Apache men. They immediately became occupied with regulation army drills and preparations related to building the new village.

An up-and-coming young army physician, Walter Reed, had been assigned to the prison camp and became quite vocal on the Apaches' behalf. His letters and monthly reports clearly show his developing concerns, particularly about the health of the children. Excerpts from several years of his letters and reports indicate his concern:

> [August 31, 1887] Relieving Ass't Surgeon J. H. Patzk, M.D. as medical officer on the 17th Inst., I found, at that time, a number of cases of lung & bronchial diseases affecting both adults and children, but more especially the latter.
>
> The cases of bronchial disease, largely confined to children under five (5) years of age, were chiefly due to exposure to the wet weather prevalent during the first half of the month.

. . . During the past ten days there have been under treatment a few cases of intermittent fever, all of which are now convalescing.

There have been three (3) births during the month. . . . [T]he hospital for Indian prisoners of war [is] located within the wall, consisting of three "hospital" and two (2) "wall" tents, properly floored. . . . It is believed that this hospital will answer every purpose for the treatment of serious cases.

[September 30, 1887] . . . The daily attendance at morning sick call has not exceeded five (5), as against a daily average of twelve (12) for the preceding month. Diarrhea, due to indiscretion in the diet of children and chronic lung diseases have contributed the majority of cases admitted to sick report. There have, also, been a few cases of intermittent fever. Three (3) children have died during the month, one (1) aged about 10 months of inflammation of the lung; one (1) 7 years of age of chronic diarrhea and ill-treatment on the part of mother, and one (1) aged 18 months, of pulmonary consumption.

. . . In this report I desire to respectfully call the commanding officer's attention to what I consider a deficiency in certain articles of the ration which these Indians are now receiving. I refer especially to sugar, coffee, beans, hominy, salt & soap. These articles, constituting a very important part of a ration, are, in my opinion, now issued in too small quantity. I feel sure that a full allowance of these would be of positive benefit to them. If it were possible, in addition, to issue occasionally onions and potatoes (articles which they have no means of procuring), a most excellent purpose would be served.

[November 30, 1887] . . . The following were the diseases most prevalent: intermittent fever 9, all adults; diarrhea 9, 1 adult and 8 children; pneumonia 4 children; bronchitis, acute 5 children. There were a few cases of constipation and muscular rheumatism in addition to the above enumerated. . . . It is believed that the ration now issued is adequate in all respects.

[December 31, 1887] . . . Bronchial affections have prevailed to a considerable extent, owing to the cold, wet weather. . . . Since the arrival of the Indian prisoners at this post on April 28, 1887, there have been twenty-one (21) deaths, of which two (2) were adult males, ten (10) adult females, and nine (9) children.

[May 31, 1888] . . . On the 23rd of May, a girl aged seven was admitted to sick report with an eruptive fever which was believed to be measles. As no cases, however, of this disease have been heard of in this vicinity, a positive diagnosis has been withheld. In the meantime, the girl's family has been removed from the main camp and quarantine established.

[July 31, 1888] . . . During the month there have been two (2) deaths, one an adult female aged about 50 of general debility & melancholia, and one (1) a female child aged about five (5) of convulsions.

[January 31, 1889] Although a large number have sought medical treatment, the affections have been, for the most part, of a trivial character. . . . The deaths were two: one adult male, aged about 40 years, the cause of death being consumption, and one child (female), aged about 3 years, the cause being tubercular ulceration of the bowels.

[March 31, 1889] . . . 3 births and 2 deaths, both children, one aged about 2 years and the other aged about 2 weeks. In both cases, death was caused by inflammation of the bowels.

[April 30, 1889] . . . 2 deaths, 1 adult female about 85 died of general debility and old age. 1 male child aged 2 years of "acute tuberculin meningitis."

[May 31, 1889] . . . [T]he health of the Apache Indian prisoners of war has continued satisfactory. Perhaps an exception to this statement should be made in the case of the young children, many of whom have been admitted to sick report for acute affections of the bowels. There have been four (4) cases of pneumonia among the children under three (3) years of age. There was one (1) birth during the month and one (1) death; the latter a male adult cause of death—old age and general debility.

[July 31, 1889] . . . [T]here were four (4) births during the month—two (2) deaths occurred, one (1) an adult male died of acute tuberculosis, and the other a child, aged about 9 months of chronic dysentery.

[August 31, 1889] . . . two (2) births and one (1) death, the latter a child about one year of age from chronic inflammation of the bowels.

[September 30, 1889] . . . three births during the month. Number of deaths was (6) six: the causes of death being as follows: consumption (2) adult females; obstruction of bowels 1 (adult female); convulsions 1 (female child, aged about 2 months); unknown 2 (female children, aged 2 and 8 months).

[November 1, 1889] . . . [D]uring the month ending this date, the health of the Apache Prisoners of War has not been as good as I have heretofore reported. In addition to the usual diseases of the bowels and skin, due to indiscretion in the matter of diet and lack of cleanliness, there has been an unusual number of bronchial affections. . . . [R]egret also to have to report that consumption has again taken hold of the Apaches. Last month there were two (2) deaths from consumption, both strong young women and this month's report shows one (1) death from the same cause (girl aged 13) and five (5) other cases under treatment; two (2) of the latter having been recently sent from the Carlisle School.

[November 30, 1889] . . . The deaths during the month have been as follows: pneumonia 2, (both young children); 6 consumption (one adult male and one adult female; poisoning 1. In the latter case, it is believed that the woman was given an overdose of an Apache medicine, although this could not be positively proven. As anticipated . . . the deaths have been caused by diseases of the lung. There are now under treatment five (5) cases of consumption, all of which will prove fatal.[17]

In the spring, summer, and autumn of 1889 Dr. Reed's reports showed increasing numbers of illness and death among the Apache adults and children. He expressed his concerns in writing about the many youngsters he was treating for acute disorders of the bowels and for pneumonia, as was his duty, but reading between the lines reveals his wish to help the Apaches more than he could at the time. Although preventive measures were instituted, such as building the new, uncontaminated homes, burning infected tents, issuing uncomplicated instructions regarding cleanliness, and policing the village daily to ensure compliance with sanitary measures, nothing seemed to reverse or even halt the continuing deaths.

In mid-November 1889 Reed submitted a long summary to headquarters in New York strongly recommending a change in climate for the Chiricahuas to put a halt to the lung diseases so harshly affecting them:

I am now convinced that the principal factor in the causation of pulmonary disease amongst the Apaches is the excessive atmospheric moisture which prevails along the Gulf and Atlantic coasts. . . . Already since their arrival they have lost more than one-tenth of their number from pulmonary disease. Add to this the large number of deaths due to the same cause amongst their children at

Carlisle, and the mortality from tubercular diseases becomes simply appalling: this too amongst a people who, in Arizona, were remarkably exempt from lung troubles.[18]

Throughout the prisoners' stay in Florida and now in Alabama tuberculosis and other serious respiratory ailments continued to infect them by contact with soldiers, students returning from Carlisle, and local citizens. At the end of 1889 and into 1890, 362 Chiricahuas at Mount Vernon were in danger of contagion. Although the numbers are not firm, it is believed that a total of 535 prisoners of war were initially removed from the Southwest and sent to Florida. Using these (possibly incorrect) counts, we can figure that 173 Apaches died during four years of incarceration from 1886 to 1890.

Reed's November 1989 special report to the assistant adjutant general corrected his previous impressions of the situation:

> In a letter dated June 12, 1889 . . . I had the honor to state that . . . the health of these Indians had improved at this post during the past two years and that their condition seemed to warrant the opinion that these Indians were at last shaking off the disease which had been such a scourge to them since their arrival on the Atlantic Coast—to wit: pulmonary consumption.
>
> A period of nearly six (6) months having lapsed since this report was made, I regret to have to state that this opinion was premature and not well founded. On the contrary, I deem it my duty to emphasize the fact that a change of location and climate is urgently needed for these people in order to stop the ravages of pulmonary disease.
>
> It may readily be imagined that such a number of rapidly fatal cases of disease would occasion anxiety and alarm amongst the Indians. Such is the case, to which is added, as a further cause of mental depression, the belief that the Government does not propose, in the near future, to improve their condition. The visit of the Division Commander in April last and his statement that he was authorized by the President to find them a home, followed by the visits of Reverend Harding, Professor C. C. Painter, and Captain Bourke, 3rd Cavalry, inspired the Apaches with the hope that they would soon be transferred to a larger reservation. Nearly eight months having elapsed, with nothing as accomplished as far as they can see, this feeling of hopefulness is rapidly subsiding. With little expecta-

tion of a change and with such a frequent occurrence of an incurable disease . . . the present condition of the Apache Prisoners of War cannot be said to be conducive to contentment.

In conclusion I beg to state that any reports that may have reached the Division Commander in that the Apaches are content to remain at Mount Vernon Barracks have no foundation in fact.[19]

President Cleveland, aware of the populace's continuing interest in the Indian prisoners, consented to find the people a more healthy, permanent place to live and tapped Captain John Bourke, a trusted acquaintance, to explore different regions of the country and make his recommendation. In a letter dated March 14, 1889, Bourke wrote,

I have the honor to submit the following memoranda in reference to the establishment of the Chiricahua Apaches upon some reservation where they may have an opportunity to work and attain the arts of civilization. . . . The following localities have been presented as possessing certain availability for the purposes of reservations for the Chiricahuas, and should, perhaps, be inspected with a view to determining just which one is best adapted.

1. Santa Rosa Island, Florida, near Pensacola, where there is said to be an abundance of land, a portion of which might be cultivated in semi-tropical fruits.[20]

2. Mount Vernon Barracks, Alabama, the present position, has a healthy climate and good water; the land is of no account whatever; shingle making and turpentine distillation are the most probable forms of industry.[21]

3. Fort Livingston, near New Orleans, Louisiana, said to be healthy and free from fever; a mile square or more of rich soil, adapted to the cultivation of every variety of farm products.

4. Fort Riley, Kansas. Climate excellent, soil fine, position central, but now occupied by the Cavalry School.

5. Fort McPherson, Nebraska, a large reservation, not suited for the growth of cereals, but an excellent hay-ground.

6 and 7. Fort Foote, Maryland, and Fort Washington, Maryland on the Potomac, below Washington, D.C., said to be malarious; neither has more than forty acres of land.

8. Hampton, Virginia, close to Fort Monroe; the records speak well for the salubrity of this place, and the Indian Normal School is here situated, and there are many advantages which present themselves to the most cursory examination.

I would respectfully recommend that each and every one of these places be carefully looked into; it would be well to inquire of the Chiricahuas themselves at Mount Vernon and ascertain their views; they may have learned some methods not known to me, by which, with a small amount of aid from the government, they may make their living at that point, although I am very much disinclined to believe in the possibility of such a thing. However, it would be proper to confer with them; they must earn their living by labor, and be contented. . . .

Santa Rosa Island and Fort Livingston are so near Mount Vernon that the one trip could include them all, without extra charge to the government, and the parties making the examination could with a very slight divergence, in returning, go to Fort Riley and Fort McPherson as well, if they be included in the scheme of inspection. The great objection to them is that the winter climate, especially of McPherson is at times, rigorous, but they are near to the Indian Territory, the ultimate destination of these, as well as all other aboriginal tribes. The law, at present, forbids the sending of wild Indians to Indian Territory, therefore, this may well be left out of consideration for the present. There are bands of Apaches already there, admitted before the passage of the law in question.[22] Hampton, Virginia, appears to my mind to be the place; the climate is equable, the well-disposed Indians would have the stimulus of civilization and could dispose of their farm-truck at profitable rates; their children could be sent to the school at that point and trained in handicrafts, and the presence of the garrison at Fort Monroe would act as a salutary check upon the refractory.

It has been urged that there is an element of colored population in this vicinity from which the Chiricahuas would be sure to obtain whiskey; the objection is a good one, but unfortunately, it obtains everywhere in our country. While I was with Mr. [Herbert] Welsh on his examination of Saint Augustine, Fla., General Ayres, the Commanding Officer, complained that his greatest trouble was to prevent intelligent tourists from giving whiskey to the Chiricahua Apaches; while I was last at San Carlos Agency, Arizona, all the vigilance of the military authorities failed to prevent Mexicans from smuggling in whiskey; consequently I attach no importance whatever to this objection, believing that no more liquor will be obtainable at Hampton than anywhere else. The Chiricahuas, men, women, and children, could be kept so busily employed learning trades (the importance of which they would be the first to recognize), that they would have very little time or inclination for debauchery.[23]

An integral part of Bourke's total assignment was interviewing the Apache headmen. He and Professor Charles C. Painter of the Indians Rights Association were charged with the task of ascertaining the leaders' views as to whether they preferred a life that was strictly agricultural or one that was partly agricultural and partly pastoral. By prior instructions the discussion was limited to

1. the locality to be selected east of the Mississippi;
2. the ability of the land to be developed;
3. the presence of a market for all that the Indians might be able to produce;
4. a healthy environment;
5. a place where no reasonable degree of objection could be voiced by the inhabitants; and
6. consideration of the Apaches' inclinations to any special form of labor.

Among the chiefs and headmen present at the discussion were Chatto, Chihuahua, Kay-e-tennay, Ramon, Noche, Naiche, Loco, Zele, Nana, Geronimo, and others—observers or participants—who were not identified. George Wratten translated from Apache into English; two interpreters named Patricio and José translated from Apache into Spanish, and Bourke translated from Spanish into English.

> *Painter:* The Secretary [of War] said we could look anywhere East of the Mississippi to find a home for you. We want to find a place healthy, with good land, opportunity to sell what you raise and make a home for yourselves . . . where you can live undisturbed, where you can be men and not Indians. We don't think there is any more room in this country for Indians, but there is room for men; no more land for hunting, but plenty for farming and making your living like the white men do. The old Indian road is all but shut up; the white man has built his railroads across it and the Indian road don't lead anywhere; it don't lead to any more game; it leads only to ruin . . . and your choice lies between utter annihilation on the one hand and the white man's civilization on the other.
>
> *Chatto* [noted warrior and army scout]: I know now for the truth that you know God's writing well, that you have read His Book well, else you couldn't talk to us in this way. God sees all things;

He sees you; He must have talked to you because you have talked so well—you understand His book so thoroughly. All of us are very thankful for your talk. It has made us all feel glad. You are right; it is true what you say about your farms; you can make your living by farming. . . . Besides a farm, if we had this grass-land, we could have some cattle and sheep; they could graze, get fat, and when large enough could be sold. I pray to God that we could once more have a farm; that someone would come to us to talk about it where we could raise cattle and crops; I pray for such a home every day.

Geronimo: I am glad to have heard your voice; I like to be like a white man. . . . I have walked in the white man's path for many days; I don't think I am an Indian any more. I think I am a white man. Look at my house and look at my clothes. We are all like white men, we are all behaving ourselves. . . . I'd like to have a good, big farm in a country where I could do something. I'd like to have you try and get it for us and we are willing to try and do what is right. When you come to a place that you think would be a good place for us, I would like to go with some of the Indians to see the place before we moved there and then I could tell you better how it would please us.

Chihuahua: It seems to me as if the earth is alive and is listening to all this talk. I know a great deal about God. I know that He is alive. He has heard this talk here today and I am glad of it. He has sent you here to talk for the people and I am glad of it. I want you to know that I have good thoughts in my head. I am glad to talk of going somewhere else. It is too hot here and there is not enough water. The ground is always thirsty. I have a family. I am very fond of them. I want the change made for their sake, as I know they'll burn up if they remain here.

Naiche: Three years ago . . . I thought I would follow in the footsteps of the white people; I saw the way they dressed, slept, ate, drank, and acted, and it seemed to me to be better than my own way. . . . At Fort Pickens I learned how to use tools, picks, spades, axes, saws to saw wood. I learned how to work. They told me that was the way to learn how to make a living. I've been longing for some one to talk to me as you have talked today. It seems as if we already had the farm, the talk has been so good. I would like to work and make my own living. I think about it every day, how hard I would work. I could buy my own clothes with money I would make myself. That's all I have to say.

Loco [Warm Springs Chiricahua Apache chief]: It's a long time since I first followed in the footsteps of the white people and I am still doing it, trying to be as much like a white man as I can. . . . I liked to be with the white people. My thoughts are more like those of a white man than an Indian. That's the reason I have been glad to grow old among them. I am so old and feeble now that I can hardly stand up. . . . I know that we can make a living off a farm, because I used to make my living farming . . . my son was taken five years ago to Carlisle school. If we get that farm, I'd like to have him sent back to me. I'd like him to come now if he could. He ought to have learned a good deal by this time, and I'll need him to help me on that farm, if we get it. I let him go to school because I thought I'd like to have him talk for me and write my letters for me, but I think he ought to be able to do all that now. I have four young relations at Carlisle. I want them well taken care of. If they get sick, let them have good doctors . . . but I want my son to come back to me now. That's all I have to say. I mean what I say. My tongue is not split.

Kay-e-tennay [noted Warm Springs Chiricahua Apache warrior]: Everything belongs to God and comes from God. The earth belongs to God. All that we wear and eat comes from God. You have no fear but all will think of what they have heard today. We've liked your talk. From today on we'll pray that though it may be hot, it may not be too hot for us. Though it may rain, there may not be too much water for us. Though the winds may blow, they may do no harm to us or our crops. . . . We would like to earn some money by our labor. . . . I would like to have some way of making money so I could take care of my family and feed and clothe them.

Nana [Warm Springs Chiricahua Apache chief]: What have I to talk about? They have all talked to you just as straight as that wall over there laid in brick and how can I say anything more? I am an old man and not going to last more than a couple of years longer.

Captain Bourke: I have known you people for just twenty years. . . . I used to think you would never come in off the warpath. . . . I want to see you get even better farms than those you owned at Camp Apache. . . . I am glad that you have learned how to use tools, because you now know how to go to work. . . . When you get on your farms and the Great Father sees that you are determined to do well, he will send your children to live with you and be instructed at home.

It is quite likely that a party of you will be permitted to go and examine the lands selected for you before the movement shall be made. . . . We have done all we could to speak clearly and have this matter fully explained to you.[24]

Many of the Apaches' comments were deliberate flattery, a skill honed in the earlier days of confinement. One cannot blame them for attempting to get into their captors' good graces, but Painter must to some degree be faulted for drawing a false distinction between Indians and "men." Even he, a sincere advocate for the Chiricahuas, fell backward into the dominant culture's stereotypical perception of Indians as less than human, as revealed in his language of colonialism. And Bourke's comment that the Great Father would send the Apaches' children back to them when they showed they could do well sounds like a veiled threat, one that reinforced the lopsided power relationship between captor and captive by implying that the government could hold the children hostage until it decided to release them. The entire statement was based on a false premise, however, and Bourke knew it: the children, ailing or healthy, were dropping out of Carlisle and returning to their parents even as he spoke. Despite the threat and the lie, Bourke wrote a report subsequent to the meeting and faithfully conveyed the essentials of what the Apache men expressed.

> They wanted a permanent home for themselves and children; they wanted an opportunity to get money for their labor, and not have to work any longer for nothing. Many of them had learned how to use tools—axes, hatchets, hammers, saws, spades, and shovels; all had built their own houses.
>
> They wanted to have their children sent back from Carlisle as soon as they themselves could be settled, and seemed to deplore deeply the terrible mortality at that school which had carried off twenty-seven out of one hundred and seven of their children. (There was at Mount Vernon during our visit, a young girl, about fourteen years old, just returned from Carlisle, who seemed to be far advanced in consumption, the seeds of which, I believe, were sewn in the damp, mouldy case-mates of Fort Marion.)
>
> They asked that a party be allowed to examine the lands selected before any action should be taken, and were promised that the propriety of such a measure should be urged upon superior authority.[25]

In the same letter, Bourke described the land he and Painter visited:

1. The country lying along the boundary of Georgia and Florida, and Florida and Alabama, is now attracting great and deserved attention. . . . Acres upon acres are laid out in pears which are shipped at remunerative rates to Chicago and New York. The water is exceptionally good—one spring being sixty-six (66) feet deep and (200) two hundred in diameter. Watermelons are raised in great quantity. . . . [W]e were informed that there was scarcely any sale of medicines [for fever and ague] in this section, but much was disposed of closer to the low-lands of the Mississippi. There are a number of tracts in this section which, if necessary, may be secured; one, of 5000 acres and one of 18,000 acres, and at as low a price as from $3 to $5 per acre.

2. The Cherokee country in the extreme Western part of North Carolina, in the Great Smoky Mountains, on the borders of Tennessee. . . . There are (1500) fifteen hundred Cherokees who own one hundred thousand acres, more or less. This land, though classed as mountainous, and hemmed in by high sierras . . . is cultivable to the tops of its loftiest hills. . . . The Cherokees have attained a high degree of advancement, live in houses, provided with many comforts, dress as white people, and are rapidly conforming to our habits. They have cattle, sheep, swine, and chickens. Orchards of peaches and apples, besides wild fruits in the greatest abundance. The valleys, where not tilled, are full of the vines of the wild grape, or fringed with the bushes of the black and other berries. Corn and potatoes, and all other kinds of vegetables, do finely. The waters are full of fish, and the speckled trout, although rarely caught close to the Friends school, is found in plenty towards the sources of the streams.

. . . It will be seen that should the Chiricahuas be established on the Cherokee land, they could get to work at once. . . . A small mill to cut wood and grind corn and wheat could be provided at a small cost and be a great benefit.

3. Bear Garden. This place . . . is accessible from Burgaw, a small station on the Atlantic Coast Line, 21 miles N. of Wilmington, N.C. . . . Heavy rains have visited all that region during the past three months, and the intervening country has been turned into a vast morass, swollen by over-loaded streams which flow into the East Branch of the Cape Fear river. In three places the road passed through water up to the mule's belly and changing depth only when it came into the buggy; one of these places was fully half a mile long.

Bear Garden contains between eight and ten thousand acres, and is about twelve miles long by an uncertain number wide. Most of it is virgin forest. Corn, cotton, peanuts, sweet and white potatoes, and other vegetables do well and the lumber, tar, and turpentine industries might be carried on profitably were the land drained and opened. There are no fruits to speak of on the place, the orchard of apple and peach trees having been allowed to die out; but, wild berries, grapes, and plums grow well in the swamps near by and could, beyond a doubt, be cultivated to advantage.

This district is classed as "malarious," but the people are generally healthy and robust and reach a great age. Consumption and rheumatism are rare, and good health would seem to be the rule.

4. Hampton, Virginia. It is a beautiful property, almost surrounded by salt water which yields a tribute of fine oysters. . . . The proximity of the Hampton School would be a great advantage. . . . In the Associated Press dispatches of late date there have appeared criticisms upon the cell used at Hampton for the incarceration of boys who got drunk and refuse to reveal the source from which they obtain whiskey. . . . The cell is built of stone, with cement floor, and closed by a door three inches thick, of double planking. . . . Ventilation is secured by eight holes in the door . . . covered with wire. . . . Regarding as I do the procuring of intoxicants by Indians as the most certain impediment to their advancement, I am not prepared to criticize the sternest measures which may be found necessary to prevent it.

I have the honor, therefore, to recommend that either the [Hampton] farm, or land on the Cherokee tract in North Carolina, be accepted for the settlement of the Chiricahua Apaches; in the former case, there would be small acreage, but great fertility, speedy returns upon produce, Hampton School for instruction, and Fort Monroe for discipline, if needed—and a contact with and stimulation by the highest form of American civilization.

In the latter, a greater area, of equally fine land, greater room for expansion, a more diversified industry, and equally certain, though perhaps slower return for products, and an intimate association with people of the same race and same habits of thought, sufficiently advanced in civilization to be a beacon-light to the new arrivals.

But, whichever of the two may be decided upon, I venture to submit the following recommendations:

1. The Chiricahuas should, for a time at least, be kept under military control and a small detachment of troops be kept near them, principally for moral effect, but also as a salutary check upon those who may not yield a unhesitating obedience to the new order of things.

2. This detachment should be supplemented by the enlistment as scouts of a small number of those who have already served faithfully and honorably in that capacity. Such enlistment, conditioned upon good behavior, would act as a reward, throw a small amount of money where it would do much good in extinguishing the embers of irritation caused by the loss of farms and property, and make the Indians feel that the reputation of the band depended greatly upon their own efficiency.

3. Send back the children from Carlisle.

4. Appoint the best one of these children interpreter upon the same salary as is now paid a white man; let the Indians see that the study of our language means something.

5. Let a suitable one of their own number act as trader; our present Indian tradership system is a blot upon our civilization.

If no Chiricahua can be found smart enough to buy wool hats for 25 cents apiece and sell them for $3.50 each, as I have seen the traders do in Arizona, the future of the band is dark indeed.

6. Let the administration of affairs, until all shall be arranged perfectly and in smooth running order, be kept under the direct personal supervision of the Secretary of War, or the General of the Army.

But, under any aspect of the case, I have no hesitancy in saying that the Chiricahua Apaches can be made self-supporting and law-abiding people in less than three years.[26]

Bourke spoke out of both sides of his mouth—one side threatened the Apaches vis-à-vis their children, and the other side told his superiors that he supported their desire to have their children returned. Given the history of the government's prior duplicitous dealings with the Chiricahuas, Bourke's transgression was trivial. Certain dishonest relations had always been part of the government's process in dealing with the Chiricahua Apaches. Deplorable outcomes were encouraged, sanctioned, and endorsed on the highest political and military levels. Years earlier the prisoners of war had been detained in Texas until the government decided what to do with them—allow them to continue on to Florida or dispose of them once and for all. The government's overt hostility toward these Indians was also obvious when it permitted them to fall ill and die in the steamy climates of the East rather than send them back to the Southwest, where they could recuperate alongside thousands of non-Indian tubercular sufferers. Such activities were dishonorable, to say the least, among representatives of a government that purportedly prided itself on upholding and practicing the moral principles of Christianity.

While government agents were exploring options, across the country public support for the Apaches had definitely reached flashpoint—a moment when a large number of Indian advocates and ordinary citizens insisted that the existing treatment of the Apaches could no longer be tolerated. It is possible that Dr. Reed found their situation so offensive that he resigned his position as their camp physician, although his biographer, William B. Bean, M.D., merely wrote that Reed felt "Mount Vernon was a stagnant backwater. So he asked for a four-month leave 'for business purposes . . . and also to enable [him] to avail [himself] of the opportunity of pursuing certain special studies in [his] profession.'"[27]

In a letter to the secretary of war, General Nelson Miles stated his thoughts about the Apaches and, true to form, about himself quite bluntly:

> I see it stated that you are going to make a visit to the Apache Indian prisoners at Mount Vernon, Alabama. I fear the fact of a great war minister visiting a band of cut throat savages would be unfavorably commented upon, not only by a hostile press, but even by journals friendly to the administration.
>
> I had made every arrangement in 1886 for the removal of those Indians . . . to some place where they would be self-sustaining and out of danger of resuming hostilities. They agreed to go to any place that I might designate [here he refers to the Apaches located at Camp Apache]. . . . At the same time the hostiles under Geronimo were hunted down and forced to surrender, and were also removed from the territory, yet when that was accomplished they were all taken out of my hands and ruthlessly banished to the fever stricken district of Florida and more than four hundred of them forced into a prison pen of less than an acre of ground where the commanding officer had already recommended that no more Indians should be sent there. From that day to this I have never been consulted or communicated with concerning the subject, except your very kind letter asking me to suggest some officer to be placed in charge of them.
>
> I have always regarded that part of their treatment, as cruel and unjust, and the officers who came back after transporting them to Florida openly stated they regarded it as simply brutal.

There appears to have been, during the past three years, efforts made on the part of certain persons to undo the good work accomplished and by hook or crook get them sent back to the mountains of Arizona where they would be a terror to the people of the country.

They are accustomed to a high altitude, having always lived in the mountains from four to eight thousand feet above the level of the sea, and, the pretense that they would be unhealthy in the bracing atmosphere of North Carolina is all nonsense. I have lived in North Carolina and Arizona and I know that the former is not an unhealthy locality, and I have no doubt but that they are at present in as healthy a locality as can be found, as it has always been regarded as a healthy resort. There ought not to be serious objection to their remaining there for a time or being placed with the Cherokees in western North Carolina, or put upon the military reservation of Leavenworth or Riley, Kansas. Any effort to move them where there would be any chance of their getting back to the mountains of Mexico or Arizona, will meet the most earnest protest of the entire populace and press of those territories as well as the entire west. While they should not be treated with cruelty or injustice, the fact should not be lost sight of that they are a body of the most cruel, treacherous savages on the continent. I presume there is scarcely a man among them whose hands are not red with innocent blood, and it is safe to say they have murdered more than three hundred men, women, and children within the past ten years. Chatto, one of them who makes the strongest protests of loyalty, was the leader of a raid in which ninety people were killed in seven days. A large number of them are under indictment now for murder and if an effort was ever made to send them back to Arizona, they would be immediately taken out of the hands of the military authorities and tried and hung, or killed without trial.[28]

Attuned to the immediacy of the situation, Redfield Procter, then secretary of war, sent a caveat to President Benjamin Harrison on January 13, 1890.

There have been two feasible plans submitted. 1st. The purchase, if authorized by Congress, of a tract of land in the mountainous region of western North Carolina, or in one of the adjacent states. 2nd. Their removal to some point in the Indian territory. However, Section 3, Chapter 87 of the Laws of 1879 provides: "And the President of the United States is hereby directed to prohibit the removal of any portion of said tribe of Indians (Indians of New Mexico and

Arizona) to the Indian Territory, unless the same shall be hereafter authorized by an Act of Congress."

If Congress will grant the necessary authority, I recommend, therefore, that these Indians be transferred to Fort Sill in the Indian Territory [in Oklahoma], with a view to their final settlement on the Kiowa, Comanche, and Apache Reservation, provided satisfactory negotiations can be consummated with these confederated tribes to that end. The military Reservation of Fort Sill comprises thirty-six square miles and is located with this Indian Reservation.[29]

So it would take literally an act of Congress to relocate the Chiricahua prisoners from Alabama to Oklahoma. As this new idea was being considered and debated in Washington, life continued routinely at Mount Vernon. Lieutenant Wotherspoon, in charge of the Indian prisoners on May 31, 1891, sent a progress report to the post adjutant. The census count showed 305 men, women, and children, not counting the 47 Apache men who had enlisted in the army. Wrote the lieutenant,

> The moral condition of the prisoners has been good, drunkenness has decreased in a very marked degree since the sellers of liquor have been under bonds; gambling, at least in public, has ceased. The experiment of introducing our sports, such as baseball and foot-ball, occupying their attention and superseding their own games, has been a great success. Work has progressed satisfactorily on the Indian village; fifty-six houses have been built with the exception of the flooring, chimneys and setting windows. The delay in building the chimneys has been due to the rising of the price of brick in Mobile to so high a figure as to make the chimneys cost more than estimated for. An arrangement has been made with a mason to build them in part from brick taken from old foundations and walls on the reserve, and work will progress. All the work on the houses has been done by Indian labor with the exception of the superintending carpenter (a white man); they have shown skill and intelligence in using tools and their work is very creditable.
>
> The Indian school has been open daily during the month, the Misses Shepard still remaining in charge of it; the attendance has been good and the intelligence of the children marked.[30]

Another report more than one year later listed 343 prisoners, not including the Indian soldiers, but counting new arrivals—46 non-Chiricahua Indians who were sent to the Alabama site from Forts Wingate and Apache. Thirty-one children had been born during the past year, and thirty-nine adults and children had died. Had the deceased Indian soldiers been included in the count, the deaths would have amounted to forty-five. Wrote Wotherspoon,

> Tuberculosis seems to be the most fatal amongst them, and shows little, if any, tendency to decrease. The people have had the benefit of constant attendance by skilled medical officers; their habitations and mode of living have been improved; and every attention has been paid to the sanitation of their surroundings. . . . I do not believe its prevalence here to be due to climatic influences, though the warmth and dampness may make it more difficult to eradicate. Almost any climate to which they might be changed would be equally detrimental to them, for it is simply out of the question that they should be sent back to the dry, hot climate of Arizona and New Mexico. . . . In my opinion, the death rate amongst these people is due to their low physical condition, to long neglect of sanitary measures and constant intermarriage and general degeneracy.
>
> . . . The greatest attention has been paid the cleanness of the houses, they being frequently and minutely inspected. Personal cleanliness has been aided by the construct of a large swimming or bathing tank, and a number of steam bath houses (sweat houses). Tubs, scrubbing boards and soap have been provided for washing of clothing and whenever a death occurred in any house, it has been closed and carefully disinfected by fumigation. The results, so far as the cleanliness of the men and children, the village, bedding and surroundings are concerned, have been most satisfactory. . . . I would therefore deprecate any agitation of the question of removing these people for the present; it would only tend to make them discontented and uneasy, and I cannot see in what way any change would be beneficial to them. They are well fed, well clothed, housed in comfortable dwellings, and, in my opinion, making steady progress. Their health condition is due more to hereditary and physical degeneracy than to any climatic condition, and the full benefits of the improved conditions under which they are living should be given a fair trial.
>
> . . . During the year a great improvement is noticeable in the matter of intoxication amongst the prisoners, due to the arrest and punishment of persons selling liquor to them. The vice of gambling has been checked in great degree by the punishment of all those caught indulging in it.

The industry, skill, and cheerfulness of the Indians cannot be too highly commended. They have been steadily at work for the twelve months past, with the best results. During that time they have almost by their unaided labor built their village of between seventy-five and eighty houses, laid out in streets with plaza. They have also built a set of company barracks for the Indian soldiers, houses for the interpreter and superintendent, a guard house, a store and issue house, bath house, swimming tank, addition to the hospital and have cultivated with skill and good results one garden and many small ones. About one hundred shade trees were planted and many days' work were devoted to leveling the ground for the village, cutting the trees, removing stumps, etc. This work was done by the Indian soldiers almost exclusively, and in addition to their regular drills, target practice, and school. Marked skill was shown in the use of tools and the buildings are most creditable specimens of work.

. . . A marked change in the past year in the mode of living and preparing food is to be noticed. Before the completion of the new village, most of the people slept upon the ground or on boards laid upon the ground. They cooked their food on open fires, and habitually sat on the ground. The way in which they used the flour ration was considered by the surgeon as particularly injurious to the children, and much sickness resulted from these two causes. They now all have bedsteads made by themselves; cook their food for the most part on cooking ranges, and serve it on tables, sitting upon chairs and stools made by themselves. Their flour ration is baked for them and regularly issued. Their houses are neat and in some cases pride is shown in this neatness and some attempts at decoration.

. . . The water for the village is obtained from four bored wells, varying in depth from 42 to 82 feet. The labor of getting water from this depth by small hand pumps is very great, and the time required so great, that only an inadequate supply is obtained. A large well with some kind of power pump, preferably a simple steam pump, which an Indian could run, with a tank, is very much needed.

Owing to the number of Indians sent here from the west during the year (46), and to the fact that the village was constructed for only those here at the time, there is not sufficient room to house all in the new village; consequently there are five families living in the log huts of the old village, exposed to all the dangers of its unsanitary condition and location. Estimates have been made for these buildings; but the state of the appropriation seems never to warrant the expenditure called for. I venture to say it never will as long as money for these Indians must be taken from the regular army appropriation, in which no special provision is made for them.

. . . The cost of maintaining these people here is very difficult to fix, as no prices are, as a rule, given for clothing supplied them and the cost of transportation is difficult to ascertain, for the same reason any comparison with previous years is impossible. Efforts will be made to get the data for a report on this subject, to be submitted at some future date.[31]

This report contains a mixture of a fair assessment and bias as indicated in the language of colonialism. Wotherspoon apparently subscribed to the same school of thought as did educator Pratt—for example, in the belief that the prisoners' poor health was owing to heredity, bad habits, and physical degeneracy—in direct contradiction of several reports submitted by Dr. Reed. However, the medical situation occurring among the Chiricahua Apache prisoners of war cannot be blamed exclusively on the factors that Pratt, Wotherspoon, and even Reed name in their interpretations and conclusions. Rather, it was caused by a combination of external circumstances—in particular confinement, an unfamiliar diet, and exposure to diseases—that were out of the Apaches' control and that conspired to affect the people adversely throughout the years of their confinement.

If the observers writing reports had taken a moment to consider carefully the Apaches' life in freedom, each would have recognized that the Apaches had been a vital and strong people, well fed with wild game and edible plants, with ancient cultural customs that reflected a healthy lifestyle in the open high desert air free of contagious ailments. The writers' biased statements served no purpose other than to denigrate the Apaches and reinforce artificially the white culture's image and opinion of itself. But, then, the jailers' responsibility was only custodial, and compassion need not be included. They were the keepers of a group of Indians who had been a ferocious, unrelenting enemy of the United States. When that past history is taken into consideration, superior attitudes and opinions take on an aura of legitimacy, as does the need to express them. However, through years of personal contact with Chiricahuas of all ages, both Pratt and Wotherspoon knew better, as did a few army officers who spoke out.

For example, Captain Marion Maus was an army officer familiar with the Apaches in their days of freedom. He was asked for his opinion regarding the upcoming relocation. In correspondence typed on the letterhead of the Headquarters Department of the Missouri, located in Chicago, Maus wrote to a Major George W. Davis, an officer assigned to the office of the secretary of war, on September 15, 1894.

> I have just returned from the west. So far have heard nothing about what they will do regarding those Indians. If they are going to move them you know it ought to be done at once, as it will soon be getting cold weather. They could pack up and move to the Territory in about ten days if it is decided to make the move.
>
> There are some very excellent pieces of land on the Indian Reservation near Sill where good water, and, I believe, good farming allotments could be given them, and where their condition would be much improved.
>
> It would be absolutely impossible, in my opinion, for these Indians to escape from that reservation, as the large body of them who are peaceable, loyal and inclined to conduct themselves properly, would do their duty, and I feel sure they would give information at once of any intention to escape. The distance to the Mescalero agency is very long, as you know, and with telegraphic communication and the assistance of the civil authorities I believe they could be easily caught should they make such an attempt. However, I am confident they are willing to remain where the Government will send them and try to improve their condition. They certainly ought to be moved. Many of them are enfeebled by disease. Forty-one, who are soldiers, will have the right of citizens to go where they choose when discharged; of the remaining (twenty-two I believe), less than half are, by reason of age and infirmity, unable to give trouble.
>
> One great reason why they should go to the Indian Territory is that they will be among their own race, or kindred races; in fact, quite a number of Apaches live near Fort Sill.[32] They would be less troublesome or objectionable to white people than at any other point and would be removed from the worst influence (that of liquor) which it would be impossible for them to obtain there, and which has, in fact, been, in almost every case, the cause of trouble among them. Those that have been rendered worthless have generally been addicted to drink which they can easily obtain where they are.
>
> I would like very much to see these Indians located, and I am well acquainted with most of them, believe that I could be of service in their location. A large number of them served as scouts under me, and a large number of them surrendered to me in Mexico.

No doubt the press of Arizona and other states will object to the transfer of these Indians anywhere. . . . They will circulate all sorts of stories about them, and what they will probably do, and in this way might influence the authorities regarding their removal at this time. If they are not moved now it is possible that the appropriation may eventually be lost or some legislation passed which will prevent their removal at all.[33]

After nearly eight years of bureaucratic ado and dozens of letters from the citizenry stating dozens of opinions, Fort Sill was eventually chosen as a more healthful home. In Oklahoma their prisoner-of-war status would not change. They would still be under the supervision of the army, but they would be physically confined to a larger area of the country and able to roam at will across the military reserve, circumstances that were expected to be more conducive to their well-being. Civilian government officials, the military, civic organizations such as the Indian Rights Association, the Boston Indian Citizenship Committee, and the Chiricahua Apache people themselves agreed on the Fort Sill site. On September 18, 1894, the action became official, and the army drew up orders for transfer. As part of the "closing out" procedures, it also prepared lists with information about some of the prisoners.

According to one unsigned military review and evaluation, the following Chiricahua men had a "disposition to improve" their records: Geronimo, Chihuahua, La-zi-yah, Kay-ih-tah, Bah-ga-do, Zee-le, Artis. Certain Apache soldiers were also included in the category: Naiche, Fatty, Nana, Nah-do-zin, Kay-dah-zinne, José First, Tzo-zonne, Chatto, Tiss-nolth-tos, Dominick, and Dah-ke-ya.

The next classification was listed as "Apache Indians surviving who were captured by General Miles in 1886, and their families." Brief comments accompanied the names:

Geronimo. Has been a good man while a prisoner. Age 60 years. One wife and five children. 1 boy over 12; 1 boy grown and one daughter married. Total number of children 5. His daughter is married to Dah-ke-ya, soldier, and has 2 children. Geronimo also has 2 sisters, 1 married and the other not. He is Justice of the Peace and does well. Has influence as such.

Naiche. Soldier. A good man since a prisoner. Has two wives, six children under 12; one boy and girl over 12, both at school, the boy at Hampton, the girl at Carlisle. Total children 8. Has two sisters, both are married. His mother is alive and with him.

Mangus. 1 wife and 2 children under 12. 1 son nearly grown who is married. Mangus has been a good and reliable man since he surrendered.

Perico. Soldier. Has been an excellent man since his capture. Has 1 wife and 2 children under 12.

Ya-n-zha. Soldier. A drinker but harmless. Has one wife but no children.

Tiss-nlth-tos. Soldier. A good man but drinks. Has one wife and one child.

La-zi-yah. Can carry a gun but not able to do much hard work; hands crippled. Has one wife.

Be-she. Old but ablebodied; industrious. Has 1 wife and 2 daughters, both married.

Chapo. Geronimo's son. Has returned from Carlisle; is now very sick in the hospital. Character "fair."

Hunlona. Now at Carlisle School.

Zhonne. Now at Carlisle School.[34]

Lists that enumerated selected men's character traits and the Apache soldiers' habits were also drawn up. No women and children were mentioned by name or described in the written material that accompanied the Chiricahua Apaches to their newest prison camp.[35]

A congressional memorial, sponsored by S. M. Brosius of the Indian Rights Association, stated the situation succinctly. "After a year's confinement at Forts Marion and Pickens, these Indians were transferred to Mount Vernon Barracks, Ala. The band was decimated so rapidly by the ravages of tuberculosis in that damp climate, it was decided to remove them, and under authority of Congress (act of Aug. 6, 1894, 28 Stat., 238) they were settled within Fort Sill Military Reservation, Okla., and told that they would not be moved again."[36]

5.
Fort
Sill

BY 1894 CONTAGIOUS DISEASES had stolen the lives of nearly 50 percent of the Apache prisoners in Florida and Alabama; the small number of surviving births in no way compensated. Something had to be done. In the autumn of that year the governmental and military authorities held hope that the decision to transfer the Chiricahuas to Oklahoma would aid their recovery and, not incidentally, demonstrate the government's goodwill.

On October 4, 259 healthy and sick men, women, and children were loaded onto ten passenger train cars—destination Oklahoma. Freight cars followed containing their baggage and most of the dismantled wooden structures that had been their homes. As a cost-saving measure, the Alabama lumber was to be used to reconstitute a new village at Fort Sill. Unhappily, fate disrupted the good intentions.

While standing on a sidetrack in New Orleans, the freight cars caught fire. When the blaze was extinguished, about eighty of the Apaches' disassembled homes and most of their earthly goods had literally gone up in smoke in the rail yard of the Louisville and Nashville Railroad. Burned beyond use were doors, window sashes, garden tools, several hundred pounds of clothing, and some stoves, along with the log walls of their former homes.

After a delay to assess the damage, the journey continued. Escorted by the Chiricahua soldiers from Company I, Twelfth Infantry, under the command of Lieutenants Allyn Capron of the Fifth Infantry and W. Ballon (also known as Ballou) of the Twelfth Infantry, the Apaches at last detrained at Rush Springs, about twenty miles from Fort Sill. Great pots of food, freshly cooked at the rail siding by military personnel, welcomed the prisoners, as did a delegation of neighboring Comanches and Kiowas. Horses and wagons had been lined up and were waiting to give the newcomers a ride to the fort. The Apaches hated wagons because of their resemblance to coffins, so quite a few chose to walk the distance. Others shrugged off their distaste and rode with sick relatives and friends. Based on his interview of Chief Loco, Shapard indicates that "Since the Apaches were superstitious of death, they would take the box section off the springs, and ride on the frame."[1]

The local press of the day reported that the "white people of the area . . . were unreconciled" to the presence of the Chiricahuas. The editor of the *Mingus Minstrel* wrote, "Yes, here we go to see the king of murderers and prince of firey destruction now made glorious by the sentimental adulation of insane freaks and misguided philanthropists. The old devil Geronimo should have been hung fifteen years ago."[2]

If the objecting Oklahomans had been afforded an opportunity to mingle with the Apaches and observe the earnestness with which some of them now faced their future, they might have changed their minds. For example, interpreter George Wratten built a trading post at Fort Sill and hired some of the younger Chiricahuas as helpers. Eugene Chihuahua was one of the youths who worked for Wratten. Said Chihuahua, "From words on boxes and bags [Wratten] taught me to read. He taught me how to write by making lists of things. And he taught me how to count and make change. I wanted to know those things that those children who were sent to Carlisle were being taught, and Mr. Wratten helped me to do that. George said to me, 'From now on I will speak English to you and you ask me what I mean if you don't understand.' After that I learned English rapidly."[3]

Charles LeBaron, a private physician under contract with the government, accompanied the Apaches from Mount Vernon to Fort Sill. In his first report to Lieutenant Hugh L. Scott,[4] the officer in charge of the Apaches, the doctor wrote, "Only one new case of sickness developed on the trip and this was due to imprudent eating. The sick stood the trip exceedingly well—one birth occurred on the train while passing through Texas (mother and child well). It is my opinion that the 24 hours they have been here has made an appreciable improvement in their spirits. They seem more bright and cheerful than usual and many have expressed to me their pleasure at being here."[5]

One month later two written updates were submitted to Scott. The first was a note about medical progress from the post surgeon, Fitzhugh Carter, listing seventy-one cases of illness treated in thirty days. In his notes Dr. Carter remarked, "A large percentage of the cases are ordinary 'bad colds' (classified as nasal and bronchial catarrh). These have been due

Chiricahua Apache prisoners of war at Fort Sill, Oklahoma, n.d. PHOTO COURTESY OF FRISCO NATIVE AMERICAN MUSEUM AND NATURAL HISTORY CENTER.

probably to the exposure incident to establishing them in camp. The cases . . . have been confined to almost entirely the younger children."[6]

The next report, written by Ballon at the same time, was general in its content:

The prisoners were transferred from Mt. Vernon, Ala. to this post, arriving here Oct. 4, 1894. Since that date the able bodied have been busily engaged in necessary preparations for the coming winter . . .

The general health has been good. . . . In my opinion, council wall tents without hoods and the brush arbors that these people skillfully construct, are far more conductive to health than houses are—One reason for this is the extreme difficulty met in the attempt to have houses kept ventilated and a second may be found in the fact that the "vick-i-up" can be burned once a month and its site thoroughly disinfected.

It may not be uninteresting or untimely to now mention some of the significant features made prominent during the last month as a result of the recent change of location of these people. In the first place they were displeased with the climate and their natural surroundings—natives of the mountains, the low, damp, wooded country was disliked. Trifles, from a white man's standpoint are often momentous to the Indian, and the Apache can not love a land where he can not jerk beef. On the other hand the present location is looked upon with favor and instead of the "Mucho malo" that formerly answered the query as to how the country was liked, the answer now is "mucho bueno" or "mucho contente–me."

In this success I foresee an element of success not to be despised. Again, at Mt. Vernon the Indian was of necessity—a pauper—subject to the same influences and vices as other paupers. Now it is to be hoped that an opportunity to become self-supportive will be afforded him. But beyond this I place the advantage that is gained by his removal from consistent contact with his worst enemy, whiskey.

The Chiricahuas can not drink moderately, but is always in trouble when an opportunity offers to indulge his appetite. In August last, the guard post shows eight persons of both sexes punished for offenses coupled with drunkenness—Not one for an offense when not drunk. It is probably safe to say that twice that number were reprimanded or suffered slight punishment for simple offenses of a less degree.

During the month of Oct. no punishments were awarded and no one was suspected of having touched intoxicating liquor. I think this fact if sustained by future experience, will double the efficiency of these Indians as laborers, and lessen by half the labor of superintending them.

On the other hand there are dangers to be guarded against— one of the greatest in my opinion being the discontent of these people at being required to work and wear the garb of civilization, while surrounded by great numbers of idle Indians, painted and blanketed and supported by the government and with no necessity for becoming self sustaining.

There will be necessary such results of labor and as will convince even the Indians that labor and civilized ways are best.

On the rolls (Oct. 1st, 1894): 17 men, 126 women, 70 boys, 46 girls. Total 259. Born in Oct. 1 boy, 2 girls. Total 3. Died in Oct. 1 girl. On rolls Oct. 31—17 men, 126 women, 71 boys, 47 girls. Total 261.[7]

The issue of liquor and drinking had haunted the Chiricahuas from their first contact with it on the Spanish colonial frontier. During the 1700s and until the middle of the 1800s, Jesuits and Franciscans had attempted to indoctrinate the Apaches into Christianity at the many Catholic missions scattered all across the Mexican states of Sonora and Chihuahua. Sacramental wine was an essential of the Catholic mass, and the Apaches, unfamiliar with the Europeans' liquor, took to it immediately. Although it cannot be shown definitively that access to the wine was one of the church's deliberate enticements to indoctrination, an informed guess would conclude just that. Unfortunately, the Apaches' relationship with liquor escalated quickly from the first taste of communion wine to the present-day high rates of consumption.

Ballon's "idle Indians" referred most likely to the Kiowas and Comanches who lived around the fort and received government subsidies. He worried that the Apaches would react negatively to the different and harsher standards set for them as compared to their Indian neighbors, but, being happy to be out of the hot and humid Southeast, the Apaches had no intention of acting up.

Shortly after reading Dr. Carter's report, Scott wrote a long letter to the assistant adjutant general on November 7, 1894, conveying the general circumstances at Fort Sill and his hopes for the future of the Chiricahuas.

> They went into camp about one mile from the Post under canvas borrowed from the post troops and companies because none of the articles ordered here for their use began to arrive until long after they did. The site of the future village has been pronounced to be a good one by all who have seen it, and has every advantage except the very necessary one of good water—it is proposed to remedy this, however, by laying the pipe ordered from Fort Supply.
>
> The Indians are encamped in the timber for the winter. . . . Lieuts. Ballon 12th and Capron 3rd Infantry, two energetic and capable young officers are on duty with superintending work and generally caring for the wants of company and prisoners. The only strictly military duty required of the company is to furnish a guard of 3 men and a non-com'd officer—which is always on duty guarding valuable property and prisoners in the guardhouse and is ready to put down any lawlessness in camp before it can gain headway.
>
> The prisoners are counted twice each day. They are given every reasonable liberty but with members of the company are usually at work getting out stone-filling lime and cutting and hauling timber for their own benefit.
>
> The purchase of any material from the especial fund has been suspended pending a decision upon the ruling of the Quartermas-

ter General to the effect that all expenses connected with these Indians must be defrayed from this fund—this ruling would seem to be misconstruent with the Act of Congress making the appr'n and appropriating the above same for their settlement—in addition to other uses.

As their current expenses last year aggregated over $2000, it is difficult to perceive how they can be . . . moved and settled with a much smaller sum.

An argument is being prepared asking for a reconsideration of this ruling. In the meantime no purchases can be made. . . .

Requisition will be made for a new supply of clothing as soon as it is determined where it shall come from.[8]

There are 56 children of school age in the camp. The Mass. Assn. which furnished two teachers for them while at Mt. Vernon has informed me thro' its chairman that it will no longer continue this practice.

Negotiations were entered into and agreement made with the Agent of the Kiowas and Comanches to have these children placed in the (Gov't) Kiowa school at Anadarko (23 miles), since . . . an offer has been made at Anadarko to receive them. . . .

Pains were taken before the arrival of the Apaches to prepare the Kiowas and Comanches for their coming and to create a friendly feeling in advance—this feeling is being strengthened in every possible way and now seems to be of the best—otherwise it would be impossible for the Apaches to remain in this country.

There is a large plain in the military reserve between Cache and Medicine Bluff about 1/4 to 1/2 mile wide and two miles long. As soon as the mules ordered from Fort Supply arrive, it is proposed to break up the sod over as large an area of this plain or creek bottom (which contains some of the most arable land in the territory) as we can cultivate—to fence it—sow it with oats which is an early crop and usually matures before the coming of the hot winds and make an effort to fill the oat contracts at this post and Fort Reno— no mules have yet arrived and it is probable that the first season will pass before the soil can be properly prepared for a crop.

It is believed that the main [illegible word] of these Indians must be in the raising of cattle—there are 36 sq. miles on the military reserve for them to graze over and especial effort will be made to save every dollar in the construction of buildings purchase . . . in order to purchase as many cattle as possible. This policy was verbally submitted to the Dep't. Commander and it is believed to have met with his approval.

It will not be practicable to purchase these cattle before next spring for the reason that they would require to be driven in and located which must be done in the summer time otherwise the driving, etc. would bring about a great loss by death. Another reason wd be that it would not be fully known what amount of money will be available for this purpose until the buildings are furnished and paid for.

If the proper policy is carried out, it is likely that a sufficient number of ponies will be presented to the Apaches by the Kiowas and Comanches—this will in itself assist in cementing their friendship.

At present the Apaches seem to be delighted with the change from Mt. Vernon Barracas—their conduct since arrival has been excellent—they are improving in health already and are looking forward to an industrious and happy future.[9]

The prisoners spent the winter of 1894, an exceptionally harsh one, living out of doors in hastily constructed traditional wickiups made of branches, boards, and tarpaulins provided by the military; several of the weakest tribal members died from exposure to the cold, and many others became ill with upper respiratory infections.

In the spring of 1895 the healthiest men built seventy-one homes. They felled timber, available some twenty-five miles away, and transported load after load by horse and buggy to the military post. Twelve small villages, in various stages of construction and development and scattered across twenty-five thousand acres of the western end of Fort Sill, soon were on the map, each settlement headed by a leader chosen by his followers to be responsible to the army for all the activities in the immediate vicinity.[10] Geronimo, Loco, Chihuahua, Naiche, Chiricahua Tom, Alfred Chato, Rogers Toklanni, Carl Mangus, Jacob Kayahtenny, Leon Perico, George Noche, and Martin and Kayitah headed up the separate settlements.

The wooden-picket homes built by the Apache men contained only two rooms—one for cooking and one for sleeping—connected by a breezeway. Each room had two doors and tile chimneys. Outdoor living was the rule, weather permitting, and it suited the Apaches perfectly.

Each family was expected to farm ten acres—eight of Kaffir corn, one of garden crops such as melons and sweet potatoes, and one of cotton. Farming took the men out into the open where their lungs breathed in clean air and where the sun warmed their bodies and hearts. Skinner points out that "The immediate concern was not the growing of food for the captives, but the providing of food for mules and horses used as work animals. At first only a few work animals were provided . . . [and] were passed from village to village, causing plowing and planting to sometimes be slow. . . . Herds of cattle were purchased as soon as the Apaches could provide for the cattle. It was agreed that in the future the Indians would repay the War Department for the cattle. During 1895, about 900 cattle were issued."[11]

But before the cattle could arrive, preparatory chores were required. Able men cut fenceposts, dug postholes, and stretched the fence wire. Some seventy thousand acres had to be enclosed lest the cows stray onto the adjoining land that belonged to the Kiowas and Comanches, and ill will arise among neighbors. When fencing was completed—a job made more difficult because the men were on foot as they had no horses yet—the Apaches next dug watering holes, located strategically in areas where the small streams could be dammed so as to form ponds for the livestock; some of these tanks—as they are called—were as large as twenty acres across.

The men quickly adapted to the physical activity, and a measure of good health returned to those not seriously ill. A few energetic Apaches hiked all over Fort Sill to find stray cattle or to repair fences. During the summer months the men formed small groups to cut and bale hay, portions of which were set aside for families' livestock and the surplus sold to the army. Any monies received as payment were put into an "Apache fund" and used to purchase additional farm implements, equipment, and more communal livestock.

The Apaches were pleased with the arrangement because this lifestyle of sharing and working together was similar to their ancestors' hunting-gathering ways. Washington authorities were happy with the reports of positive accomplishments.

As noted in chapter 3, on November 1, 1895, J. D. Glennan, an assistant army surgeon who provided medical care to the prisoners, wrote an annual report to the surgeon general. During the first year of their incarceration in Oklahoma he treated 655 individuals, of which the majority, 349, were children, 178 were women, and 128 were men.

> During the year twelve children were born and thirteen died. The causes of this mortality are such as obtain among all Indians—bad and improper food and exposure—added to the tubercular infection common among the Apaches.
>
> The principal cause of the death rate, and of the diminishing numbers [of all the prisoners] has been tubercular diseases.

Chiricahua Apache children prisoners of war at Fort Sill, ca. 1913.
Left, *Mildred Imach Cleghorn.* Right, *Myrtle Cleghorn.*
PHOTO COURTESY OF FORT SILL NATIONAL HISTORICAL LANDMARK.

They have lived under canvas, and during the greater part of the year, the camp has been on a hill, open to plenty of air and sunshine, well policed, and, as far as possible, cases of phthisis have been isolated and disinfection of sputa practiced.

Many cases of pulmonary tuberculosis do not seem to be originating here [at Fort Sill]. . . . [O]nly two cases have been under treatment which were not treated before being removed to this post. Records of cases of pulmonary and laryngeal tuberculosis show that twelve prisoners [ten women and two children] arrived ill with the disease from Mount Vernon, three males were transferred from the Carlisle School in advanced stages of tuberculosis, and two new cases were newly diagnosed at Fort Sill. Of these seventeen, ten died and seven were still living at the time of this report.[12]

Dr. Glennan's year-end summary also noted that "bad and improper food and exposure" added to the unusually large incidence of tuberculosis among the prisoner population, but he failed to mention the specific gastrointestinal effect of these foods or to connect it to the respiratory problems. Even though the prisoners received the same type and roughly the same amount of rations issued to the soldiers, the variety of Euro-American foods and their preparation were physiologically foreign to Apache bodies and caused much physical distress.

Until the 1886 surrender the Chiricahuas had lived a hunting and gathering lifestyle, eating foods high in animal protein and fat as well as fresh natural foods that were metabolically compatible and well suited to their excellent physical health. Earlier sporadic and limited ancestral contact with Europeans and Mexicans on the Spanish colonial frontier had introduced foods high in carbohydrates and sugars into their diet, which caused random complaints at the time. However, under the artificial conditions of confinement in Florida, Alabama, and Oklahoma with its forced dietary change, the Apaches ate each day what was provided; some of the government rations were so physiologically disruptive that digestive disorders resulted. No doubt the struggling of their bodies to process and accommodate the unfamiliar nutrition lowered their resistance to disease in general, and then opportunistic diseases such as respiratory afflictions galloped in and caused life-threatening situations.

Coupled with the contagion, access to alcohol and its abuse contributed to debilities and demoralization. At Fort Sill this situation improved, as noted in a December 11, 1895, report to the adjutant general of the army from George M. Sternberg, a physician employed by the War Department.

An important element in the improvement and prosperity of these people has been the prevention of access to alcoholic liquors. They have not been allowed access to the post exchange bar, and their distance from the reservation line, and the vigilance of the officer in charge, have prevented whiskey peddlers from reaching them. No case of alcoholism has occurred. They lead regular lives, working steadily in the open air, with a prospect of homes and property interests ahead, all of which is conducive to cheerfulness and good health.

I think that their condition already shows the wisdom and humanity of their removal to this territory.[13]

Although Sternberg's optimism regarding the Chiricahuas' sobriety seems well founded, digestive diseases were increasing, and tuberculosis was still the cause of many deaths. These serious medical conditions oddly were not mentioned in a long report Major Maus made to the War Department on December 23, 1895.

About one year ago the Apache Prisoners were all transferred to Fort Sill, and in every respect their condition is greatly improved. The climate is dry and salubrious. They have, or will, as soon as a few more are erected, comfortable houses, one for each of the 70 odd families in groups of 4 to 6, on the Military Reservation, scattered over many miles' extent of the beautiful hill and valley country, west of the post. The soil is fertile, promising good crops of corn, especially of the South African variety,[14] which has recently been introduced with marked success in the semi-arid regions of the West. In years when the rain fall is above average some other cereals and some vegetables can be grown. A herd of 500 cattle, have been purchased for their use, and they are daily herded by the Indians on the excellent ranges near the post. Hay in almost unlimited quantities can be stored for winter use.

They have now a promising future, but must be guarded and controlled by the military for a year or two more, or until all danger of their outbreak is passed, and the adjacent population is convinced of this immunity from danger. They are hard at work in house and stable building, fencing, well boring, ploughing and seeding, herding their stock and feeding with hay they have themselves harvested.

. . . They told me they liked this work for they now saw a promising future. None have arms or ammunition, and they have no opportunity to obtain intoxicating liquor.

While they were in Alabama and Florida, there was no opportunity for them to make any substantial industrial progress. There disease carried off two or three hundred of their number, but now the Surgeon reports a marked change for the better, though their numbers are not increasing.

All wear the clothing of civilized communities. Their houses are neat and tidy. They have good medical attendance, and all the rising generation will be able to speak and write the English language.

These Apaches, who were formerly so wild and intractable, have made great progress towards a self-sustaining basis, and have a better opportunity for quickly attaining the end sought than any Indians I have knowledge of. Fifty of the men are still bourn on the rolls as soldiers and are under strict martial law, but they have been relieved from many routine post duties so they can practically devote all their time to labor under due personal direction of the officers assigned to their special charge.

The Chiefs of the band expressed to me the wish that all their absent children return to them, and that school opportunities be made available at or near their home. I would suppose that there are about seventy children of school age and physically able to attend school, which they should do. . . . As respects education of the young, I would remark that while the Carlisle training would fit them for competing with our own people in securing a livelihood, considering the change in conditions that has recently taken place, I do not believe that it is wise to send any more of these youths to distant educational establishments, nor to retain any now at those places if it be the ultimate purpose to return them to their people. . . . So much of the instruction at Carlisle has resulted in teaching obedience, thrift, cleanliness, a knowledge of the English language, arithmetic, and the trade of carpenter, shoemaker, harnessmaker, and perhaps some others, is valuable, but as I see the present situation, all this can now be done in the vicinity of the post, and with very much less expense than at a remote school.

The Indian Department now carries on a school for the Comanches near Fort Sill. It is understood to be the policy of the Indian Department to increase the capacity of this school, so that all Apache children can be instructed there. . . . It seems to me that a clearly understood policy as respects these Indians should be determined upon between the War and Interior Departments.[15]

So soon as there is no longer any military necessity for holding this band as prisoners, the War Department should end their status as such. When this is done, it will be impossible for any further issues to be made of food, clothing &c. procured from Army appropriation. Their control will naturally fall to the Indian Office of the Interior Department.

I beg to suggest that as respects the Indians still at Carlisle, instructions be given to the effect that all these Apaches must now elect whether they wish to return to their tribe or to take employment elsewhere. Those who wish to return should be permitted to do so, and the others informed that should they elect to take private employment, they cannot return to their people for any help or assistance or for Governmental support anywhere.

Status of Returned Students

It appears, then, that there are now at Fort Sill with the Chiricahua Apache prisoners, and enrolled as such, some 25 men and women who in past years have rejoined at Ft. Sill & Mt. Vernon Barracks.

There are two men now at Sill who were dismissed from the Carlisle School, who were again dismissed from the tribe by orders of the War Department, but who have again joined their tribe in Oklahoma, and are now being rationed, &c.

There are also two other Indians reported to be now with their kindred who ran away from the Carlisle School in January last. These men it is assumed are now enrolled as prisoners and rationed.

The students who returned early last month are 5 women and 14 boys—the women it is reported having promised to return to Carlisle, but who now prefer to remain with the rest at Fort Sill.

Then there are 23 Indians whose status is undetermined officially, and some 25 others who it appears reverted to the prisoner class without any direction or instructions from the War Department.

With respect to the two former incorrigibles who are now with the tribe, and also as regards the two others who ran away to rejoin their people, it seems to me that in view of the changed conditions it would be the most expedient course to direct that they be enrolled as prisoners and held under strict discipline as such. If they be turned adrift they may become vagabonds or tramps, and as such a danger to the community. They are certainly as dangerous as any others and if any should be restrained of their liberty, these should be.

. . . Their parents certainly wish them to be at Sill and Capt. Scott has recommended such a course, giving as a reason the need of the help of these vigorous young people in assisting the old in the manual labor necessary, especially at this time in establishing themselves in their new country. While I concur in this recommendation of Capt. Scott, I am not unmindful of the fact that their opportunities to rise in the social scale will be unfavorable, or less favorable than they would be if they remained east permanently, yet I do not see any hope to do more for these people than to effectually neutralize their power to do harm and at the same time to give them a fair opportunity to work out their industrial future on as favorable a basis as exists for other Mountain and Plains Indians who were recently hostile.

. . . Capt. Scott should also be instructed that no Indian under his charge should be permitted to leave the Military reservation for any purpose except [to] visit their children at the school near the post, or to make short pleasure or hunting excursions within a radius of a few miles. This should not preclude the sending of these Indians out of the post on duty, nor to prevent those whose conduct and abilities would warrant, from taking public or private employment near Fort Sill, with the consent of the officer in charge.[16]

Maus's concerns and opinions about the students are clear, but he is undecided about whether the adults will break out of the prison, so they still "must be guarded" and "their power to do harm " neutralized. These sentiments contrast with his statement as to whether their "status [as prisoners should] end," for if they still needed military monitoring, their incarceration obviously should continue. As a result of being involved in various experiences with the Apaches, Maus and other high-ranking military officers were conflicted regarding how they felt about them. Officers and enlisted men who had been fighting the people in the field were often unable or unwilling to let go of their early impressions of Apaches at war in favor of the new look of Apaches at peace. All would have had less trouble and a better understanding if they had been cognizant of a primary Chiricahua cultural attribute—pragmatism.

The year 1896 was characterized by hard work among the healthiest of the Apache prisoners and by bureaucratic machinations in Washington regarding several issues pertaining to the Chiricahuas. One of the topics extensively discussed was future plans, or, in other words, what to do about these Indians. The secretary of war in Cleveland's administration, Daniel Lamont, suggested to Secretary of Interior Hoke Smith that an Indian Service officer travel to Fort Sill to discuss the options with the officer in charge. Lamont recommended that June 30, 1897, be designated the date when the Interior Department would take administrative control of the Apaches from the War Department and turn over the western end of Fort Sill to the Apaches as their permanent residence site. Smith was unhappy with the idea. According to historian John Turcheneske Jr., "Interior had not only no interest in retaking charge of the Chiricahuas, but also no intention of doing so."[17] Especially delicate was the matter of the fort becoming the Apaches' permanent home, a subject that would be debated exhaustively for a number of years, both inside and outside of political circles.

For the present, the long-term goal was to make the "Chiricahuas self-sustaining by the summer of 1897."[18] Independence appeared possible when Scott wrote, on August 1, about the Apaches' attitudes. They seemed "happy, contented, and pleased with the country and their prospects for the future. [Not] one complaint . . . has been lodged against them for a wrong committed against a white man or an Indian since their arrival. [Furthermore, newspapers] of this section which opposed their coming here most bitterly, [now] having seemingly forgotten their existence [and lack any] mention of them whatever."[19]

Near the end of 1896 Scott sent a favorable report to the War Department:

> When the prisoners first arrived they were quartered in tents on the open prairie. The outdoor life seemed to have a beneficial effect on health and they have been encouraged to live outdoors for two years with the hope of stamping out the tuberculosis rife among them. They are all now in dwelling houses constructed by themselves with the assistance of one white carpenter as foreman. Since arrival 500 acres of prairie sod have been broken and fenced. Their conduct has been so uniformly good that almost everybody has forgotten that they are here and no white man or Indian in the vicinity of this reservation has had the slightest just cause for complaint against them. They work eight hours a day except Sundays and holidays, and usually with considerable faithfulness. All the younger ones speak English so as to be readily understood. They are somewhat more thrifty than the Kiowas and Comanches but they have little idea of taking care of themselves and unless prevented would dispose of their crops for anything they can get, no matter how small the sum, and use up the results of a year's work in less than a week.[20]

In December 1896, while Scott was furloughed in Washington, D.C., Lieutenant Allyn Capron reported

> one death of an old woman. No new cases of consumption and the old (cases) doing well. During the month the people moved into their houses and the camp (was) broken up. All have stoves (probably the same ones they had at Mount Vernon). All the Indians have made beds and tables, and purchased chairs, china-ware, etc. . . .
>
> Sanitary conditions of each village [are] excellent and inspections made weekly. Each village has a chief or other prominent man in charge and he reports and is held responsible. Now they think

that the white man's medicine is "heap good." Hogs have been purchased and each house has its own pen. Turkeys and chickens also
have been given to each family. Conduct most exemplary.[21]

Scott's report mirrors the basic fairness that characterized most of his
dealings with the Apaches, but his observation that they "have little idea
of taking care of themselves" and would "use up the results of a year's work
in less than a week" reflects a profound ignorance of the Chiricahuas' cultural values. The Apaches did indeed take care of themselves but in ways
that were dissimilar to the prevailing American ethos of that day, which
Scott used as a measure. The forced cultural changes and exposure to the
white man's diseases, not their inability to take care of themselves, were
decimating the people. It appears from Scott's next statement that the
Chiricahuas had not yet "caught on" to the white man's idea of saving
something for the future. It is hard to believe that after at least two hundred years' exposure to Euro-American ways, the Apaches did not understand that concept any better, especially considering that their ancestors'
contact with Europeans on the Spanish colonial frontier had introduced the
idea of preserving surplus crops. Similarly, Capron's phrase "heap good" was
likely a figment of his imagination. No Apache spoke that way. The need
to create stereotypes and to express them verbally through putting others
in their place enforces the writer's sense of superiority, deserved or not.

By this time, late 1896, a hospital had been built especially for the Chiricahuas and was receiving patients. Capron worried that the Apaches would
reject the facility, which they did at first, but then they warmed to the idea
and presented themselves for treatment of routine ailments. In a report
Capron stated to the adjutant general, "these Indians depend nearly as much
upon the hospital and doctor as do whites. The old way of 'drawing out
the devil that caused the illness' by means of Indian medicine—a concoc-
tion of herbs gathered from the woods, the use of which almost invariably
resulted in death from narcotic poisoning has been generally given up and
they now think that the white man's medicine is 'heap good.'"[22]

Scott sent a report to the adjutant general, dated February 12, 1897,
describing the Apache hospital and expressing a couple of his immediate
concerns:

A new porch has been built on the south side [of the hospital] and
three small rooms added on the north side . . . by an appropriation
authorized by the surgeon general. The work of the hospital is not
satisfactory. . . . It is under the control of the surgeon at the post
who is not entirely in sympathy with the Indians or with the officer

in charge of them. As there is only one surgeon here, he has but little time for the Indians. Of the 22 Indians who have died in the past
year, only three have died in the hospital—the others have died in
their villages without civilized care or medical attendance.

The opening of the surrounding country to settlement by whites
has made whiskey easy access to them and whiskey is the cause of
nearly all the troubles and disorders that arise among them. Whiskey
is sometimes brought on the reservation and given to them and they
have no difficulty getting it in the town nearby. It is not apparent
that the officers of the law make any genuine effort to suppress the
sale of liquor to these Indians. I have made complaint against one
white man for introducing liquor on the reservation and against two
for selling whiskey to the Indians. These complaints have not so far
resulted in the punishment of anyone.[23]

Problems with liquor continued to plague the Chiricahuas during their
confinement at Fort Sill. Associates such as Scott and others who were gen-
uinely interested in helping the people must have been disheartened by
the difficulties alcohol abuse caused, particularly because so many other
distressing situations, especially the numerous deaths among the prisoners,
were also occurring.

For example, early in 1897 interpreter Wratten wrote a letter to a Miss
Richards, a teacher at the Hampton Normal School in Virginia, about a
death at Fort Sill:

I have sad news for one of your pupils, Miss Richards, and write to
ask if you will please break it to him.

Paul's mother (Nah-de-yole or Mrs. Spitty) died here on the
night of the 24th of Dec.—of pneumonia.

She was well cared for but of no avail. . . .

I thought his father "Pauls" had written to the boy, hence my
delay.

A letter came for her in Paul's handwriting the other day and
then only I knew he had not been informed.

Pauline and Josephine are here. Pauline is married and Josephine
rapidly becoming an Indian.

How sorry I felt when I saw them for the first time, after their
return.

I believe I could have attended their funeral with a lighter heart.

I would like to see the old Indian ways and customs abrogated
to the attic, never again to be brought to light.

Pauline has some, but Josephine no will at all to resist the many temptations that are bound to be in their path.

They were very much improved by their short stay with you. I only wish it could have been longer.

I shall try to keep them from falling into their old ways again, but they have so many examples that it will be, I fear, next to impossible.

Please remember me with a kind world to Sophie, Alice, Paul and [illegible word].[24]

Capron conveyed more bad news in a February 1898 letter to the adjutant general, proclaiming that the Apaches' health was worsening owing to "contact with civilization" and the fact that "these people are so thoroughly saturated with the germs of consumption and scrofula [tuberculosis of the lymph nodes] and are so closely intermarried that nothing can save them."[25]

In contrast, Chiricahua men continued the hard work on the farms and running cattle, despite Capron's denigrating remarks to the contrary. As was often the case, circumstances were evaluated by individuals who felt an obligation to color their remarks to suit their superiors.

In August 1898 the first Protestant missionary, Reverend Frank Hall Wright (son of Chief Allen Wright of the Choctaw Tribe) of the Dutch Reformed Church in America (now the Reformed Church in America), sought access to all the Fort Sill Chiricahua Apaches, including the youngsters. As far back in time as 1628, the philosophy of the Dutch Reformed Church in the New World had been to concentrate on winning over the children, and Wright hoped to continue that practice through the Chiricahua children.

This minister had been successfully evangelizing for four years among the nearby Comanche children and adults, during which time he lamented that the Apache prisoners of war at Fort Sill lacked any guidance from local religious authorities. The current situation was not an oversight. Ever since the Apaches had arrived in Oklahoma, the U.S. War Department had for reasons unknown consistently denied all churchmen's requests to visit and speak with the prisoners. Wright's efforts, however, bore fruit; how that happened despite government wishes to the contrary is uncertain. It is known only that Wright held a conversation with a Lieutenant Francis H. Beach, Seventh Cavalry, a young officer who was Capron's assistant. Shortly after that discussion the Apaches expressed a strong desire—it could even be considered a demand—to have a mission established and to begin receiving religious instruction. The mysterious spark that ignited this response was apparently so overwhelming that the War Department atypically reversed itself and agreed to allow the minister and designated members of his faith to evangelize the Chiricahuas. The prisoners' earlier exposure to Christianity in Florida and Alabama had been minimal and not intense enough to have made serious seekers of most of them,[26] so there had to be a compelling reason behind their wish at this point, but it must remain in the realm of speculation only.[27]

Nonetheless, Wright's words, others' periodic reports, and several church publications have been preserved regarding this change among the Apaches. In an 1899 report the minister described his first meeting with Lieutenant Beach:

> Driving across the Apache reservation and coming to a gate that opened on Nahwat's [a Christian Comanche] lands, I saw a cavalry officer with a white helmet, just closing it after passing through. He saw me coming and courteously opened the gate for me. I recognized Lieutenant Beach and he said, "In passing, preach to my people." That was truly the Macedonian cry to us.
>
> Sunday mornings, young and old come together for Sunday School. The older people do not understand the words that are spoken, but the bright pictures on cards and charts appeal to them, and their children sing the beautiful hymns which are familiar to them. Here is a class of young people, returned students from Carlisle. How happy they are to have this Mission as a refuge, a place where they receive encouragement and help in their hard fight to sustain the standard they have known in the school.
>
> On Saturday evenings Miss [Maud] Adkisson [a teacher] invites the older men of the villages and, through James [Kaywaykla],[28] tells them Bible stories. They listen eagerly and always promise to come again. During the week Miss Adkisson and Dorothy [a Comanche girl] drive about the villages, inviting the women to come to a cooking or sewing lesson and before they separate a Bible story is told and explained by the bright colored picture roll.[29]
>
> Now there is a bright atmosphere of hope here. There is constant testimony of our Christian teachers, the instruction of the children, the noble efforts of Miss Adkisson in the villages. The result so far is the winning of the good will of parents and children. Good seeds are being sown, and when I hold a two day's meeting this Summer I expect to see an ingathering. Already one man is a candidate for baptism.[30]

Teacher Adkisson was clever in taking the orphaned Comanche girl Dorothy with her to the Apache villages, even though the girl did not speak a word of the Apache language. From the authorities' perspective Dorothy served as a living, breathing example of the obvious benefits of life with the missionaries; archival photos published in later newsletters show her dressed immaculately in a starched white dress with a big bow holding back her hair. By her appearance alone, especially the big, happy smile on her face, she communicated to everyone—adults and children alike—one of the Euro-American values related to coming to Christ: cleanliness. However, a number of adult Chiricahuas of all ages probably did not see anything worthwhile in imitating their captors and were content to ignore the outsiders' ways. More than likely they saw no reason to be dressed uncomfortably in starched outfits, no reason to learn English, and no reason to associate with people so thoroughly unlike themselves. Yet the young adult children who returned from the Carlisle School were bringing change, and they would not be ignored.

As Wright had written, the returning students who resumed life with their families were happy to have the missionaries at Fort Sill, for the religious workers represented all that was familiar to them, now that they were no longer part of the traditional culture. After years at Carlisle, they resembled members of the dominant society rather than their parents. And they were not about to revert to the traditional culture's ways.

As the new century arrived, health problems were still of great concern. An anonymous staff member at the fort wrote in a report,

> lately there has been an alarming amount of illness in the camps, and the people are uneasy and sorely distressed, feeling as though there were no secure foundation beneath them. They sent a message to the Christian Indians to meet them at a certain time and place. When they were gathered together, the people said: "We are blind. Give us the road. Help us to save our friends and children from so much sickness and death."
>
> They were told the plan of salvation and also how they had disregarded the laws of health. They listened patiently, and it may be that this is the beginning of a great awakening.[31]

This information is difficult to believe. The writer's imagination most likely conjured up this picture of Chiricahuas' appealing to Christian tribal members for help in avoiding sickness and death. Their ancestors' historical experience with contagion on the Spanish colonial frontier and the inability of Christianity then to immunize or protect them had been long established in tribal memory and likely had been incorporated into a story or two. Also, this anonymous writer's belief that Apaches were responsible for their own ill health through careless neglect is reminiscent of Pratt's accusation that venereal taint rather than tuberculosis was the causative factor for the students' illnesses at Carlisle. The truth was that most of the prisoners had no immunity against the white man's diseases no matter which religion—traditional, Catholic, or Protestant—they practiced.

During the Dutch Reformed missionaries' efforts at proselytization, many of the prisoners continued to practice traditional religious observances as best they could. However, some of the ancient practices relied on situations no longer extant, such as warfare, so they slowly began to fade into history; others remained viable. Angie Debo records a ritual at Fort Sill in which Geronimo was called upon to cure coyote sickness:

> This ceremony was held in an arbor outside Geronimo's house as soon as darkness fell. Geronimo faced east and had the patient in front of him. The man's relatives were in the background, sitting in a semicircle behind the arbor shelter. In front of Geronimo was a basket tray, holding an eagle feather, an abalone shell, and a bag of pollen. Geronimo started the ceremony by smoking a cigarette he rolled himself and sending the smoke toward each of the four directions. Then he rubbed certain parts of the patient's body with the pollen, praying to the north, south, east, and west at the same time. Each of his prayers referred to Coyote. Then the famous healer sang and beat his drum with the traditional curved stick of the Chiricahuas. His songs praised Coyote and asked his help in healing the patient before him. Geronimo continued singing each night for four nights, every ceremony a repetition of the one before.[32]

But the young Chiricahua adults were setting modern examples for their parents, and Christianity in the form of Protestantism started to take hold among prisoners of all ages. At the end of June 1902 Scott's report to the adjutant general listed 60 men, 86 women, 18 boys over twelve years of age, 36 boys under twelve years of age, 11 girls over twelve, and 32 girls under twelve—for a total of 243 Chiricahua Apache prisoners of war. Absent from Fort Sill were 2 men and 2 boys over twelve away at school and 3 men supporting themselves by their own labor, for a total of 7. Thirteen Indian scouts were on duty and counted separately, according to Scott. Added together, there were 263 Apaches in his charge. Wrote Scott,

> There have been 22 deaths during the year and but 10 births and there is consequently a decrease in the number of the tribe. The

health of the tribe has been in general much better than during the preceding year. This is accounted for partly by the fact that they have been prohibited from having dances in cold and inclement weather during the past year. Some of their dances the preceding winter were noticed to be followed by episodes of colds and pneumonia and there has been noticeably less of these diseases during the year just passed.

The death rate is large on account of the fact that a number of infants died with intestinal troubles during hot weather of last summer. The Indian women cannot be prevented from feeding their babies condensed milk undiluted and in too large quantities and it is frequently fatal.

These people draw the same rations as a soldier for those men over 12 years of age. The matter of a reduction of these rations was seriously considered but no reduction has been made on account of the almost total failure of their crops. Issues were changed however during the month of February from once in five days to once in ten days. . . . The change has resulted in much greater economy of labor and is thought to be a benefit.[33]

Preventing the infants' deaths would have involved withholding condensed milk from a family's rations, a simple adjustment. Also, it seems odd that the Apache women accepted and favored condensed milk for their babies rather than breast milk or cow's milk, but there might have been an overriding factor, such as a belief that tuberculosis was spread through an ailing mother's breast milk.

Six months after Scott's report was submitted, the missionaries must have thought that a miracle had occurred when Geronimo indicated his willingness to be accepted into the church. Reverend J. T. Bergen, a minister visiting Fort Sill from Holland, Michigan, wrote in January 1903,

Geronimo's means of grace is the Fort Sill Mission of the Reformed Church in America. If he has a spiritual father, it is the Rev. Frank H. Wright, minister of that church and missionary to the Indians of Oklahoma, who for a long time has made Geronimo an object of special prayer, and who has often pointed out to him the way of salvation.

Geronimo came into camp on Sunday morning, but did not attend the afternoon meeting. However, he sent word that he was tired, had traveled all night and must sleep—he says that he is over eighty. Toward evening Mr. Wright walked over to Geronimo's tent and had a long, earnest talk with the old man, one of his family, a nephew or grandson interpreting. Mr. Wright reported that the old chief's heart was good toward us and we made him a special object of desire and prayer.

Geronimo came early and sat with bowed head during the sermon. Then Mr. Wright made an appeal and the Indians began to come and give him their hand, thus declaring the renewal of their consecration and their personal acceptance of Jesus.

Then came one of those thrilling experiences when God's spirit moves upon the human emotions and hearts melt. Geronimo gave way. Even while the leader was speaking and we were singing "Jesus is tenderly calling," Geronimo began to speak in that strange Indian way—an undertone—and in the midst of all the other voices, yet heard and understood by every Apache present. "What is he saying?" I asked Asa [Daklugie, Geronimo's nephew and interpreter]. "He says that the Jesus road is good, and he is telling people to go right into it," replied the scout. Then the old chief came out. Leaping to his feet, he fairly rushed to where we stood, clasped us by the hands, then turned to his people and held his finger up toward heaven, striking his breast with the other hand. When those who came forward remained for personal prayer, Geronimo stayed with them, seated on his chair.

After the meeting I talked for some time with Geronimo. We would have received him into the church if he had given satisfactory evidence of his repentance. But this he did not give, nor did he ask for baptism, as did nine other Indians that day. This is his confession as he gave it to me, requesting, at the same time, that the Christian people of America might pray for him. He says that his heart is good toward the white people. Many of them who are in the Jesus road have told him that they love him, and he loves them. He says that his heart is good toward Jesus, that he wants to be in the Jesus road. Geronimo will not be left to himself. Mr. Wright will see him again in two weeks and the ladies at the Fort Sill Mission of the Reformed Church will be near him if he wants instruction. He is a weak character because of his sinful life, and since that meeting has given evidence that the power of sin over him is not yet broken.

But God's grace can save him. Why should we doubt concerning Geronimo? As I lay that night in the mission at Medicine Bluff, and looked up into the starlit sky, so clear and pure, over the Oklahoma hills, I thought of the Holy Being who died for and saved me, and I must believe that the same sovereign grace will save Geronimo.[34]

Geronimo a "weak character"? Hundreds of Arizonans, New Mexicans, and Mexicans who felt Geronimo's wrath would have testified to the contrary. But when viewed within a religious framework by Christian church officials, the description is easy to understand.

Geronimo was baptized ten months later, in October 1903. Rev. Wright provided the information about the event in one of his periodic written reports:

> As to the results [of the camp meeting], one of the most remarkable was the baptism of Geronimo. When we thought of his previous reputation and character as the bloody, wily chief, it required faith to accept his profession of faith as genuine. But he made a most impressive statement of his earnestness in the step which he took. He professed his faith in Christ and determination to follow Him. He said, "You must help me. Pray for me. You may hear of my doing wrong, but my heart is right." The old man had fallen from his horse and was badly hurt, but it may have been the means of his conversion. Prof. Bergen clung to him, and it was touching to see his old time friend, Naiche, the war chief, sit by him and prompt him—once councillors in awful raids and wearisome flights—now the younger prompting and explaining to the elder.
>
> Pray for Geronimo, Christian friends. God is able to save; Jesus saves to the uttermost. All these children of nature, just learning to walk on the new way, need your most earnest sympathy and prayers.[35]

Wright was mistaken in noting Geronimo as chief and Naiche as war chief; their rankings were just the opposite, but the excitement of writing about Geronimo's baptism into the faith might have so affected the minister that all else was extraneous. One cannot blame him for that, and one can also understand the tinge of doubt he expressed: Did the fall from a horse cause Geronimo to examine his own mortality and to become a Christian, or was it something else? Was he sincere? These and other questions were likely on the minister's mind even as he wrote his report.

During the same period of time three arenas of activity were occurring simultaneously. In the first, the majority of the Chiricahuas could be seen leading routine lives of hard work, prayer in the traditional or Christian way to stay healthy, and amazement regarding the changes they saw in their children who had returned from the Carlisle School.

In the second, the national newspaper spotlight was shining more and more on Geronimo. The public's curiosity about the Apache prisoners of war had not significantly diminished over the years, and, true to their task, reporters from all over the country were still paying attention. Readers always welcomed news about Geronimo, whose legend had grown dramatically. In addition, Fort Sill's military officials scrutinized and usually rejected many invitations for the celebrity Geronimo to attend various public functions.

But in 1903 Captain Farrand Sayre,[36] the officer who followed Scott in being responsible for the Apaches, negotiated a deal with S. M. McGowan, one of the promoters of the Louisiana Purchase Exposition at St. Louis (also called the World's Fair). Sayre answered McGowan's request for Geronimo's presence by writing,

> [I] talked the matter over with Geronimo . . . and he was pleased with the proposition. . . . I know that he will be dissatisfied with the $15.00 or $20.00 per month . . . but I know that he wants to go . . . and I will not give my consent to his going with anyone except you.
>
> In regard to Geronimo's family—his wife is a chronic invalid—(Zi-yeh) has tubercular lupus and I would not recommend her going—or her daughter, Eva. Geronimo has a grandson, Thomas, about 12 . . . and he would probably want to go. Geronimo would very much like to have a tent or house and I could send a man who could act as interpreter and his wife to live with Geronimo and Thomas. I should like to have the Apache interpreter, a white man, Mr. G. M. Wratten, to go with the party to St. Louis and have his fare paid going and returning but it would not be necessary to keep him there after he saw the Apaches established.[37]

Geronimo attended the exposition and, of course, was a big hit. Afterward McGowan reported to Sayre, "He really has endeared himself to whites and Indians alike. With one or two exceptions, when he was not feeling well, he was gentle, kind and courteous. I did not think I could ever speak so kindly of the old fellow whom I have always regarded as an incarnate fiend. I am very glad to return him to you in as sound and healthy condition as when you brought him here."[38]

In the third arena events happening in Washington, D.C., involved a tug of war between the War Department and the Interior Department as to which agency would have jurisdiction over the Apaches when they were released from incarceration, a pending possibility. A special agent named

Geronimo. Rare photo taken at St. Louis Exposition in 1904 by unknown photographer.
PHOTO COURTESY OF FRISCO NATIVE AMERICAN MUSEUM AND NATURAL HISTORY CENTER.

Frank C. Armstrong had conducted an investigation and concluded that although the Chiricahuas had made excellent progress in their agricultural endeavors (despite years when the crops failed) and had learned trades, they required another two years under military control, which would then "place them in a condition to be released from the nominal captivity they now undergo without realizing the change."[39] Armstrong also believed that if the Apaches were released sooner than two years hence, they would become demoralized owing to the surrounding white settlements and their vices.

Armstrong's language of colonialism is of an odd variety in that he apparently does not blindly consider the Anglos who live in the Fort Sill area to be superior to the Apaches and indeed notes "their vices." Still, he believes the Apaches would not be able to resist the white men's "vices" and thus recommends incarcerating the prisoners for two more years, during which time they ostensibly would develop the willpower or whatever else required to resist the locals' moral turpitude.

Always on the alert to rumors that might affect their status, the Chiricahuas were aware of the Washington machinations concerning their future, especially the gossip that told of Fort Sill being turned over to them as their reservation upon their release from confinement.[40] This possibility was exciting and motivating; it suited them very well as it meant they would continue living in the homes they built, continue running their cattle, continue building their horse and mule herds, and continue farming the lands around their villages. They had come a long way from the moment in their history when, in September 1886, a telegram sent by President Grover Cleveland stated, "All the hostiles should be very safely kept as prisoners of war until they can be tried for their crimes or otherwise disposed of."[41]

Despite the rosier outlook, including the fact that the Chiricahua men had formed three baseball teams and one football team, Captain Sayre was worried about the prisoners' health. Even though the number of new cases of tuberculosis had decreased, he fretted about whether the increasing presence of civilians on the military reserve would expose the prisoners to alcohol. He wrote, "On account of the Indians, greater precautions should be observed to prevent the introduction of intoxicating liquor on the reservation than are thought necessary on other posts."[42]

Diligence and recently enacted substantial penalties for selling alcohol to the Indians kept most liquor peddlers away but did not keep some of the Indians from attempting to obtain liquor illegally in Lawton, the town immediately abutting Fort Sill. Periodically an Apache, including Geronimo, would convince a white man to buy a bottle or two, but that practice was growing less frequent in 1904.

That same year interpreter Wratten became intimately involved in the now highly charged bureaucratic issue of removing the prisoners from Fort

Sill. Late in 1903 government officials had suggested that the Apaches be relocated to the southern part of Fort Sill, an area known as "Reserve Pasture No. 1." Sayre and Wratten opposed the move, leading Wratten to write a letter to the Indian Rights Association.

> The Apaches were brought here in Oct. 1894 and given to understand this was to be their home, to get to work and give up all thoughts of Arizona because this was to be their reservation. That when the gov. was through with the land it would be turned over to them.
>
> . . . when the reservation was enlarged in 1896 it was enlarged as they were told to give more room for their cattle and give enough land for each individual to have 160 acres. Now, after almost ten years of incessant toil, after undergoing hardships and privation breaking up the land, building houses and fences, building large storage reservoirs to catch summer rains in order that the cattle could have water close, after accumulating close on to 4000 head of cattle and some 200 head of horses it seems to have been about decided to remove these people to another place and give them one township of 23,040 acres of land. . . . [That] would do if the grass was good . . . to support year in and out no more than 2500 head of cattle. Now they will have here next Spring or rather this Spring after branding time, close to 4500 head of cattle. Now what are they going to do with these cattle and some 200 head of horses on 23,040 acres of land?
>
> Now there are 267 of these people and to give each 160 acres of land which they are entitled to would require 42,720 acres.
>
> . . . I think it is a shame—after all the promises that have been made these people to remove them out of here. Never again can they be induced to put forth the efforts that have characterized them for the last 10 years. They will be left utterly without hope, and a man without hope had just as well be dead.
>
> . . . I firmly believe that when they do move these Indians from here that from that time on they will go down hill, that in a short time the gov. will have to support them. If let alone, it will be a matter of a few years 'till they can support themselves.
>
> Knowing your sympathies to be with these people and that you have always been glad to help them, I write in this one hour of need hoping you can enlist the sympathies of your friends in the Indian Rights Association in behalf of the Apaches.[43]

Regardless of the swirl of events around him, Geronimo kept his visibility high, which was especially apparent during President Theodore Roosevelt's inauguration in 1905, to which he was invited as a "celebrity." On the way to Washington, wherever the train stopped at a station, people crowded the car and bought his autograph for fifty cents apiece. When his party changed trains, interpreter Wratten had difficulty pushing him through the throngs who wanted his autograph.

A few hundred Indians from different tribes had been invited to participate in the festivities, and the government wanted them to be seen especially in the parade. The Indians were grouped together in the section right behind the grand marshal and other marching soldiers. A reporter from a Florida newspaper sent back a dispatch about the occasion:

> In this class was the band of three hundred and fifty real Indians, headed by a half dozen chiefs from the West, riding their war ponies and ferocious in feathers and paint. These chiefs were brought here at the expense of the (Inaugural) Committee and everyone has a reputation. They were led by no less a warrior than Geronimo, that headman of the Apaches, whose name was a terror until [Lieutenant Colonel Henry Ware] Lawton ran him down. Bowed and aged, this most famous Red Man of them all rode his little pinto pony up the avenue today and never lifted his saturnine old face from the folds of the blanket around his shoulders.[44]

Several days after the parade Geronimo and other notable Indians were taken to see Roosevelt. In an unusual opportunity to address the highest U.S. government official Geronimo began with words of great respect.

> Great Father, I look to you as I look to God. When I see your face I think I see the face of the Great Spirit. I come here to pray you to be good to me and my people. . . . Did I fear the Great White Chief? No. He was my enemy and the enemy of my people. His people desired the country of my people. My heart was strong against him. I said that he should never have my country. . . . I defied the Great White Chief, for in those days I was a fool.
>
> I ask you to think of me as I was then. I lived in the home of my people. . . . They trusted me. It was right that I should give them my strength and my wisdom.
>
> When the soldiers of the Great White Chief drove me and my people from our home we went to the mountains. When they followed us we slew all that we could. We said we would not be captured. No.

We starved but we killed. I said that we would never yield, for I was a fool.

So I was punished, and all my people were punished with me. The white soldiers took me and made me a prisoner far from my own country. . . .

Great Father, other Indians have homes where they can live and be happy. I and my people have no homes. The place where we are kept is bad for us. . . . We are sick there and we die. White men are in the country that was my home. I pray you to tell them to go away and let my people go there and be happy.

Great Father, my hands are tied as with a rope. My heart is no longer bad. I will tell my people to obey no chief but the Great White Chief. I pray you to cut the ropes and make me free. Let me die in my own country, an old man who has been punished enough and is free.[45]

Roosevelt rejected Geronimo's wish. Nevertheless, the old warrior had sufficient freedom to attend various regional celebrations in Oklahoma. The temptation to return to Arizona, with or without permission, apparently got the best of him in the summer of 1907, however, as noted on the front page of an Oklahoma newspaper. Headlined "Apache Warrior Seeks Freedom: Geronimo Said to Have Attempted to Escape into Mexico," the item was quite succinct:

The report that the Apache warrior, Geronimo, recently went out from here [Lawton, Oklahoma] stating he had attempted to make his escape to Mexico while attending a celebration at Cache [Oklahoma] on the fourth [of July] is confirmed today by a newspaper correspondent writing from Cache.

He says that Geronimo left Cache as if to return to the Fort Sill reservation but that he turned southward after leaving town and was in hiding during the night on a stream while several soldiers were hunting for him. The next day he was captured and taken back to Fort Sill.

Geronimo is credited with saying: "Apache tired all time stay here. Me go big plain help brothers get killed."

It is believed that he was headed for the Apache reservation near El Paso.[46]

It is doubtful that Geronimo spoke in the anonymous reporter's quoted vernacular, but the language of colonialism persisted and was apparent again in October of that year, when Geronimo, representing the Chiricahuas, was invited to a gathering of Oklahoma notable Indians in Colinsville, north of Tulsa. A Shawnee chief, Spybuck, sponsored the get-together to celebrate the coming Oklahoma statehood. In a news item the following week, written again by an unnamed staffer, Geronimo was quoted as referring to himself in the third person:

> Geronimo has religion now. The blood of the men whom me, big chief, kill is before me. Geronimo is sorry. But the big God—Him who is friend of the white man and Indian—He forgive.
>
> In the paper, write a letter to the great white father in Washington. Say to him: Geronimo got religion now. Geronimo fight no more. The old times he forget. Geronimo want to be prisoner of war no more. He want free. Tell the great white father that—tell him in the paper.
>
> Me want to go out in Arizona. Plenty deer and plenty things to hunt out there; plenty good water; no big houses. Indian want to live like Indian used to live, but Indian kill no more.
>
> Geronimo getting old and he want peace. My people and me not bother big white father, if he only let us go out where the Indian get lots of air and good hunting.[47]

His request was not granted and would not be addressed again as he died of pneumonia two years later, still a prisoner of war, on February 17, 1909. The *New York Times* published an obituary:

> Geronimo, the Apache Indian chief, died . . . today in the hospital at Fort Sill. He was nearly 90 years of age, and had been held at the Fort as a prisoner of war for many years. He will be buried in the Indian cemetery to-morrow by the missionaries, the old chief having professed religion three years ago. . . .
>
> The career of Geronimo, Chief of the Apaches, gave point to the proverb that a good Indian is a dead Indian.[48] Geronimo, aged nearly 90 years, is dead. Crafty, bloodthirsty, incredibly cruel and ferocious, he was all his life the worst type of aboriginal savage. Even his so-called religious conversion was not without cunning. He embraced the Dutch Reformed faith, which is President Roosevelt's in the hope thereby of obtaining executive clemency and freedom. In his terrible raids on the Mexican borders, terminated by his capture, in the Apache Campaign of 1886, by Gen. Miles and Surgeon Leonard Wood, who was then in command of the infantry scouts, Geronimo had confessedly murdered hundreds of men and women. Gen. Miles showed him the white men's use of the steam engine,

of the heliostat, of the telegraph; and he acknowledged the useless-
ness of contending further against the military authorities of the
United States.

His white captors were more merciful than Geronimo or than his
tribe and its redskin foes. Those who decry the modern and more
deadly refinements in the art of war forget that when the rifle succeeded the bow and tomahawk, and the telegraph outdistanced the
signal smokes, internecine strifes upon this continent were ended.[49]

On the very next day the same newspaper published a column, written
anonymously, entitled "Geronimo Was a Great Man."

Now that all the obituaries of Geronimo have been printed, and
everybody has been reminded of what a cruel and bloodthirsty
wretch he was, it is only fair to recall the fact that while all the
charges made against him are true, they are so only from the white
man's point of view, and that justice requires judgment of him as
what he was, an Indian. So regarded, the old cutthroat was not
without certain attributes of greatness.

Not wholly without cause, Geronimo thought that the land over
which his ancestors had hunted as masters belonged to him and
his people. The white settlers in the Southwest were not for him, as
for us, brave frontiersmen carrying civilization into the wilderness,
engaged in innocent and commendable occupations of agriculture
and stock-raising. Instead they were invading aliens, ruthlessly appropriating a country to which they had no claim or title, and, making life itself impossible for the Indians—in short, enemies to be
driven away if possible and to be killed if necessary. That is exactly
the way we or any other race would have felt in like circumstances,
and beyond any question we would have proceeded to make war
on the invaders in whatever manner was in accord with our instincts
and customs.

That is all Geronimo did, and in doing it he showed military
ability of the highest order. With only a handful of men under his
command, he defied for years all the forces which a great Government found it convenient to send against him. Again and again, he
rose superior to crumbling defeat, and had success been for him
among the physical possibilities, he would have ranked in history
with its greatest conquerors and patriots. Knowing of his opponents
and their strength only what he saw, his expectations of ultimate
victory were due to lack of information, not to sanguinary madness,

and he yielded at last when somebody had belated wisdom to show him the size of the task he had undertaken.

Of course he had to be suppressed, and too high praise cannot be given to the final campaign conducted with matchless courage and determination by that magnificent soldier, Lawton, who was to die for us later in the Philippines, doing like work against a hardly less average and not at all less "murderous" foe.[50]

Among the tributes to Geronimo was a poem by George Wratten:

In days of old
When time was gold
And Apaches held their sway
An Indian chief, a wily thief
Sat waiting for his pony—
Geronimo.[51]

Geronimo's death invigorated the Washington bureaucrats, now convinced once and for all that any prospects of a Chiricahua rebellion were buried with the old warrior. Feeling safe from their imagined possibility of strife with the Apaches, they turned their attention to debating the prisoners' fate seriously. Should they be allowed to remain at Fort Sill, or should they be released from incarceration? Turcheneske writes, "By the end of 1910, the Bureau of Indian Affairs publicly stated what it viewed as acceptable justice for the Chiricahuas. Because many were successful stock raisers who became attached to their lands, those so desiring were to be permitted to remain at Fort Sill permanently and be allotted lands at this location."[52] The War Department responded negatively by protecting its interests in the fort, which ensured its viability as a military installation and not the permanent home for the Chiricahua Apaches.

S. M. Brosius, an agent for the still active Indian Rights Association, endorsed a U.S. Senate Memorial on February 15, 1910, in support of allotting lands at Fort Sill to the prisoners. Part of the memorial contained references to acts of Congress, previously passed, that Brosius believed showed intent:

Further recognition of the right of the Apache prisoners to the permanent use and occupancy of these lands is made by Congress in the act approved June 28, 1902 (32 Stat., 26) appropriating funds for the erection of buildings and repairs to same, purchase of draft animals and live stock for breeding purposes, farm and household utensils, blacksmith and wheelwright tools, and repairs to same, and all other necessary articles absolutely needed for the support and maintenance of the Apache prisoners of war permanently established at Fort Sill, Oklahoma, under control of the War Department.

The act approved February 18, 1904 (33 Stat., 26), makes a similar provision for their permanent establishment at Fort Sill. . . . The Government has promised a permanent home for these prisoners within Fort Sill Reservation. This obligation should be carried out by allotting the lands heretofore referred . . . to any of the Apache prisoners who desire to remain on the lands. . . . [T]he allotment should be made without further delay and coincident with allotment of land these Indians should be released from their bondage under the military and be given the rights of freemen.[53]

Bureaucratic processes began soon that would result in the Chiricahua survivors' freedom from prisoner-of-war status, but years were to pass before they were actually released from incarceration.

6.
Starting Over

THE WAR DEPARTMENT CONCLUDED that the Chiricahuas should participate in the decision making as to where they would be permanently located, and it designated Lieutenant Scott to travel to Fort Sill and determine their wishes. The meeting with several leaders occurred on September 21, 1911. True to their respect and recognition of Naiche as their chief, many of the Apache men kept silent and let him speak for them.

> *Scott:* General [Leonard] Wood sent me down here to find out what you were thinking about and whether you are happy or not . . . to meet with you and to look into your faces and see and hear what you have to say. . . . If anyone wants to open his heart and talk with me, this is a good thing.
>
> *Naiche:* It is not right that I should talk to you first, to tell you what we are thinking about, and what we want, and what is in our hearts. You came down here to see us and there is something in your mind. . . . It is not right that we should talk to you first.
>
> *Scott:* I am sent here to get information and not to deliver any orders. I have come down here to find out what is needed. I am not empowered to take any steps other than to get information for General Wood. General Wood wants to know how you feel. He can't find out unless you tell me. Whatever you say I will take and see that General Wood gets it.
>
> *Naiche:* We don't know very much. None of us are very smart but we thought that maybe you came down here to tell us what was going to be done. . . . We want to be given land somewhere that would be our homes and now we thought you had come down here to tell us about that. We don't think of anything else. All we want is to be freed and be released as prisoners, given land and homes that we can call our own. That is all we think about.

You took us a long time ago and they took this land from us . . . that is enough now. Half or more than half of these people here talk English, half or more than half can read and write. They all know how to work. You have held us long enough. We want something else now.

We have learned to work. That is generally the way when they take anybody to learn. After they have taught them for a while they will look at them and look them over and see how much they have learned and think, well now these people have learned so much. I will give them some kind of work that they will like. Are we going to work here for you as long as we can move our hands? Work until we are so old we can't work anymore?

They told me when I was a boy that my mind and my way of living was no good . . . yours is not good, throw it away.

I am an old man now. You took me with you from place to place and brought me here. I have listened to what you have told me and I have watched you people and I think that I have learned a whole lot and all of these young people have learned to do good work and I think that you ought to give us homes to ourselves where we can be ourselves.

We are not a rock. You set a rock down in one place and it will stay there and it will not get old and there will be no children. Give us our homes to ourselves where we can take care of ourselves and make our own living.

We are brothers now, your God is our God. We want to be just like you are now, all of us. That is what we all think. That is all for me.

Mithlo:[1] We are not little children.

Kaywaykla: It is right that they should set us free and give us our homes right here.

Jozhe:[2] Do we not have any rights in the United States? Are we not human beings? If not, what are we?

Gooday:[3] What will you do with us? Haven't we got any sense?[4]

Shortly after that conference, on October 8, a group of about five Chiricahua men, accompanied by Scott, traveled to the Mescalero Apache Reservation in south-central New Mexico to meet with the Mescaleros and get an idea of the terrain, its suitability for farming and ranching, and the Mescalero people's attitude toward the Chiricahuas, who possibly would be relocated there from Fort Sill. At this meeting with Scott, Asa Daklugie,[5] one of the young leaders who much earlier had returned from the Carlisle School, presented a lengthy report of his visit, and finished by saying,

> You white people, when a family is poor and unable to earn a living, others will give them something to feed them, also to build a house. We are that way now ourselves. The meanness that was in us is all out now, all gone; none have any more.
>
> A great many years ago the government commenced feeding us and clothing us. Do they want to keep it up until our children's children and their children's children are old men and women? No, we do not want it! We think we have been given enough rations and clothing. We want to be free! . . . Those who want to stay here, let them stay! Those who want to go, send them!

Rogers Toclanny[6] argued for being released to the Warm Springs Apache Reservation (also known as Ojo Caliente), his home. "These people who want to go there will get old pretty soon. They want to be there and get settled so their children can grow up there. The soil is good there—you can raise anything. . . . Do not send me any place but there! . . . That is why I have always been a friend to the white people. I thought that when the time came and I would ask for something, I would not be refused."

Talbot Goody added his words and his name to Toclanny's on an informal list of Apaches who wanted to return to Warm Springs.

> Ojo Caliente has always been my home. All of my people, as far back as I can remember, have lived there. It has been a great many years since I was taken away from there. Whatever officer comes to talk with the Apaches, I have always spoken of that, my country.
>
> It has been a great many years that the government has been our father. We are still looking up, and it doesn't matter where they put us, what they do with us; we still belong, in a sense, to the government.
>
> We are getting along all right here, but we pine for our old homes. Put us there!
>
> The government goes according to law. If a man owns a piece of property or an allotment is given to him, it cannot be taken away from him. Even if he should kill somebody they cannot take away his land. The government has been good to us, but we want land like that, land that nobody can take away.
>
> We have been moved around for twenty-six or twenty-seven years; have been taught to do all kinds of work; have done as we

have been told to do; and now we want to be sent back to our old homes and be given land that cannot be taken away. If the government will put us back at Ojo Caliente, we will stay there and be happy.

Jason Betzinez spoke first for those Apaches who wanted to remain at Fort Sill and receive allotments of land there. "We are poor, and want something for ourselves. That is why we want to stay here. I talked with President Taft, when he was Secretary of War, and asked to be left here. He made a note on paper of what I said and may have it yet."

James Kaywaykla added his support for remaining at Fort Sill:

The Indians assembled here have no home, no place they can call their own. Today it appears as if it was right in front of us waiting. I know this country around Fort Sill. I know the land because I have seen it. We have thought of this land here, and want it. We do not ask for something we have not seen, something that is over the hill and out of sight. We do not want that. What we ask for is land that we have seen and is right here in front of us. If a man lives he must have something to live on. If I am here I know I have something to live on, something that will take care of me. Make a strong plea for this land for us!

Lawrence Mithlo also spoke in favor of Fort Sill:

We have worked very hard on this reservation. Why should we go away and leave it without making something from that labor? Please give it to us and make it so that it is ours, nobody else's. We think that you think it is time for us to be free. That is why we want this land upon which to make our living. The white people around the country here have farms, and they came here since we did. But already they have many things and we have nothing. The white man has his farm, has a home on it, a barn and chicken-home close by, and fields not far from the house. That is the way you want us to be![7]

After full consideration approximately 150 Chiricahuas expressed a desire to be relocated to the Mescalero Apache Reservation, but approximately 90 preferred to remain in Oklahoma.[8]

Scott next asked for the views of others having frequent contact with the Chiricahuas. Major George W. Goode, the new officer in charge of the Chiricahuas, suggested that the prisoners be freed, placed under Department of Interior control and be given a "liberal allotment in some place where suitable land is available."[9] Reverend Walter C. Roe of the Reformed

Church in America agreed with Goode's first two suggestions and then recommended that the Chiricahuas be "allocated 30,000 acres at Fort Sill east of Cache Creek."[10]

Armed with these messages, Scott traveled to Washington and reported to Major General Leonard Wood, recommending that

> legislation be obtained . . . to move such of the Apache prisoners of war at Fort Sill to the Mescalero Reservation, New Mexico, who may elect to go to live there (now approximately 150) and that an appropriation be obtained to carry this into effect, of one hundred thousand dollars. That upon arrival . . . they be released as prisoners of war and turned over to the jurisdiction of the Honorable, the Secretary of the Interior; that their property, horses, farming implements, etc., be transported for them by rail; their cattle to be sold for them slowly, as opportunity offers to effect the sale to the best advantage and the money re-invested in cattle in New Mexico and that the Apaches be fed and clothed until they can realize on their first crop.
>
> That those who elect to remain at Fort Sill be permitted to do so as prisoners of war under their present status, retaining their share of cattle and implements with the exception of Jason [Betzinez], Benedict [Jozhe], and a few others who will be found not to exceed ten, who have trades, are sober, industrious and are considered by the officer in charge . . . as able to make their way among white men; that these have the option of being allotted land in severalty unalienable for 25 years in the northeast of the reservation away from the vicinity of the post, and where they will not interfere with the military use of the reservation, or, in case they so prefer, that allotments belonging to the estates of deceased Kiowas and Comanches be purchased for them and an appropriation be obtained therefor; these allotments to be put in as good condition as to improvement as their present location. That they be released as prisoners of war and turned over to the jurisdiction of the Honorable, the Secretary of the Interior, to be fed and clothed until they can realize on their first crops. If those others, who elect to remain at Fort Sill hoping for allotment there, were to be treated in the same way they would in all likelihood pawn or sell their property in the near future for drink and continue in the neighborhood of the post a reproach to the War Department as long as they live, but their best chance of survival is with the others who have elected to go with the Mescalero Apaches, for the reasons stated within.

> In case any allotments are made for Apaches anywhere, it is considered right that George Wratten, Martin Crab, and E. I. Welch, all of whom have devoted themselves to the Apaches for more than 20 years and are now old and broken and have no other means of livelihood, should be mentioned by name for allotment, wherever they elect, in the bill.[11]

Scott surprised many Apache advocates by recommending that those who elected to remain at Fort Sill should retain their prisoner-of-war status. Also, his worry that some would pawn their property to buy liquor appeared to be in contradiction of his previous apparently sympathetic position. The anonymous writer of an Indian Rights Association report noted with regret that Scott had showed no interest in the "advancement of the Red Man," and although Scott recommended removal of the larger portion of the tribe to New Mexico, he failed to suggest that a provision for individual allotments of land be made for them. The writer also commented on Scott's recommendation that

> the ninety or more (intelligent) members of the tribe who do not desire to remove, shall not be allotted lands, but shall be retained as prisoners of war while remaining at Fort Sill. This is so palpably unjust to this more progressive class that it should be condemned as unworthy of serious consideration. . . . All friends of these Apache prisoners should petition that the portion of the band desiring to remain at Fort Sill should be allotted lands there, and immediately thereafter be relieved as prisoners of war and placed under the care of the Department of the Interior.[12]

After all of the meetings, discussions, debates, and arguments, Scott's final proposal was to enact legislation to resettle most of the Chiricahuas in New Mexico, where they would receive their freedom. Turcheneske explains that Scott's noted exceptions to this idea were those Apaches who could easily adjust to white society—mostly the young, educated people. In Scott's opinion these Chiricahuas should receive allotments either on Fort Sill's northeast quadrant or on the estates of deceased Kiowas and Comanches. Then they would be freed but fed and clothed by the government until they harvested their first crops.[13]

To this day the Chiricahua Apaches hold various opinions about the events that occurred while determinations were being made regarding who would stay in Oklahoma and who would go to the Mescalero Apache Reservation; Ojo Caliente was not being considered. Turcheneske points out that of the ninety-three prisoners who wanted to remain, "only fourteen would be permitted to do so" because of the stringent criteria Scott had developed. On October 4, 1912, Hendrina Hospers, a Reformed Church missionary among the prisoners of war, told a church official of the existence of a list (Scott's?) of fourteen Apaches who did not gamble or drink and who could run a farm or make a living in the trades; these men were offered a choice. All others had to leave for Mescalero. Mithlo was not listed among the favored and wanted to know why. "Col. Scott gruffly told him he was worthless [and] not to say a word. Mithlo had set his heart on staying, is a good worker, [and] has been doing right. He is all broken up over it," Hospers stated. According to Turcheneske, "Not only was it apparent that . . . Scott did not intend to assist the Chiricahuas in attaining freedom, but as Talbot Goody [also known as Gooday] bitterly summed up . . . there was only one way out—either remove to Mescalero and become free, or remain as prisoners of war at Fort Sill."[14]

The pending release of the prisoners caused Henry L. Stimson, the new secretary of war in President William H. Taft's administration, to transmit a report to the U.S. Senate, enumerating 257 incarcerated individuals— 138 males and 119 females. Only 30 of the men were identified as having been engaged in hostilities. Of the warriors on Stimson's list of those who had surrendered with Geronimo in 1886, only the first 6 were still alive; the other warriors from his group had passed on.

> Tiss-nolth-tos, age 47; health good; conduct fair.
> Calvin Zhonne, age 47; health fair; conduct fair.
> Leon Ferico [Perico], age 60; health fair; conduct fair.
> Beche, age 75; health fair; conduct good.
> Yar-no-zha [Yah-n-zha], age 47; health good; conduct fair.
> Christian Noiche [Naiche], age 56, health fair; conduct has been
>   very good for about a year past.
> Too-is-gah, age 51; health good; conduct fair.
> Jasper Kanseah, age 39; health good; conduct good.
> Kay-dah-Zinne, age 51; health good; conduct fair.
> Nah-do-Zinne, age 51; health good; conduct fair.
> Kay-ih-tah, age 51; health good; conduct fair.
> Mithlo, age 48; health good; conduct good.
> Ky-zah, age 48; health good; conduct fair.
> Tah-ni-toe, age 57; health good; conduct fair.
> Tse-de-kisen, age 51; health good; conduct fair.
> Martine, age 54; health good; conduct fair.
> Binday, age 54; health good; conduct good.
> Fatty, age 54; health good; conduct fair.

Dexter Loco, age 48; health good; conduct good.
Harold Dick, age 69; health good; conduct fair.
Paul Gey-dil-Kon [Guydelkon], age 52; health good; conduct fair.
Nah-nal-Zhuggie, age 51; health good; conduct fair.
Jose, age 53; health good; conduct fair.
Kah-ah-te-nai [Kayetennae], age 51; health good; conduct fair.
Coonie, age 56; health good; conduct good.
As-toy-eh, age 50; health good; conduct fair.
Tzozonna, age 52; health good; conduct fair.
Jason Betzinez, age 51; health good; conduct good.
Chiricahua Tom, age 62; health good; conduct fair.
Chatto, age 58; health good; conduct fair.

Stimson concluded, "There is no military necessity for continuing to hold these Apache Indians as prisoners of war if provision can be made for their location elsewhere than on the Fort Sill Reservation and if the Indians desire to remove therefrom."[15]

As the release of prisoners became more and more politically complex and frustrating, Reverend Roe wrote, "It will literally be true that the iniquity of the fathers is visited upon the children unto the third and fourth generation, if this thing goes on much longer. . . . Shall innocent babies be born prisoners, and harmless, laughing children grow up in captivity, because their grandfathers fought against or possibly for—think, of it, possibly for—the United States Government?"[16]

During these trying times Scott Ferris was Oklahoma's representative to the U.S. House from the Fifth Congressional District, a political entity encompassing Fort Sill and the town of Lawton. He and other Lawtonians were unopposed to releasing the Chiricahuas but would never have agreed to the military's abandoning Fort Sill and turning it over to the Apaches. After months' long machinations Ferris introduced a bill on January 3, 1912, authorizing the secretary of war to grant freedom to certain of the Apache prisoners of war.

> Sec. 1. Be it enacted by the Senate and House of Representatives of the United States of America in Congress assembled, that the Secretary of War is hereby authorized to grant freedom and free release to such individual members of the Apache prisoners of war on the Fort Sill Military Reservation, in Oklahoma, as may desire to return to the Apache Mescalero Indian Reservation in New Mexico, and to convert their proportionate part of such tribal moneys and proper-

ty into money as soon as may be practicable, the same to be covered into the Treasury of the United States as the Fort Sill Apache prisoner of war fund, until such time as it may be feasible to reinvest it for their use and benefit.

Sec. 2. That immediately upon the payment into the Treasury of the United States of such funds and the granting to said Indians their full release and freedom by the War Department, the Interior Department shall at once acquire full jurisdiction over said Indians, the Indian fund, and all property, and the status of said Indians so freed shall be that of all other restricted Indians.

Sec. 3. That the Secretary of the Interior is hereby authorized to remove such of the Apache Indian Tribe as desire to return to their tribesmen in the Mescalero Apache Indian Reservation in New Mexico, and there establish them as nearly as may be, on equal terms and equal footing with the other Mescalero Apaches: provided. That the Secretary of the Interior shall have full power to reinvest the moneys of such Apache tribesmen so removed in property similar to the property owned by them as nearly as may be deemed practicable and feasible.

Sec. 4. That for such of the Apaches as do not desire to return to the Mescalero Apaches, they may remain on the Fort Sill Military Reservation under such rules and regulations as the War Department may prescribe.

Sec. 5. That there is hereby appropriated, and made immediately available, out of any money in the Treasury of the United States not otherwise provided for, a sum of money, not exceeding one hundred thousand dollars, sufficient to carry out the provisions of this Act.[17]

The wheels of government moved swiftly, an unusual occurrence, and appropriation bills, an example of which was H.R. 16651, were passed usually without too much opposition. The only sticking point continued to be who among the prisoners would be permitted to remain in Oklahoma and who would be assigned to Mescalero. Scott still believed that only fourteen were suitable to live within the dominant society in Oklahoma without problems. Dutch Reformed missionary Hendrina Hospers spoke out against Scott's list, stating that it was unjust "because there were others who, equally able to earn a living, were most anxious to remain."[18] She clearly spelled out her objections in a letter to Reverend Roe, who forwarded her comments, with exclamations of his support, to the Board of Indian Commissioners. Roe was steadfast in his belief that every Chiricahua head of family and single adult should be allowed to decide freely where he or she would live. Roe's written and verbal objections to Scott's list and to the credibility it was receiving grew stronger and stronger—so extreme were his pronouncements that it seemed he was harassing the board with his continual letters and public objections. Once again as in days long past, the government took careful notice because it was vulnerable to negative publicity.

By late 1912 the complex bureaucratic dispute within the Department of War and the Department of Interior had been settled—upon release the Apaches would be supervised by the latter—and a decision was reached to allow the prisoners to vote their preferences for settlement in New Mexico or Oklahoma. On December 2, 1912, the board certified the results: 176 elected to go to Mescalero, and 88 would stay in Oklahoma. Those opting for New Mexico would be provided with additional clothing, blankets, tents, heating stoves, and lumber upon their arrival. On Wednesday, April 2, 1913, a Rock Island Railway special train carrying the soon-to-be-released Chiricahua Apache prisoners of war departed Fort Sill for Tularosa, New Mexico, the nearest depot to the Mescalero Apache Reservation. On April 4 at Mescalero, Major Goode, who had accompanied the Chiricahuas, officially transferred custody to Agent Clarence R. Jefferis. The Chiricahuas' prisoner-of-war status was finally terminated.

From a secure, protected environment at Fort Sill, where they had established farms, run cows for twenty years, and attempted to recuperate from all that had befallen them, these Chiricahua Apaches were suddenly thrust into yet another way of life and were nervous about starting over again. No doubt their worries were confirmed when they discovered that the government housing they had been promised at Whitetail, a remote site atop a mountain within the reservation's borders, was not ready. To compensate for the setback, Major Goode promised that it would not be long before everyone was comfortably settled. The Chiricahuas moved into temporary tents erected not far from the agency headquarters to await transfer to their homes.

A month later Goode returned to Mescalero to inspect the progress made by the Apaches in establishing an independent way of life in their new surroundings. Imagine his surprise when he discovered them still encamped around the agency and learned that nothing of any significance had occurred.

Yet again, on October 8, 1913, Goode returned and found the Apaches in desperate need of heavy clothing. Only blankets and shoes had been distributed since their arrival from Fort Sill six months earlier. By this time winter was closing in fast, and frantic preparations were being made at Whitetail. At seven thousand feet above sea level Whitetail usually felt the full blast of winter earlier in the season than did homesites at lower altitudes. Also because of the altitude, the growing period was short, and the Apaches had already lost the opportunity to plant and harvest one season of crops as they waited for permission to function on their own. The outlook was bleak for getting everyone settled at Whitetail before the first snow, especially because many houses were only partially constructed or not even started. The rough road up the twenty-mile stretch from the agency was not totally ready, nor were the wells or stock tanks. Worst of all, there was no health facility, and many Apaches had caught pneumonia.

Thirty families were sent to Whitetail to get through the winter as best they could in the half-built homes. Those without adequate shelter, regardless of whether they were sick or well, had to spend the winter in tents. It would be a long time—nearly ten years—before the people were finally settled and in a better position to become self-sufficient or even adequately provisioned.

In January 1914 William H. Ketchum, a Jesuit priest and member of the Board of Indian Commissioners, visited the reservation, talked with the Chiricahua leaders, and later urged Congress to appropriate approximately $200,000 for both the Mescaleros and Chiricahuas to breed and raise cattle. Ultimately, a $75,000 lump sum was awarded, not enough by more than half to start up a herd, but the Chiricahuas—no strangers to challenge—dug in their heels once again and were prepared to manage their fate. Farming and cattle ranching seemed to the Whitetail Apaches to be good opportunities for self-sufficiency, so with the appropriated federal money they bought livestock and prayed to accomplish their goal. By this time families started to grow as they had in days of freedom; all ages and sizes lived together or nearby, shared a little or a lot, but were pleased to be with each other. Surely there were disagreements, but most of them kept their eyes on the future and worked toward the day when they hoped the tribe would be totally reconstituted in population and much more than a shadow of its once mighty self.

In the meantime they relied on government-supplied furnishings that were in sad condition—torn couches, battered tables, and wobbly chairs filled the small houses. While women hung curtains in some windows and put down throw rugs to make their homes look attractive, the men shored up the sagging lumber and reinforced the walls and ceilings.

Fueled by abundant wood from the surrounding forest, potbelly stoves provided heat; only a very few homes had propane. Most houses had an indoor sink in the kitchen, but pipes froze routinely during cold weather, and then the people had to walk to the school to fill buckets and cans with water from the only protected tap.

Kitchens contained just a few pots and pans, but that was not a problem. Reflecting traditional practices, the Apache preferred cooking outdoors around an open fire and eating on dishes that often were only tin pie plates; empty jelly jars and old cans served as glasses. A few elders ate with hunting knives wiped clean on pants or sleeves, as their ancestors had done in days long gone.

Outhouses were prominent and permanent fixtures across the landscape, and personal cleanliness required heating water on the stove or over an outdoor fire and pouring it into a large metal tub. To conserve precious water and fuel, bathing was often a family affair, with children using the same water one after another until everyone was clean.

The homes at Whitetail had been constructed so shoddily or were built of such poor materials that James O. Arthur, a Dutch Reformed missionary among the Chiricahuas at Whitetail observed, "When the high winds from the west . . . sweep down the canyon, every crack and knot-hole is discovered to admit the cooling breeze."[19]

Regardless of the poor conditions, the housing at Whitetail offered more protection than what was available to relatives and friends still living in the tents surrounding the Mescalero agency buildings. Several families were still there five years after they arrived on the reservation.[20]

The situation was so serious that in 1918 Scott paid a visit to Mescalero in his new role as a member of the Board of Indian Commissioners. Seeing the deplorable condition firsthand, he apologized to the Chiricahuas. "I am sorry," he said. "I am personally responsible for your people moving here."[21] He offered to escort anyone who wanted to return to Oklahoma. Several agreed to go, but they may have regretted their decision once they arrived.

Most of the Whitetail Apaches were content with their difficult lives despite the hardships. Government teachers at the new school, the Dutch Reformed missionaries, and the minister and priest from the main churches down the mountain were helping the people become comfortable with the ways of the dominant white culture. Contagious diseases, especially tuberculosis, were on the wane, and good companionship usually filled the rarefied air.

When government housing projects in the center of the reservation started at Mescalero during the 1950s, all the Chiricahuas—one or two families at a time—moved over time from Whitetail toward the center of the reservation. Transportation, paved roads, and electricity had not been available high on the mountain, and the people had concluded it was time for them to enjoy access to America's modern amenities. They simply vacated the housing at Whitetail—abandoning it much as their nomadic ancestors had left their temporary brush shelters in northern Mexico when they were on the move. One or two large oval, metal water troughs were left in the fields, no longer filled with refreshing water for the cattle and horses, but now containing discards: old high-button shoes, a lunch pail, a child's mattress, broken crockery. The barns were emptied, too, left to the snakes, birds, and other creatures to occupy.

Today, most of those old government-built drafty homes have fallen to the earth, dead from the changing values of the Apache way. Living on the New Mexico reservation, whether at Whitetail or closer to modern facilities, slowly accustomed these Chiricahuas to being a free people, and they remained a tight-knit group. They preserved their language, some of their ceremonies, several of their sacred stories, and much of their history, even though quite a few of the former prisoners of war were loathe to discuss or pass on to their descendants their experiences while confined. In time social interactions with members of the surrounding communities and cultures modified even more of what remained of most of the traditional customs, but there was always great pride in being a Chiricahua or a descendant of the notable Chiricahuas.

The grandchildren of these imprisoned Chiricahuas are now in their late sixties, seventies, and eighties and have seen and felt the impact of American society on old Apache ways. Many of these elders worry that their ancestors' customs, experiences, and lifestyles will soon be unimportant memories to the next generation or will be lost altogether, and that their children and grandchildren will be completely acculturated into the anonymity of the American melting pot.

In the face of that fear, one ancient ritual is held every year around July 4: the puberty ceremony, a rite that publicly marks the passage of a girl from her youth to early adulthood. Everyone is invited. Private ceremonies are also periodically held, and attendance at those is limited to invitation only. Some celebrations may be held at Whitetail, not far from homes the girls' ancestors occupied.

Another tradition that remains strong is the Dance of the Mountain Spirits. Today it is performed publicly and privately. Author Clifford Coppersmith states that the dance "has lost much of its spiritual significance for most members of the tribe [but] still projects a powerful political and cultural symbolism which personifies the survival of Chiricahua . . . identity."[22]

The Apache language is still spoken freely at Mescalero among the elders; some members of the younger generation also understand, but English is the main language of communication. Elders are part of the reservation school system and speak in their native language to children in the early grades in order to keep the language alive. A dictionary of the Chiricahua/Mescalero vocabulary has been compiled and published; it is arranged by topic. Unfortunately, an audiotape demonstrating pronunciation of this difficult language is not available with the dictionary.

Many Chiricahuas of all ages still practice certain cultural customs, such as healing ceremonies with the medicine people. However, the presence of mainstream medicine is unmistakable. Staffed by young physicians who move quickly on and off the reservation, the Public Health Services' Mescalero Indian Hospital sits on a hill within sight of the administration complex and provides emergency services, follow-up examinations, clinics, and health counseling such as nutrition instructions and care for diabetes. For surgery or complicated medical conditions the Chiricahuas are referred to area hospitals.

Although the majority of Chiricahuas are practicing Christians—Catholics or Protestants—many elders compartmentalize these organized ways of worship with the old, traditional religion and see no conflict. The attraction of pow-wows—once an essential social, political, and religious ingredient in most Indian societies, but not in the Chiricahua community—is growing among Chiricahua young men and women. Like the puberty ceremony, the pow-wow is an opportunity for socializing and in some cases for the excesses of youth. Occasionally a pow-wow is held on the reservation, but a main attraction is the annual Gathering of Nations, easily accessible two hundred miles to the north in Albuquerque, New Mexico.

Contemporary acculturation at Mescalero may be likened to a sieve through which the traditional ways of life have been filtered. Those customs that have successfully passed through the separator are then further sorted and ranked according to subjective categories such as the intensity of their meaning throughout Apache history. All in all, despite the impact of both the forced cultural changes and the voluntary cultural adaptations, the closed Chiricahua community within the borders of the Mescalero Apache Reservation has managed to maintain a degree of cultural identity and allegiance to several of their ancestors' traditions while participating in the dominant society's activities as well.

Not so in Oklahoma, however. In the growing farm towns around Fort Sill in 1914 initial conditions for the remaining Chiricahuas were not much better than those experienced at Whitetail. Freedom for the prisoners who had opted to remain in Oklahoma was delayed for more than a year. The promised allotments of land were so slow in being bureaucratically processed that at the end of 1920, seven years after the majority of Chiricahuas went to New Mexico, thirteen Apaches were still waiting and depending on friends and relatives for shelter and sustenance. Another problem was that the farming and ranching achievements realized by the prisoners during twenty years at Fort Sill could not be transferred to the new living arrangement. It is true that the Apaches were paid the proceeds from the sale of their livestock and crops, but beginning anew required energetic initiatives from each family, some of whom were very ill and unable to manage a farm or run cows. Moreover, no longer could these Oklahomans count on support from friends and relatives, as they had been doing as prisoners for decades. Now each family was on its own and had to struggle for a livelihood. These Oklahomans were dropped into the middle of an agrarian society that regarded them as suspiciously as they regarded their neighbors. To make matters worse, many of their loved ones, on whom they should have been able to count for cultural, physical, and emotional support, were far away in New Mexico, having their own serious difficulties with adjustment to freedom.

In order to survive, the Oklahoma Chiricahuas struggled with farming, trying to eke out a living by raising pigs or crops. Some also labored in the neighbors' fields for day wages, while others found work with the army at Fort Sill. A new generation of educated Apaches took leadership, as was happening at Mescalero, while the former adult prisoners of war grew older. "Life in the scattered family allotments around the small rural communities of Apache, Fletcher, and Elgin [all Oklahoma towns] differed from the kinship-based and tight-knit village life at Fort Sill," concludes Coppersmith.[23]

No longer were the Apaches easily able to communicate with one another, as they had to travel by hack and horseback over country roads to visit friends all over the environs. Even though many lived in the town of Apache or on its outskirts and could visit with each other when time permitted, tribal allegiance was breaking down as the farmers had to pay more attention to their livelihood than to the larger community. And then there was the situation regarding the allotted lands, promised to be 160 acres per person. "No one got 160 acres," said Mildred Cleghorn, former tribal chairperson:

The closest they got was 158 acres and the least amount they got was twenty-three. A majority received eighty acres apiece. My father [Richard Imach, child prisoner of war] got eighty acres and my mother [Amy Wratten, born a prisoner of war in Alabama] got eighty acres and I live on my fifty acres. Yes, we were promised 160 acres apiece, but Uncle Sam doesn't follow through. . . . We in Oklahoma stayed [at Fort Sill] one year longer [than those who went to Mescalero]. Because we had to find a place to live. It was about 1923 that the last Apache got an allotment.[24]

Actually, by December 23, 1920, twelve minors and one adult (the thirteen mentioned earlier) had received neither their promised rations of food (until they could raise a crop) nor their allotments. Three Apache men wrote an open letter "to those who Believe in a Square Deal for the Indians" about the situation. After a brief one-page history and background of their reason for writing, the men stated:

It will be seen that thirteen members of the band are entitled to allotments not yet obtained by the Government for them. For the almost seven years which have elapsed since these people were supposed to receive their allotments, they have lost the use or rental which would have been derived from the lands . . . and which would have been accruing to the credit of said minors. The rations were not issued nor were they paid in lieu of the failure of their issuance, so there has been real and painful deprivation in this matter. It is true that these Indians are not farming, and are doing creditably, but they had to take money from the sale of their cattle to buy provisions with, which money otherwise could have been invested in stock or needed implements.

We are not asking any favors, but only that the promises of the government to us be fulfilled by the Congress if possible. Will you, in the name of what is fair and square, do what you can to help us in this matter? We who sign this letter are hard-working farmers, asking only what white men would ask, that we be paid what is owed us, and that we be paid now.

Thanking you for your assistance, we are

Jason Betzinez
James Kaywaykla
Talbot Goody[25]

Filled or unfilled, the government's promises to these Fort Sill Apaches formed the basis of a community that surprisingly is still connected today and focused in a tribal complex located north of town on an allotment of land that once belonged to Dorothy Naiche Kaywaykla—granddaughter of Cochise, daughter of Naiche, and wife of James Kaywaykla. The tribe purchased property from her descendants, built its administrative offices on it, and then added several outbuildings over time, including a gymnasium and a facility that houses social programs. Nearby are dance grounds where an annual celebration is held each September to honor and commemorate the tribe's heritage. Attended by members of various area Indian tribes, close non-Indian friends, and rarely by local Anglo residents, the event might be misconstrued as a "mini-pow-wow."

The puberty ceremony is almost never held among the Oklahoma Chiricahuas. Coppersmith reports that Michael Darrow, the tribal historian, informed him that the

> tribal elders made a conscious decision not to practice this rite for a number of reasons. First, to be practiced correctly and in its entirety the Coming Out ceremony is expensive. It could become a significant burden for a people struggling to survive . . . in the decades after their release from Fort Sill. Second, to be practiced correctly, elements of the ceremony require commodities such as lodge poles which were not available, again without a great deal of expense, from the local area. For the ceremony conducted in Apache in 1994 cedar poles and mescal leaves were trucked in from New Mexico. In essence the tribal elders from the early post-allotment period decided not to practice the Coming Out ceremony. Therefore, it receded from its preeminent place in Chiricahua . . . Apache life.[26]

The Dance of the Mountain Spirits is performed by Oklahoma Chiricahua men and is a highlight of the annual September festival. Chiricahua and Mescalero friends and relatives are always invited, as are some of the New Mexico dance groups; many make the five-hundred-mile trip to renew tribal and family connections.

During these visits one may occasionally hear snippets of the ancestral language, but today many Oklahoma Chiricahuas are unable to speak as their ancestors did, a casualty dating back to days following release from incarceration. Many of the young adults back then were already able to speak English because of their Carlisle School education. As young married people, they spoke English at home, and when their children heard and began to use the language, English gradually became the family's first language.

When an elder dies, families of all ages may gather for the burial at the Apache Prisoner of War Cemetery on the grounds of Fort Sill. There, the

Geronimo's grave at Fort Sill Apache Prisoner of War Cemetery. PHOTO BY THE AUTHOR, SEPTEMBER 1998.

tribe's history cannot be ignored. Hundreds of graves of the prisoners of war and their descendants cover a vast expanse of military headstones, prominent among which is Geronimo's unique marker, a pyramidal-shaped mix of stones and cement five to six feet high and topped by a cement eagle.

The mold for the eagle is in constant use because the symbol is periodically broken off its base and stolen by souvenir hunters. A tree close to the gravesite is usually festooned with ribbons, balloons, and notes to the famous warrior who was buried in a Christian ceremony.

The history of this great people and their relations with the surrounding dominant cultures has always been the stuff of legends, and the passage of time has not dimmed that history. Yes, certainly the outside culture has had an impact and has caused many changes, but the Chiricahuas' traditional vitality—their power and strength—has refused to surrender. Whether jailers punish them with imprisonment as in the past, or current detractors lambaste them in the media for their newly acquired riches through casino gambling, the mighty Chiricahua Apache spirit, so evident in the bones and blood of the people, can be neither totally captured nor totally compromised.

"We're not like the other groups," says Kathleen Kanseah, great-great-granddaughter of the warrior Clee-neh. "We're Chiricahuas, and we will never give in, not as long as one drop of Apache blood flows in our veins."[27]

Notes

Introduction

1. Born near Dayton, Ohio, on September 8, 1930, George Crook graduated from West Point in 1852. He participated in the Civil War, was breveted major general of volunteers in July 1864, and was put in command of the Army of West Virginia. In late February 1865 Crook was captured by Confederates and was exchanged the following month. He was breveted brigadier and major general on March 14, 1865, thereafter distinguishing himself in several campaigns against Indians. He died on March 21, 1890, at Chicago while in command of the Department of the West. He was originally buried in Oakland, Maryland, but was moved to section 2 of Arlington National Cemetery on November 11, 1898. For more information, see primarily Schmitt, ed., *General George Crook: His Autobiography*, and Bourke, *On the Border with Crook*. Lamar includes a long biography of Crook in *The New Encyclopedia of the American West*, pp. 275–76, as does Thrapp in *Encyclopedia of Frontier Biography*, pp. 348–50.

2. Born on August 8, 1839, near Westminster, Massachusetts, Nelson Appleton Miles joined a company of volunteers in 1861. He was commissioned as a captain and served on General Oliver O. Howard's staff. Miles served as commanding general of the U.S. Army from October 5, 1895, to August 8, 1903. For more information, see Thrapp, *Encyclopedia of Frontier Biography*, p. 986, and Lamar, *The New Encyclopedia of the American West*, p. 699.

3. A remote site on the Arizona-Mexico border.

4. Mangus, son of Mangas Coloradas, headed up the last Chiricahua group to surrender about a month after Geronimo did. Mangus and his followers were also imprisoned in Florida.

5. Debo, *Geronimo*, p. 259.

6. An inspiring slogan based on a core concept that "Americans are destined by divine providence to expand their national domain" (Lamar, *The New Encyclopedia of the American West*, p. 676).

7. Thrapp writes that the "Apacheria was enormous in extent. It stretched from the willow thickets along the Colorado into the broken mountains beyond the Rio Grande, and from the great canyons of the north southward for a thousand miles into Mexico, excepting of course the agricultural empire of the peace-

ful Papagos and Maricopas along the Gila and other streams tributary to it. The tribes of Apacheria were a product of their habitat, harsh, cruel, and pitiless" (*The Conquest of Apacheria*, p. x).

Chapter 1

Note: Known originally as the Castillo de San Marcos, Fort Marion is the oldest masonry fortress in North America. In the year 1672 a Spanish military engineer named Ignacio Daza drew the plan and organized work crews to start building a strong fort. Castillo de San Marcos has served not only Spanish, but also British and U.S. military forces as the key defense of early Florida and its capital city, St. Augustine (from public relations literature handed out at the fort). Protected by a moat, the fort has walls that are thirty feet high and up to fourteen feet thick. A drawbridge is lowered across the moat to allow tourists access.

1. Born around 1822, possibly in the Dragoon Mountains of southeast Arizona, Chihuahua was a courageous warrior and an outstanding leader. By the 1880s he had become prominent in the Chiricahuas' major activities. By 1883 he was living on the San Carlos Reservation, where he stayed until May 15, 1885, when he went out with Geronimo. He was the first important leader to surrender, in March 1886, to General George Crook. Chihuahua lived through the early years of imprisonment; he died at Fort Sill on July 25, 1901. For more information, see Thrapp, *The Conquest of Apacheria*, and Thrapp, *Encyclopedia of Frontier Biography*, p. 262.

2. Fort Bowie was first established on July 28, 1862. Located in the Chiricahua Mountains on the eastern approaches to Apache Pass, the post was intended to protect travelers and to guard the important spring that provided water to the area. In 1868 the post was moved from its original site to a new location on a nearby hill. The fort was abandoned on October 17, 1894, after the Apaches had been removed from the area. It has been brought back to life and is a popular tourist attraction today. See Frazer, *Forts of the West*, p. 4.

3. Born in New York (?) in 1831, Philip H. Sheridan graduated from West Point in 1853. In *The New Encyclopedia of the American West*, Lamar calls Sheridan "The pre-eminent figure in the frontier army" (p. 1043). In *Encyclopedia of Frontier Biography*, Thrapp calls him "something of a sycophant, not markedly original in thought . . . [someone who] found it difficult to correct his own erroneous views, was often harshly inflexible when compromise might efficiently accomplish desired ends, and on the whole, while attractive to many was less appealing to others" (pp. 1295–96). The literature about Sheridan is abundant. For more information, see primarily Hutton, *Phil Sheridan and His Army*, and Rister, *Border Command: General Phil Sheridan in the West*.

4. Born a Warm Springs Chiricahua, Kaahteney fought under Chief Victorio. When Victorio and his band made their last stand at Tres Castillos, Mexico, in October 1880, Kaahteney was in the rear guard and escaped death. He enlisted as a scout for General Crook on March 20, 1884. He survived imprisonment and died on the Mescalero Apache Reservation, date unknown.

5. Crook, "Résumé of Operations Against Apache Indians, 1882 to 1886," pp. 576–77.

6. The full text of the conversation among Chihuahua, Geronimo, and General Crook may be found in *Conference Held on March 25 and 27, 1886*, Senate Exec. Doc. 88 (51-1), pp. 11–17.

7. Born in 1856, Naiche was the younger of Cochise's two sons. His mother was Dos-teh-seh, a daughter of Mangas Coloradas. During the 1861 Bascom affair Naiche was a child captive of the U.S. Army, held at Fort Buchanan, but shortly released. He was with his father in 1872, when Cochise surrendered to Brigadier General Howard at Council Rocks in Arizona. When Cochise died in 1874, his eldest son, Taza, became the leader, but upon Taza's death two years later Naiche took over. Thrapp states that Naiche "was less able than Cochise or Taza, but was a fine warrior and held the respect of his people . . . [remaining] nominal leader during Geronimo's campaigns, deferred to by the other who was a war leader but himself never a chief" (*Encyclopedia of Frontier Biography*, pp. 1037–38). Naiche fully participated in all the Chiricahuas' attempts to remain free but surrendered with Geronimo in September 1886 and was sent to prison in Florida. He survived incarceration and was released to the Mescalero Apache Reservation in 1913. Naiche married three times; his first and second wives died at Fort Sill. He fathered eight sons and six daughters; six of the sons and two of the daughters died at Fort Sill. Suffering for years from tuberculosis, Naiche died of influenza on March 16, 1919, at the Mescalero Hospital.

8. *Conference Held on March 25 and 27, 1886*, U.S. Senate Exec. Doc. 88 (51-1), pp. 12–16.

9. Crook, "Résumé of Operations Against Apache Indians," p. 578.

10. Crook to Sheridan, telegram, March 31, 1886, Chiricahua Apache Collection.

11. Crook, "Résumé of Operations Against Apache Indians,," p. 581.

12. Born March 1, 1859, in Lynn, Massachusetts, Charles Lummis was educated at Harvard. In 1884 he walked from Ohio to Los Angeles, sending articles to the *Los Angeles Times* all along the way. He worked for the newspaper for two years, after which he lived at Isleta Pueblo in New Mexico for five years to recoup his health. He traveled widely all across the United States; founded many organizations, including the Southwest Museum; was a member of many archeological, literary, and historical organizations; and, according to Thrapp, "did much to shape the culture of the southwest. And to better orient it toward respect for its varied past" (*Encyclopedia of Frontier Biography*, pp. 884–85). He died on November 25, 1928.

13. Thrapp, *Dateline Fort Bowie*, p. 33.

14. The Tribolet (spelling varies) brothers were liquor dealers in Tombstone, Arizona. They apparently had had prior contact with the Geronimo band because one of them, Robert, was able to gain access to the Apache camp at Cañon de los Embudos and there to peddle his whiskey to the people. The Tribolet mentioned in Lummis's article could have been worried that if Geronimo and the others surrendered, it would mean that the soldiers—some of his best customers—would leave the area, so it was in his best interest to keep the Apaches free. Lummis stated that General Crook told him, "That man Tribolet is the cause of this whole trouble now. If it had not been for his whisky, those renegades would never have decamped, the whole thing would now be settled and we would be reaping the

results of nearly a year's arduous work. . . . Oh, no, there's no way of dealing with Tribolet. He has been tried before, but bought his way out. If we had shot him down like a coyote, as he deserved to be, it would have raised a terrible row. Why, that man has a beef contract for our Army. . . . Now this man Tribolet may be, through that action of his, the cause of death of a thousand people. There is no knowing where this thing will end, now. And such fellows as he can undo the whole work of a great government, without recourse" (qtd. in Thrapp, *Dateline Fort Bowie*, p. 75). A customs officer named George M. Green told Lummis, "Tribolet has told me he didn't want the hostiles captured. 'Why,' said he, 'it's money in my pocket to have those fellows out.' He bragged to me how much whisky he had sold them, and how he had given Geronimo a bottle of champagne" (p. 76). After Geronimo's final surrender in September 1886, Robert Tribolet established a ranch or farm near Fronteras, Sonora. He was arrested for robbing a stagecoach and apparently shot while trying to escape. Thrapp states that Tribolet family members remember that he was lynched by mistake after a cattle or horse robbery. Mexico then is alleged to have paid the family fifty thousand U.S. dollars for the mistake. Thrapp reports, however, that "The facts of the case have never been researched out" (*Encyclopedia of Frontier Biography*, p. 1441).

15. Born in Maryland in 1850, Marion Maus graduated from West Point in 1874 and joined the First Infantry. He became a captain in 1890. In 1885–86 he was second in command to Captain Emmet Crawford on an expedition penetrating the Sonora Sierra Madre in pursuit of Geronimo. When Crawford was killed by Mexican irregulars, Maus assumed command and eventually arranged for the March meeting between Geronimo and Crook. He died at New Windsor, Maryland, in 1930 (Thrapp, *Encyclopedia of Frontier Biography*, p. 960). For more information, see Miles, *Personal Recollections*, pp. 450–71.

16. Thrapp, *Dateline Fort Bowie*, pp. 50–51.

17. Ibid., pp. 35–36, 65.

18. Lummis is probably referring to Kaahteney here.

19. Thrapp, *Dateline Fort Bowie*, pp. 62–63. Chihuahua's continued references to his family illustrate the love and high regard Apaches had for their immediate and extended families. Many observers commented on this cultural trait.

20. Cleveland was elected president twice and served 1885–89 and 1893–97.

21. *Repair of Fort Marion*, U.S. Senate Report 184, and *Repairing Fort Marion*, U.S. Senate Report 189. Needing repairs were the lookout towers, the parapet walls, the chapel entrance, the counterscarp walls, and steps to the ditch (which also needed regrading), the breast-height wall of the covered way, the glacis, and the drains in the seawall.

22. Stockel, *Survival of the Spirit*, p. 69.

23. Born in New York and appointed to West Point from New York, Loomis Langdon was made brevet second lieutenant on July 1, 1854; second lieutenant First Artillery on August 21, 1854; captain on August 28, 1861; and brevet major on February 20, 1864, for gallantry and meritorious service in the Battle of Olustee, Florida. He was made brevet lieutenant colonel on September 29, 1864, for gallant and meritorious service in the attack on Fort Gilmer, Virginia. He became a major of the Second Artillery in March 1879.

24. *Education of the Apaches in Florida,* U.S. Senate Exec. Doc. 73 (49-2), pp. 5–6. Attention must be called here to Langdon's worry about "evil-disposed people" of St. Augustine gaining access to the Chiricahuas. Similar statements appear several times in other examples of military correspondence.

25. This reference is to Captain Richard Henry Pratt. Born in Rushford, New York, on December 6, 1840, Pratt enlisted as a corporal in the Ninth Indiana Infantry on April 20, 1861. He became a sergeant in the Second Indiana Cavalry on September 18, 1861; was commissioned a first lieutenant of the Eleventh Indiana Cavalry on April 20, 1864; and then was made captain on September 20, 1864. He was commissioned a second lieutenant of the Tenth U.S. Cavalry on March 7, 1867, and a first lieutenant on July 31, 1867, and was promoted regularly after that, finally reaching the rank of brigadier general on April 23, 1904. Pratt participated in winter campaigns against the Cheyennes, Comanches, and Kiowas in 1868–69 and again on the Southern Plains in 1874–75, when he led Indian scouts. He was placed in charge of Cheyenne and Comanche prisoners, taking them to Fort Marion, where he began to educate them. He eventually became the superintendent of the Carlisle Indian School in Pennsylvania. His papers are at Yale University and span his long career as an army officer, educator, and advocate for Indian causes. It was as he was fighting Indians on the frontier that he developed the theories that were to guide him throughout his life. He believed that the American Indian, although leading an "uncivilized" life, was fully capable of being educated and absorbed into American society. Thrapp, in the supplemental volume to *Encyclopedia of Frontier Biography* (p. 422), devotes nearly a full page to Pratt's biography. Lamar, in *The New Encyclopedia of the American West* (pp. 910–11), is not as generous. Thrapp states that Pratt "believed that the solution of the Indian problem did not lie [in preserving or developing] Indian culture but was rather in teaching the Indian to make a place for himself in the world" (*Encyclopedia of Frontier Biography,* p. 422). Lamar agrees, stating that "Pratt believed that the only satisfactory way to educate and assimilate Indians was to remove them from the reservations as children and surround them with Euro-American influences" (*The New Encyclopedia of the American West,* p. 910). Literature about Pratt and the Carlisle School is abundant. Pratt and the children's experiences at the school are discussed more fully in chapter 3.

26. *Education of the Apaches in Florida,* U.S. Senate Exec. Doc. 73 (49-2), pp. 5–7. Communiqué dated August 23, 1886. Many writers and researchers have commented on the Chiricahuas' great love for their children, whom they regarded as the future of the tribe, a most important consideration, made more so because the circumstances of imprisonment cast doubt on the people's destiny.

27. *Report of the Treatment of Certain Apache Indians,* U.S. Senate Exec. Doc. 83 (51-1), p. 18.

28. Ibid.

29. Darrow, conversation with the author, May 1991.

30. *Message from the President of the United States,* U.S. Senate Exec. Doc. 35 (51-1), pp. 34–35.

31. Born in 1854, Chatto was among the earliest Chiricahuas to make peace in 1883. He became a sergeant of a scout company under Lieutenant Britton

Davis and took part in the pursuit of Geronimo following the 1885 outbreak. According to Thrapp, Davis called Chatto "One of the finest men, red or white, I have ever known." Thrapp says Chatto was embittered by the prisoner-of-war experience (*Encyclopedia of Frontier Biography*, p. 259). He survived imprisonment and lived on the Mescalero Apache Reservation until August 13, 1934, when he died in an auto accident.

32. Named after Brigadier General Henry Leavenworth, the fort was originally designated Cantonment Leavenworth in 1827 and renamed Fort Leavenworth in 1832. It was quite important to the settlement of the West during the frontier period. Today the fort hosts the U.S. Army Combined Arms Center and the General Staff College.

33. *In Response to the Resolution of February 11, 1887,* U.S. Senate Exec. Doc. 117 (49-2), p. 67.

34. Lamar characterizes the Indian Rights Association as a "humanitarian reform group." The group was open to all for membership, "but Welsh deliberately solicited support from elite Philadelphians who would bring both money and personal connections to the association." It was a watchdog group that employed a full-time lobbyist in Washington. "The association aggressively supported Indian assimilation, particularly programs . . . which would bring an end to the reservation system" (*The New Encyclopedia of the American West*, p. 530). The University of California at Berkeley houses a great deal of information on the Indians Rights Association.

35. Herbert Welsh and other Americans found this situation outrageous. In his report entitled "The Apache Prisoners at Fort Marion," Welsh describes this situation as "the injustice with which the good behavior, the fidelity and, in some instances, the distinguished services of these imprisoned Chiricahua Indians have been rewarded by the government of the United States. I hold that in this case a fundamental principle of just and wise policy in the treatment of Indians has been violated, for not only have the innocent been condemned unheard, but the meritorious have received the punishment of the guilty" (p. 20). If Washington officials read the report, they turned a deaf ear to Welsh's objections, and the imprisonment continued. Professor Charles Painter, an Indian Rights Association agent, had a meeting with President Cleveland regarding this unusual matter. According to Welsh, in a brief written statement for his files, "The President told Prof. Painter that no discrimination had been made between the guilty and the innocent among these Indians because of necessary haste in their removal. Five months have elapsed since their imprisonment. The President also said he did not believe that they were so crowded as to endanger health" ("Welsh to file," n.d., Chiricahua Apache Collection).

36. *Message from the President of the United States,* U.S. Senate Exec. Doc. 35 (51-1), p. 34.

37. Numbers are not firm.

38. A member of a prominent Philadelphia family, Herbert Welsh founded the Indian Rights Association in 1882 and served in various leadership positions until his death in 1941. According to Lamar, the association directed itself toward "abolishing the reservation system, which humanitarians deemed the cause of

Indians' poverty, ill health and lack of civil rights" (*The New Encyclopedia of the American West*, p. 530). The association's lobbying activities in Washington distinguished it from other Indian advocacy organizations of the day. See also Hagan, *The Indian Rights Association: The Herbert Welsh Years, 1882–1904*.

39. Welsh to War Department, letter, n.d., Chiricahua Apache Collection.

40. Two bathtubs for approximately five hundred people.

41. *Education of the Apaches in Florida*, U.S. Senate Exec. Doc. 73 (49-2), p. 8. It is perhaps difficult to believe that statement.

42. This reference is to the Chiricahuas from Fort Apache. Those from Chihuahua's group apparently were free from malaria on arrival.

43. Webb, M.D., "Apaches at Castillo San Marcos," speech, September 1887. Born on December 19, 1840, in Clinton, New York, DeWitt Webb graduated from the New York College of Physicians and Surgeons. He was elected to a two-year term at the New York State House of Representatives, from 1903 to 1905. He then moved his family to Florida, and from 1911 to 1912 he served as mayor of St. Augustine. Webb was president of the staff of Flagler Hospital and for fifteen years was special physician in charge of the State School for the Deaf and Blind. For a number of years he was superintendent of the Sunday School of Flagler Memorial Church, where he also served as an elder. During his tenure as acting assistant surgeon and medical officer at Fort Marion, he gained the friendship of the Indians imprisoned there and acquired a great deal of knowledge that served him well some years later when the government sent him into the Everglades to investigate conditions among the Seminoles. Webb died on April 14, 1917.

44. There were twelve births among the Apaches at Fort Marion, one of them being Geronimo's daughter Marion, named for the fort. Welsh, "The Apache Prisoners at Fort Marion," pp. 14–15.

45. Probably Chatto's delegation.

46. Edwards has the wrong date. By October 26 Chihuahua's people had been imprisoned for six months.

47. Edwards, "Waiting for the Indians," pp. 1–3. These oral histories must be read with full acknowledgment of the writers' perceptions and the social climate of the times. I especially refer to the writer's use of the word *negro*. Also, some dates may be incorrect.

48. The Apache children had not yet returned from the Carlisle School, so Sabate could not have known that they were intelligent and learned rapidly.

49. Is Dick Hicks the same individual the Apache woman at the well encountered? There is no empirical evidence that a black man was part of any Apache group.

50. Sabate, "Apaches Were Here," pp. 1–2.

51. Johnston, "Saved by an Apache," pp. 1–2.

52. *Florida Times-Union*, April 15, April 19, and April 21, 1887.

53. *Education of the Apaches in Florida*, U.S. Senate Exec. Doc. 73 (49-2), p. 11.

54. Ibid., pp. 2, 5, 7, 11, 13, 16, 17, 19. The children initially were taught in the dark and dank casemate that was immediately off the fort's courtyard. They came under the direction of a young French nun, Mother Alypius, and Sister Jane

Francis. Instructions in reading, writing, drawing, and singing were conducted daily from nine o'clock in the morning until noon (Stockel, *Survival of the Spirit*, pp. 116–17).

55. *Education of the Apaches in Florida*, U.S. Senate Exec. Doc. 73 (49-2), p. 17. The nuns accommodated sixty-eight youngsters.

56. Welsh, "The Apache Prisoners at Fort Marion," p. 12.

Chapter 2

Note: Fort Pickens occupies the western tip of Santa Rosa Island at the eastern entrance to Pensacola Harbor. The pentagonal stone structure, built in 1834, is now part of the Gulf Islands National Seashore. In 1886 it was unoccupied, had not been cared for in many years, and was badly in need of a cleanup. See Bearss, *Historic Structure Report*.

1. *In Response to the Resolution of February 11, 1887*, U.S. Senate Exec. Doc. 117 (49-2), p. 2.

2. Ibid., pp. 2–3.

3. Located in southeastern Arizona within sight of the Dragoon and Chiricahua Mountains, Fort Huachuca sent out regular patrols to attempt to keep peace in the area. In the final months of the Geronimo campaign, the 290-acre fort served as advance headquarters. In time it became the location of the Buffalo Soldiers and today specializes in information technology, electronics, and communications. See Swartly, *Old Forts of the Apache Wars*, pp. 35–36.

4. *In Response to the Resolution of February 11, 1887*, U.S. Senate Exec. Doc. 117 (49-2), p. 3. Born March 17, 1843, near Toledo, Ohio, Henry Lawton enlisted in the Ninth Indiana Infantry in 1861 and became a first lieutenant of the Thirtieth Indiana, serving with Sherman's forces. He rose to the rank of lieutenant colonel, winning a Medal of Honor at Atlanta. After briefly studying law at Harvard, he accepted a commission in the Forty-first, later the Twenty-fourth Infantry, a black regiment. In 1871 he was transferred to the Fourth Cavalry, serving under Ranald S. Mackenzie in West Texas, mainly as a quartermaster. Thrapp writes, "In 1886 under General Miles, Lawton headed a fruitless search of the Sierra Madre in Sonora for Geronimo and received his surrender after it had been arranged by Lieutenant Charles B. Gatewood" (*Encyclopedia of Frontier Biography*, pp. 821–22). During service in the Spanish-American War, he was killed instantly while he was directing troops opposite San Mateo, east of Manila, on December 19, 1899.

5. *In Response to the Resolution of February 11, 1887*, U.S. Senate Exec. Doc. 117 (49-2), p. 4. The acting secretary of war forwarded this telegram the next day, August 20, 1886, to President Cleveland, who was vacationing at the Saranac Inn, Bloomingdale, Essex County, New York, and to the secretary of war, at Salem, Massachusetts.

6. Ibid., p. 4.

7. Born November 8, 1830, at Leeds, Maine, Oliver Otis Howard attended West Point and was commissioned a brevet second lieutenant of ordnance on July 1, 1854, and a second lieutenant on February 15, 1855. He served at various arse-

nals until 1857, when he operated against the Seminole Indians in Florida. He became a first lieutenant in 1857 and had a distinguished career during the Civil War. He lost an arm at Fair Oaks and won a Medal of Honor and the thanks of Congress for his services at Gettysburg. He ended the war as major general of volunteers, a brigadier general of the army, and a brevet major general. In 1872 President Ulysses Grant named him a special Indian commissioner and directed him to go to the Southwest to deal with "Apache unrest and hostility," according to Thrapp. "Howard was honest, compassionate and of undoubted personal courage and on the whole his career on the frontier was distinctly positive" (*Encyclopedia of Frontier Biography*, pp. 683–84). Lamar writes about Howard's relationship with Cochise, with whom he reached an agreement to surrender in 1872: "Howard's work was criticized on the grounds that it was a verbal agreement and thus open to interpretation" (*The New Encyclopedia of the American West*, pp. 500–501). Nonetheless, Cochise honored the agreement. Howard was nicknamed the "Christian general" owing to his religious faith. He died at Burlington, Vermont, on October 26, 1909. See also Thrapp, *The Conquest of Apacheria*. Literature about Howard is abundant.

8. "Unconditional surrender" was not what Crook had offered the Chiricahuas when they met in March in Cañon de los Embudos. At that time he promised the Apaches that they would be imprisoned for a period of two years and then be permitted to return to Arizona. Miles's instructions were different, but they were not known to the Chiricahuas, who assumed Crook's offer was still valid when they surrendered to Miles in Skeleton Canyon.

9. *In Response to the Resolution of February 11, 1887*, U.S. Senate Exec. Doc. 117 (49-2), p. 5. The acting secretary of war forwarded this telegram to the president and to the secretary of war on August 25, 1886.

10. Born on April 6, 1853, near Woodstock, Virginia, of a secessionist family, Charles Gatewood attended West Point and on graduation in 1877 was assigned to the Sixth Cavalry. He then "embarked upon a singular career in the Apache country as commander of Indian scouts," reports Thrapp. "His experience in the numerous Apache outbreaks was perhaps more extensive and more indispensable than that of any other officer . . . although Gatewood never received any particular recognition for his intrepidity and devotion to duty on the part of Miles or other officers of the Miles faction. This is not only to Miles' eternal discredit, but also to that of his country" (*Encyclopedia of Frontier Biography*, pp. 543–44). Gatewood had many physical ailments and was in poor health, which forced him to retire from active duty. He died at Fort Monroe on May 20, 1896. Literature about Gatewood is abundant. One of the most recent works is Kraft, *Gatewood and Geronimo*. A classic is Debo, *Geronimo: The Man, His Time, His Place*. Miles had approached Gatewood to be his "peace emissary" to Geronimo, revealing to Gatewood that Chiricahua scouts Martine and Kayitah had already consented to search for Geronimo in Mexico. Gatewood agreed and organized a small party at Fort Huachuca consisting of himself, the two scouts, courier Tex Whaley, packer Frank Huston, and the official interpreter George Wratten. This group came across Lawton and his men at their main camp on the Arros River and learned that they had not seen Geronimo. So the Gatewood party moved on, leaving a frustrated Lawton and his group of forty-five soldiers behind.

11. These negotiations put Gatewood and his group, rather than Lawton, at the center of the event.

12. Haozous, "Personal Reminiscences Concerning Geronimo," pp. 25–26. Ruey Darrow, Sam Haozous's daughter, loaned the original tape to the American Indian Institute so that it could be copied for the Oral History project. Members of the Haozous family made the tape in 1956 in order to preserve some of the reminiscences and experiences of their father, who was more than ninety years old at the time. As a young man, Sam Haozous, a relative of Geronimo, had witnessed firsthand many of the experiences of Apache groups in the Southwest and had known Geronimo before his final surrender to General Nelson Miles (American Indian Oral History, the Duke Collection).

13. Miles, *Personal Recollections and Observations*, pp. 520–21.

14. In his autobiography Geronimo says that General Miles told him, "I will take you under Government protection; I will build you a house; I will fence you much land; I will give you cattle, horses, mules, farming implements. You will be furnished with men to work the farm, for you yourself will not have to work. In the fall I will send you blankets and clothing so that you will not suffer from cold in the wintertime. . . . While I live you will not be arrested" (Barrett, ed., *Geronimo: His Own Story*, pp. 154–55). Geronimo believed that Miles never fulfilled his promises.

15. Skinner, *The Apache Rock Crumbles*, p. 71.

16. *In Response to the Resolution of February 11, 1887*, U.S. Senate Exec. Doc. 117 (49-2), p. 7.

17. Ibid., p. 8.

18. Ibid.

19. Ibid. p. 10.

20. Ibid.

21. Ibid., p. 11.

22. Ibid., pp. 12–13.

23. Ibid., p. 13. In volume 2 of his recollections, Miles included one sentence about this event: "These Indians were for a time detained at San Antonio, Texas, but were subsequently forwarded to their destination in Florida" (*Personal Recollections and Observations*, p. 528). Miles's reluctance to give Gatewood and his party the credit for finding Geronimo in Mexico, preferring instead to credit Captain Lawton, has been one of the enduring topics of discussion in the history of the American West. Kraft presents an accurate description of the events leading to Geronimo's surrender and immediately thereafter (*Gatewood and Geronimo*, pp. 149–72); Lawton is mentioned peripherally and only after the surrender.

24. *In Response to the Resolution of February 11, 1887*, U.S. Senate Exec. Doc. 117 (49-2), p. 13.

25. Ibid., p. 14. Geronimo, Naiche, and their followers were held at Fort Sam Houston, established in 1879 following San Antonio's donation, in 1870, of enough land for a permanent post; additional land was donated in 1871 and 1875. Erection of the post began in 1876; permanent quarters for headquarters staff were added in 1881. In 1885 construction of housing was begun. The fort was

known as the Post of San Antonio until September 10, 1890, when it was named Fort Sam Houston (Frazer, *Forts of the West*, pp. 159–60).

26. Debo, *Geronimo*, p. 292.

27. Ibid., p. 303.

28. *Frank Leslie's Illustrated Newspaper*, September 25, 1886.

29. Born on January 31, 1865, at Sonoma, California, George Wratten moved with his parents to Florence, Arizona, when he was fourteen. He became associated with the Apaches at the San Carlos Reservation and learned to speak their language fluently. In 1881 Wratten was named chief of scouts, doubling as an interpreter, and served as superintendent of pack trains. He was with Gatewood when Geronimo surrendered, and he volunteered to go east with the prisoners of war. He remained with the Chiricahuas for the rest of his life, marrying a Chiricahua woman at Mount Vernon and fathering two daughters with her. One of the daughters, Amy, became the wife of Richard Imach. The other daughter, Blossom, became the wife of Sam Haozous. Their descendants live in Oklahoma today. Most of the descendants of the five children of his second marriage, to Julia Cannon of Mount Vernon, Alabama, live in Texas. He died of tuberculosis on June 23, 1912, while with the prisoners of war at Fort Sill, Oklahoma. Wratten is one of the unsung heroes of Chiricahua Apache history.

30. Young Jasper Kanseah, Geronimo's nephew, recalled, "We had tents and blankets, but no arms. We had food. But every minute we expected to be taken out and shot. Nobody said it aloud" (qtd. in Wratten, "George Wratten," p. 102).

31. Ball, "Interpreter for the Apaches," p. 36.

32. *In Response to the Resolution of February 11, 1887,* U.S. Senate Exec. Doc. 117 (49-2), p. 26.

33. Ibid., p. 29.

34. *The Pensacolian*, October 23, 1886.

35. Fit-A-Hat, an elderly man, died en route to Florida. His body was left at Fort Union, New Mexico.

36. Langdon to assistant adjutant general, letter, March 24, 1887, Chiricahua Apache Collection. Goso (or José) was eventually sent to the Carlisle School, although he was still at Fort Pickens a month later, in April. Most wives and children did indeed join their husbands and fathers at Fort Pickens.

37. Letter given in Skinner, *The Apache Rock Crumbles*, pp. 151–52. To an Apache, one's word is one's bond, and Geronimo kept believing Miles's statement that the families would be kept together. Geronimo's reference to Chatto is probably owing to Chatto's betrayal of the people. Wratten's translation of the Chiricahua word for God, which is Ussen, should not be misconstrued to indicate that the Chiricahuas were Christians. Their indoctrination into Christianity would come later in the period of their incarceration. In other words, while dictating this letter to Wratten, Geronimo probably said "Ussen," and Wratten wrote "God." Herbert Welsh of the Indian Rights Association entered the controversial topic of the conditions of surrender by stating in an 1887 report, "Geronimo and 16 of his men are confined in Fort Pickens, on the West Coast of Florida. The wives and

children of these men are in Fort Marion. *This separation is a direct violation of the terms on which Geronimo surrendered to Miles"* (Welsh, "The Apache Prisoners in Fort Marion," p. 16, Welsh's emphasis).

38. Langdon to commanding officer, March 3, 1887, Chiricahua Apache Collection.

39. *Pensacola Commercial,* December 22, 1886. By "locked-up" this reporter meant that the gates to the fort were locked.

40. Mount Vernon, Alabama, is where the entire group, minus many youngsters, would be incarcerated. See chapter 4.

41. Langdon to Welsh, letter, June 23, 1887, Chiricahua Apache Collection. There is no indication of a response from Welsh.

42. *The Pensacolian,* June 11, 1887. The "wooden crosses" should not be construed as representative of Christianity. In the Chiricahua Apaches' religion prior to their indoctrination into Christianity, the form of a cross was always used to symbolize the four sacred directions. See also Bearss, *Historic Structure Report,* pp. 780–81.

43. Langdon to assistant adjutant general, letter/report dated June 28, 1887, Chiricahua Apache Collection.

44. Langdon to commanding officer, August 9, 1887, Chiricahua Apache Collection.

45. *Mobile Register,* April 23, 1887.

46. Langdon to assistant adjutant general, letter/report dated August 7, 1887, Chiricahua Apache Collection.

Chapter 3

1. *Education of the Apaches in Florida,* U.S. Senate Exec. Doc. 73 (49-2), p. 6. These were the children of Chihuahua's band. Langdon's fears that the children might leave the classroom if their parents walked away from the casemate that served as a school were unfounded. The Apache men stood outside the casemate and looked on, so impressed with what they saw that they began to learn the lessons and sing the songs.

2. Atkins to secretary of interior, letter, January 10, 1887, ibid., p. 19. Was the organization known as the Catholic Indian Missions the parent organization of the Sisters of St. Joseph, or were the sisters acting independently? This confusing situation needs to be clarified for better understanding. The government documents do not offer any further information.

3. Stockel, *Survival of the Spirit,* pp. 117–18.

4. Welsh, "The Apache Prisoners in Ft. Marion," p. 13.

5. *Education of the Apaches in Florida,* U.S. Senate Exec. Doc. 73 (49-2), p. 9.

6. Ibid., p. 11.

7. Ibid., pp. 14–15. Pratt was an arrogant and self-confident individual who was completely convinced that he knew exactly what had to be done to civilize the children of America's Indian groups and did not hesitate to broadcast his opinion. Because of his excellent reputation in dealing with Indians, both allies and antag-

onists alike listened to him. Pratt's interest in Indian education started in April 1875 while he was a U.S. Army captain. Seventy-two warriors from the Cheyenne, Comanche, Kiowa, and Caddo tribes were imprisoned under his military supervision at Fort Marion. He viewed these captives as military adjuncts, issued them old army uniforms, and forced them to cut their hair, polish their buttons, press their trousers, and clean their shoes. He eventually taught the men how to read and write, and by the end of their incarceration three years later seventeen of the prisoners expressed a desire to go on with their schooling. At Pratt's request the all-black Hampton Institute in Virginia enrolled them. Hampton was founded in 1868 as the Hampton Normal and Agricultural Institute, a private, nonsectarian coeducational institution of higher education that aimed to prepare promising young African American men and women to lead and teach their newly freed people. The school was located on the banks of the Hampton River in Hampton, Virginia, near Chesapeake Bay. It was later renamed Hampton Institute and still later, in 1984, became Hampton University. After studying Hampton's philosophy of training students to return to their communities as leaders and professionals, Pratt formulated a similar model for Indians only. His goal was to take children from the reservations; send them to a school far away from home, family, and tribal influences; and transform them into Christians and honorable, productive U.S. citizens. Pratt made no secret of his intentions, believing that the more he publicly stated them, the more support his pronouncements would engender. He trusted that America was ripe for the idea of Indian education. In an address to a convention of Baptist ministers, Presbyterian Pratt proclaimed, "In Indian civilization, I am a Baptist, because I believe in immersing the Indians in our civilization and when we get them under, holding them there until they are thoroughly soaked" (qtd. in Landis, "Carlisle Indian School History").

8. Stockel, *Survival of the Spirit*, p. 115.

9. Born July 4, 1860, near Monticello, New Mexico, Jason Betzinez was Geronimo's second cousin. He participated in military ventures first as a boy, then as an apprentice warrior, and finally as a full-fledged warrior until the surrender of the Geronimo band in 1886. Betzinez entered the Carlisle School on April 30, 1887, and subsequently became a blacksmith for the prisoners at Fort Sill. As Thrapp says, "He was the last Apache scout on duty at Fort Sill, 1914" (*Encyclopedia of Frontier Biography*, p. 103). In 1919 he married a white missionary, but the couple had no children. Betzinez died at the age of one hundred as a result of an auto accident.

10. Betzinez, *I Fought with Geronimo*, p. 149. Some modern Chiricahuas have criticized Betzinez for being too accommodating to the authorities. His cooperative behavior, however, could have been an example of Apache pragmatism—making the best of any situation. Like most of the students at Carlisle, Betzinez acquired his name from a teacher, Flora F. Low. His only Apache name had been Batsinas. According to Betzinez, "She said that Jason was some man who hunted the golden fleece but never found it. I thought that was too bad but it didn't mean anything to me at that time so I accepted the name. In the intervening years I believe that the story of Jason and his search for the golden fleece has set a pattern for my life" (p. 154). This conclusion was never subsequently explained.

11. Adams, *Education for Extinction*, pp. 21–24.

12. Tatum, *Our Red Brothers*, p. 361.

13. Each Indian tribe's traditional religion was unique and reflected its special spiritual beliefs; there was no one all-encompassing Indian religion before contact with Europeans or Americans.

14. Resistance was minimal as Pratt's constant supervision and peer pressure worked their magic.

15. The Chiricahuas' traditional belief was the reverse of the generally held idea that heaven was "up." The Apaches believed that upon death good people went into the earth—underground—where an idyllic new life was imminent.

16. The graveyard at Carlisle today holds the remains of 106 children from various tribes.

17. Qtd. in Stockel, *Survival of the Spirit*, pp. 126–27. Here again the numbers are not firm. In an earlier statement Pratt claimed there were 112 Chiricahua children at Carlisle. Also, Pratt's reference to "venereal taint" was a transparent attempt to lay blame for the illness among the children on conditions beyond his control. His statement about "sifting" the Chiricahuas and disposing of "the unhealthy ones" is chilling.

18. Qtd. in ibid., p. 127.

19. Cochran to assistant adjutant general, letter, July 1, 1889, Chiricahua Apache Collection.

20. Both letters qtd. in Stockel, *Survival of the Spirit*, pp. 129–31.

21. *The Indian Helper*, September 16, 1898.

22. Ibid., September 23, 1898.

23. Ibid., October 7, 1898.

24. Ibid., October 14, 1898.

25. Dewey to secretary of war, letter, February 21, 1895, Shapard Papers, Alabama. The last sentence of this letter seems incongruous, given the previously described medical conditions of the children.

26. Wratten to Pratt, letter, July 25, 1895, Shapard Papers, Alabama.

27. Glennan to adjutant general, letter, November 1, 1895, Chiricahua Apache Collection. Glennan's letter actually went up the chain of command to his superior officer, George M. Sternberg, M.D., the surgeon general of the U.S. Army, and was then forwarded to the adjutant general on December 11, 1895. Nothing happened as a result of this correspondence.

28. Pratt to Major George W. Davis, letter, December 13, 1895, Chiricahua Apache Collection.

29. Adams, *Education for Extinction*, p. 52.

Chapter 4

1. Known today as Searcy Hospital, a mental institution, the former two-thousand-acre prison camp is still enclosed with the same wall that was present during the Apaches' incarceration.

2. Ball, *Indeh*, pp. 138–39.

3. Patzk, M.D., to post adjutant, letter, June 30, 1887, Shapard Papers, Alabama (hereafter SPA).

4. A number of houses for the prisoners were built in 1890. For three years prior to that, the Apaches lived in canvas tents.

5. Skinner, *The Apache Rock Crumbles*, p. 235.

6. Kellogg to adjutant general, letter, November 17, 1889, SPA.

7. *New York Times*, May 11, 1890.

8. Bowman to Welsh, letter, July 26, 1887, SPA.

9. This disproportionate ratio of males to females indicates the toll of warfare and disease.

10. *Message from the President of the United States*, U.S. Senate Exec. Doc. 35 (51-1), pp. 37–40.

11. Shapard, "Prison Life Continues in Alabama," p. 158. No official document exists that describes the Apaches' reaction to this clothing or to the vaccinations.

12. *Mobile Register*, April 19, 1894.

13. Shapard, "Prison Life Continues in Alabama," p. 171. As with all information recorded by government or military officials, the description was written by non-Indians and thus possibly does not reflect the activity or event as the Chiricahua Apaches saw it. It is questionable that old cultural customs such as polygamy and "divorce" would be surrendered easily.

14. Skinner, *The Apache Rock Crumbles*, p. 295. Chihuahua's initial exposure to American Christianity likely came while he was confined to Fort Marion and saw the nuns teach the children. He also may have learned about European Christianity through oral history, passed among his ancestors who had experienced the Jesuit and Franciscan teachings on the Spanish colonial frontier as far back as the middle 1600s.

15. Shapard, "Prison Life Continues in Alabama," p. 175. In 1888 the fee was a dollar and fifty cents for a sixty-mile round trip from Mobile to Mount Vernon. When the steel wheels of an excursion train ground to a halt in Mount Vernon, dozens of tourists peered out the windows to catch a glimpse of Indian prisoners. A few seconds later, Geronimo and several other Chiricahuas, heavily attended by soldiers, stepped into the sun from beyond the shade of the big trees. Geronimo usually strolled confidently toward the train, arms weighted with goods for sale. Anything the Apaches owned had become popular collectors' items. During the next hour negotiations for payment between buyers and sellers were conducted by gestures: one finger held up meant one dollar and two fingers crossed meant sixty cents. For more information see Stockel, "Geronimo and the Chiricahua Apaches: The Alabama Years."

16. *Presidential Message on Trespasses on Indian Lands*, U.S. Senate Exec. Doc. 41 (51-2), p. 3.

17. Reed, M.D., to assistant adjutant general, letters and reports 1887–89, SPA. Reed was the U.S. Army bacteriologist renowned later for his work on yellow fever.

18. Reed, M.D., to assistant adjutant general, report, November 18, 1889, SPA.

19. Ibid.

20. This is the same location as Fort Pickens.

21. No records exist in regard to shingle making and turpentine distillation.

22. He means the Kiowa Apaches, a tribe not linguistically related to the Chiricahua Apaches.

23. Bourke to secretary of war, letter, March 14, 1889, SPA.

24. Bourke to adjutant general, report appended to letter, July 5, 1889, SPA.

25. Ibid.

26. Ibid.

27. Bean, *Walter Reed*, p. 44.

28. Miles to secretary of war, letter, December 6, 1889, SPA.

29. Procter to Harrison, letter, January 13, 1890, SPA.

30. Wotherspoon to post adjutant, report, May 31, 1891, SPA. The financial balance sheet with this report showed expenditures of $269.46 for the month, which included items such as sweet potatoes, hatchets, seventy-six quarts of milk, and the cost of freight on goods from Mobile.

31. Wotherspoon to commanding officer, report, July 26, 1892, SPA.

32. This reference is to the Kiowa Apaches.

33. Maus to Davis, letter, September 15, 1894, SPA.

34. Unsigned and undated letter, SPA.

35. Ibid.

36. *Memorial from S. M. Brosius,* U.S. Senate Doc. 366 (61-2), p. 1.

Chapter 5

Note: Fort Sill was established in January 7, 1869, at the junction of Cache and Medicine Bluff Creeks near the eastern base of the Wichita Mountains in southern Oklahoma. Major General Philip Sheridan decided that a post there was necessary to serve as a base of operations against the Cheyenne and Kiowa Indians. At first called Camp Wichita, the post was renamed on July 2, 1869, after Brigadier General Joshua A. Sill, killed on December 31, 1862, in the Battle of Stone River, Tennessee. "The post became the center for the control of the southern plains Indians, and the headquarters for the agency for the Comanche, Kiowa, Kiowa-Apache, Waco, Wichita, Kicahi, and Caddo Indians" (Frazer, *Forts of the West,* p. 124). Fort Sill is still operative today as an artillery post.

1. Shapard interview with Raymond Loco, June 20, 1966, first Loco file (1/2), D-5, Shapard Papers, North Carolina.

2. *Mingus Minstrel,* October 3, 1894, qtd. in Wratten, "George Wratten," pp. 113–14. Wratten remained with the Apaches at Fort Sill until he died on June 23, 1912, of tuberculosis. His son Albert wrote, "His last days were spent in deep frustration because of his failure to help his Apaches remove their chains as prisoners of war. He never stopped resenting General Miles' broken promises, the

NOTES TO PAGES 102-111

notoriety given to Geronimo to the exclusion of Naiche, the real chief, and others. . . . He could have written a true account of the Apaches and their history and set the record straight, but he would never talk about such matters and would never write or allow to be written his views on the entire sordid story of the treatment of the captives. . . . [H]e undoubtedly had his deep convictions, but he also needed to keep his job as interpreter and supervisor at Fort Sill. . . . George Wratten's efforts to help his Indians were certainly not in vain. After devoting the best part of his short life to their welfare, he was laid to rest in an honored part of the Fort Sill Post Cemetery, with a red granite marker to remind visitors that though he was not given the place in history commensurate with his contributions, he had done his best" (Wratten, "George Wratten," pp. 121-23).

3. Qtd. in Ball, *Indeh*, p. 166. Eugene Chihuahua was excused from going to the Carlisle School when Pratt recruited the boys and girls at Fort Marion. At the time, special courtesy was afforded to Chief Chihuahua to select one of his children to remain behind with him while the others were sent away. The chief chose Eugene.

4. Born at Danville, Kentucky, on September 22, 1853, Hugh Scott graduated from West Point and was commissioned a second lieutenant of the Seventh Cavalry on the day after the Custer fight on the Little Big Horn. In 1877 he was sent with others of Company I of the Seventh to rebury the dead from that battle. In 1888 he was sent to Fort Sill, where he was in charge of monitoring any ghost dance disturbances on the southern plains. From 1894 until 1897 he had charge of the Chiricahua prisoners at Fort Sill, having gone to Mount Vernon in 1894 to confer with the Apaches and to record the proceedings of the council at which some of the prominent Chiricahua men spoke about relocation. In 1911 he began to help the Apaches make arrangements for their release. He was chief of staff from 1914 to 1917, retiring from the military in 1919 and then becoming a member of the Board of Indian Commissioners. Scott died in Washington, D.C., on April 30, 1934. See Thrapp, *Encyclopedia of Frontier Biography*, pp. 1281-82.

5. LeBaron to Scott, report, October 5, 1894, Shapard Papers, Alabama.

6. Carter, M.D., to Scott, report, November 1, 1894, Shapard Papers, North Carolina.

7. Ballon to Scott, report, November 1, 1894, Chiricahua Apache Collection.

8. The Apaches had only the clothing they wore during transfer and other items donated by the soldiers and their families.

9. Scott to assistant adjutant general, report, November 7, 1894, Chiricahua Apache Collection.

10. This was a very smart move. Allowing villagers to designate their leader assured a trouble-free group of Apaches.

11. Skinner, *The Apache Rock Crumbles*, p. 398.

12. Glennan, M.D., to Sternberg, M.D., report, November 1, 1895, Apache Prisoners of War Archives.

13. Sternberg, M.D., to adjutant general, report, December 11, 1895, Apache Prisoners of War Archives.

14. Kaffir corn is a sorghum grain.

15. Turcheneske has written about this bureaucratic nightmare in *The Chiricahua Apache Prisoners of War,* pp. 53–66.

16. Maus to War Department, report, December 23, 1895, Shapard Papers, Alabama.

17. Turcheneske, *The Chiricahua Apache Prisoners of War,* p. 55.

18. Ibid., p. 57.

19. Scott to adjutant general, August 1, 1896, qtd. in ibid., p. 58. Turcheneske adds a quote from Francis E. Leupp, an agent for the Indian Rights Association who visited Arizona and Fort Sill during the summer of 1897: "To travel through Arizona and hear people talk of Geronimo, the Apache archfiend, who, if he sets foot in the Territory, would be hanged for murder without the formality of a trial is impressive. But to pass into Oklahoma and find the same Geronimo putting in his honest eight hours of daily work as a farmer in the fields, and at intervals donning his uniform as a U.S. Scout and presenting himself with the other scouts for inspection, is still more so" (p. 203 n. 17).

20. Qtd. in Skinner, *The Apache Rock Crumbles,* p. 404.

21. Qtd. in ibid.

22. Qtd. in Stockel, *Survival of the Spirit,* p. 212. This information may not be totally correct. Legend tells that the Apaches thought of the hospital as a "death house" and were reluctant to enter.

23. Scott to adjutant general, report, February 12, 1897, Shapard Papers, Alabama.

24. Wratten to Richards, letter, January 11, 1897, Paul Naiche file in the Hampton Institute Archives. Paul died in 1898 from unknown causes after attending a Comanche festival.

25. Qtd. in Stockel, *Survival of the Spirit,* p. 231.

26. Chief Chihuahua and his family are the exception. The chief had a child baptized in the Roman Catholic faith while he was imprisoned in Alabama.

27. In 1899 the mission church and school for the prisoners were established about a mile north of the site known as Medicine Bluffs. Five buildings eventually formed the compound: a grade school and laundry; the orphanage and kindergarten, including dormitory and mess hall; a laundry; the mission church; and a camp meeting tent. The church had a curtain down the middle of the center aisle in observance of the old Apache custom that men should never look directly at their mothers-in-law. The young people sat on one side, and the mothers-in-law and grandmothers sat in the back. James Kaywaykla often interpreted from English to Apache. The grade school served as the church in the early days, before money was appropriated for permanent buildings.

28. James Kaywaykla was born in 1877 into a Warm Springs Chiricahua family. His father was killed in an 1879 battle near Deming, New Mexico. His mother, Gouyen, then married Kaahteney, a noted Warm Springs leader. As a small boy, James was with his mother and stepfather in the rear guard at Tres Castillos when Victorio and many of the group were massacred. They escaped with their lives. James entered the Carlisle School in 1887 and stayed until 1898. He married

Dorothy Naiche, the daughter of the chief. Upon release from incarceration, James and Dorothy remained in Oklahoma and reared a family. The Fort Sill Chiricahua/Warm Springs Apache Tribe's complex stands on their land today.

29. "Bright pictures" were exactly what the noted Jesuit Eusebio Kino held out to the Indians of northern Mexico two hundred years earlier as he proselytized. Despite those Indians' inability to understand the Jesuits' language, the strange, never-before-seen material was impressive to the beholders and elevated in their eyes Kino's status and his wish to baptize. At Fort Sill centuries later a repeat of the situation was based in a similar expression of perceived religious power and authority.

30. Wright, report, 1899, to the Women's Executive Committee of the Board of Domestic Missions of the Reformed Church in America, Western Theological Seminary of the Joint Archives of Holland.

31. Anonymous, report, 1901, Western Theological Seminary of the Joint Archives of Holland.

32. Debo, *Geronimo*, pp. 434–35. According to Debo, another one of Geronimo's patients was an old woman who had chased a wolf. When the wolf ran into a hole, the woman seized its leg to pull it out. Then, according to Debo, "she became violently ill, with her body shaking, her lips twisted, her eyes crossed. Geronimo sang over her and cured her" (p. 435).

33. Scott to adjutant general, report, June 30, 1902, Shapard Papers, Alabama. In an attempt to control the degree of contagion the Apaches were experiencing, Scott issued the "Special Regulations for Government of the Apache Prisoners of War at Fort Sill, Oklahoma." An excerpt of the undated regulations reads, "The houses . . . and water supply of the Apaches should be frequently inspected—kept in a sanitary condition, the houses fumigated with formaldehyde gas at least once every quarter for tuberculosis germs and the walls whitewashed with . . . sulphuric acid."

34. Bergen, report, January 1903, Western Theological Seminary of the Joint Archives of Holland. Daughter Eva Geronimo Godeley and wife Zi-yeh had been baptized Catholic while in Alabama.

35. Wright, report, October 1903, Western Theological Seminary of the Joint Archives of Holland.

36. Sayre assumed charge of the Chiricahua Apaches for four years, beginning in 1900. He was succeeded by Lieutenant George Augustus Purington, who was followed for a short time by Major George Scott. When Scott resigned because of poor health, Major George W. Goode replaced him and remained until the Apaches were released in 1913.

37. Qtd. in Skinner, *The Apache Rock Crumbles*, p. 418

38. McGowan to Sayre, report, October 3, 1904, qtd. in Debo, *Geronimo*, p. 415. Debo quotes Geronimo's reaction to a puppet show, writing that he said, "In front of us were some strange little people who came out on the platform. They did not seem in earnest about anything they did; so I only laughed at them. All the people around where we sat seemed to be laughing at me." He was also treated to a ride on a Ferris wheel with enclosed cabs, and when he looked out, he saw

that "our little house had gone high up in the air and the people down in the Fair grounds looked no larger than ants." At the end of the experience, Geronimo said, "I am glad I went to the Fair. I saw many interesting things and learned much of the white people. . . . I wish all my people could have attended the Fair. . . . [I] wrote my name and kept all of that money. I often made as much as two dollars a day and when I returned I had plenty of money—more than I had ever owned before" (pp. 416–17).

39. Qtd. in Turcheneske, *The Chiricahua Apache Prisoners of War*, p. 78. Turcheneske goes into detail about this bureaucratic competition and its ramifications. See especially chapters 7 and 8 in his book.

40. Turcheneske, "The United States Congress and the Release of the Apache Prisoners," p. 202 n. 3. Turcheneske writes, "A document which leaves no doubt that these lands were intended as a permanent home for the Apaches is a December 23, 1910 memorandum of Judge–Advocate General George B. Davis. Davis cites the Kiowa-Comanche agreement of March 15, 1897 which added 26,987 acres for the use of the prisoners, and the acts of August 6, 1894, February 12, 1895, Sundry Civil Act of June 28, 1902 and the urgent Deficiency of February 18, 1904—all of which envisioned permanent establishment of the Apaches at Fort Sill through the appropriation of funds for buildings, stock, farming implements, seeds, household utensils and other necessities" (p. 202 n. 3). The added acreage was the result of the Jerome Agreement, which was later challenged in the Supreme Court because it allegedly violated the Treaty of Medicine Lodge (1867) in Article 12; according to Prucha, in *Documents of the United States Indian Policy*, that article "provided that no part of the Kiowa-Comanche Reservation could be ceded without the approval of three-fourths of the adult males. When Congress, after allotment of the reservation in severalty, approved the sale of excess tribal lands without the three-fourths approval, action was taken to enjoin the implementation of the act. The Supreme Court declared that Congress had plenary authority over Indian relations and that it had power to pass laws abrogating treaty stipulations" (p. 202). So the Jerome Agreement stood; the Kiowas and Comanches surrendered their lands, ostensibly to become a portion of the Chiricahuas' reservation, which never occurred because Fort Sill remained open as an artillery post with more than 25 million newly added landholdings. For more information see Prucha, *Documents of the United States Indian Policy*, pp. 202–3.

41. Qtd. in Davis, "Our 'Prisoners of War,'" p. 356. Davis wrote in 1912, "How well they have done is shown by the fact that now these Indians own about 10,000 head of fine cattle worth approximately $150,000. They enjoy the reputation of having the best cattle in Oklahoma. They raise good mules and fair horses. They have constructed fifty miles of fence and are well supplied with wagons and other farming implements. Besides their cattle, they have probably $25,000 worth of stock and other property. Most of the cattle are held in common, but some of them are owned by different families. Those owned in common are branded 'U.S.' Those owned individually are branded 'U.S.' with the Indian's [census] number. Cattle are marketed only by the supervising officer. The proceeds are divided and each Indian receives just what is due him and his family" (pp. 363–64).

42. Sayre to adjutant general, report, August 8, 1904, qtd. in Stockel, *Survival of the Spirit,* pp. 221, 306 n. 47. Sayre took an interest in the Apaches' money-making efforts, in particular raising cattle and harvesting hay. The Apaches had been putting their profits into a special fund, and Sayre began adding to these monies in a determined manner. The funds were used to purchase farm implements, vehicles, and horses. He imposed rules on the prisoners, especially one that forbade the dances during cold weather. He was convinced that sharing dance masks spread contagion. And he stopped the gambling, at least overtly. Captain Purington, Sayre's successor, was also interested in the Apache cattle-raising project and in helping the fund to grow. He lifted the ban on dancing, and soon afterward two young men died from pneumonia. During the short time that Major George L. Scott (no relation to Hugh Scott) succeeded Purington, liquor became a factor, and gambling made a comeback. When Major Goode succeeded Scott, he set rules and made the Apache scouts responsible for carrying out his orders. He controlled gambling and booted the liquor sellers off the reservation. Goode was involved in selling the prisoners' herd of ten thousand cattle to the highest bidders when the Chiricahuas were eventually released from confinement.

43. Wratten to Indian Rights Association, letter, 1904, qtd. in Skinner, *The Apache Rock Crumbles,* pp. 448–49.

44. *Pensacola Daily News,* March 4, 1905.

45. Qtd. in Debo, *Geronimo,* pp. 420–21. Wratten interpreted.

46. *The Daily Oklahoman,* July 9, 1907. The reference to "a reservation" is probably to the Mescalero Apache Reservation in New Mexico, now about a two-hour drive from El Paso.

47. *The Daily Oklahoman,* October 13, 1907. On July 29, 1948, the *Collinsville News* ran a news item about a Mrs. Thomas Lee, who remembered the Collinsville event so many years earlier. Said Mrs. Lee, "The guard shackled Geronimo at night when he stayed in our home but during the day the famous Indian ate his meals with us and was very much a gentleman. . . . The Indian chief was a picturesque individual, dressed in a long fringed buckskin jacket, a white loincloth looped around his stomach and hanging to his knees. Tight trousers were tucked into soft handmade boots. His hair was long, reaching to his shoulders, while around his head was tied a bright red scarf. . . . Geronimo had his first automobile ride while he was here. They put him in the car and rode him around and around the race track. He enjoyed it enormously and was loath to climb out when the ride was over." On March 10, 1977, the *Collinsville News* ran a letter to the editor from Amy Sanger of Midland, Texas, who also remembered the 1907 event. Referring to Geronimo, she wrote, "he was the main attraction at the celebration. I was sixteen years old and remember it well. He was dressed in full Indian regalia—his War Bonnet was beautiful—and was sitting in his teepee. I don't recall what we paid to see him, but everyone bought a post card picture of him for five cents."

48. Actually not a proverb but a statement: "The only good Indians I ever saw were dead," by General Philip Henry Sheridan in 1869.

49. *New York Times,* February 18, 1909, editorial.

50. *New York Times,* February 19, 1909.

51. Qtd. in Skinner, *The Apache Rock Crumbles,* p. 462.

52. Turcheneske, *The Chiricahua Apache Prisoners of War,* p. 115.

53. *Memorial from S. M. Brosius,* U.S. Senate Doc. 366 (61-2), pp. 2–3.

Chapter 6

1. Lawrence Mithlo was born in 1864 and married four times. His third wife was his stepdaughter. He lived through all the years of imprisonment and died in 1938.

2. Benedict Jozhe was born in 1872, the youngest child in the family. His brothers were said to be the warriors on whom Geronimo depended the most. Jozhe was among the children removed from their families and sent to the Carlisle School; he arrived with the second group on April 30, 1887. He married Mabel Nahdoyah, a fellow student who had one child from a previous marriage. Together they had three children. Jozhe died in 1918.

3. Talbot Gooday was born in 1865, the grandson of Mangas Coloradas and Chief Loco. He and his wife entered Carlisle on April 30, 1887. She gave birth there; both mother and baby died at Carlisle. He married four times. Gooday died on February 26, 1962, survived by his widow, five children, seventeen grandchildren, twenty-eight great-grandchildren, and two great-great-grandchildren.

4. Fort Sill Apaches, 1915–present, Shapard Papers, North Carolina. "Proceedings of Conference with Apache Prisoners of War," September 21, 1911. See also Turcheneske, *The Chiricahua Apache Prisoners of War,* p. 122.

5. Asa Daklugie was born in 1871 in the vicinity around Fort Bowie, Arizona, to Chief Juh of the Nednhi band of Chiricahuas and his wife, Ishton, said to be the first cousin of Geronimo. He was a member of the small group led by Mangus, who surrendered last. He entered the Carlisle School on December 8, 1886, and eventually married Ramona Chihuahua, the daughter of the chief. Daklugie often functioned as Geronimo's interpreter and became a leader of the group who elected to live on the Mescalero Apache Reservation. Daklugie was one of author Eve Ball's major informants for *Indeh: An Apache Odyssey.* He died in 1955.

6. Born in 1863 into the Warm Springs band of the Chiricahuas, Toclanny was one of a handful of older survivors of the original prisoners. He never at any time bore arms against the United States. He served as a scout for the army and helped track down his friends and relatives. Toclanny married Siki, the daughter of Chief Loco, and then went to Mescalero in 1913. He died there on January 6, 1947.

7. The remarks by Daklugie, Toclanny, Gooday, Betzinez, Kaywaykla, and Mithlo are in Davis, "Our 'Prisoners of War,'" pp. 364–67.

8. Controversy continues to surround this decision. Many Chiricahuas complained that the army, not they themselves, designated those who would be relocated to New Mexico and those who would remain in Oklahoma. In its "Twenty-ninth Annual Report" the Indian Rights Association declared, "The educated and intelligent members of the tribe are desirous of securing allotments at Fort Sill, while those who are inclined to follow tribal customs feel that Mescalero offers most favorable opportunities for continuance of communal relations." Did the writer really mean to imply that those who chose Mescalero, or who had Mescalero chosen for them, were less intelligent than the others? Or does

the writer mean to imply that those who chose to remain in Oklahoma or had that choice decided for them did not wish to continue tribal customs? In any case, the decision to split the Chiricahuas into two groups and locate them five hundred miles apart from each other ensured once and for all that no putative rebellion would be successful. The government could rest easy at long last.

9. Goode to Scott, October 17, 1911, qtd. in Turcheneske, *The Chiricahua Apache Prisoners of War*, p. 125.

10. Roe to Scott, October 6, 1911, qtd. in ibid., p. 127.

11. "Twenty-ninth Annual Report," pp. 50–51. Wratten died in 1912 and is buried on the Fort Sill Post Cemetery. His widow was allotted the land of Kiowa allottee number 2207, Mabel Emouah, deceased. Instead of living on the Oklahoma allotment, however, she and her five children returned to their old home in Mount Vernon, Alabama (Skinner, *The Apache Rock Crumbles*, p. 478).

12. "Twenty-ninth Annual Report," pp. 51–52.

13. Turcheneske, *The Chiricahua Apache Prisoners of War*, p. 128.

14. Turcheneske, "'It Is Right That They Should Set Us Free,'" pp. 13, 19–20.

15. *Inquiry Concerning Apache Indians at Fort Sill, Oklahoma*, U.S. Senate Doc. 432 (62-2), pp. 1–2.

16. Roe, "Apache Prisoners of War," pp. 10–11.

17. *A Bill Authorizing the Secretary of War to Grant Freedom to Certain Apache Prisoners of War*, U.S. House of Representatives, H.R. 16651 (62-2).

18. Qtd. in Turcheneske, *The Chiricahua Apache Prisoners of War*, p. 156.

19. Qtd. in Turcheneske, "Disaster at White Tail," p. 121.

20. Ibid.

21. Qtd. in ibid., p. 125.

22. Coppersmith, "Cultural Survival and a Native American Community," p. 185. I do not agree with Coppersmith that the dance "has lost much of its spiritual significance," either in Oklahoma, which is the focus of Coppersmith's dissertation, or in New Mexico, but many Chiricahuas may disagree with me.

23. Ibid., p. 181.

24. Cleghorn, interview by the author, August 8, 1989.

25. Betzinez, Kaywaykla, Goody, letter, December 31, 1920, Hugh Scott Papers.

26. Coppersmith, "Cultural Survival and a Native American Community," p. 184. An attempt at reviving the puberty ceremony was held in 1994 but, according to Coppersmith, was "full of political and cultural complexities." Many elders at Mescalero perceived it as inappropriate and incorrect in its procedures, but the maiden's family members saw it as a "legitimate expression of a sacred and important ritual . . . also as a powerful statement of Chiricahua identity and cultural maintenance. Ironically, one of the reasons family members chose to practice the rite in Oklahoma was in order to escape the alcohol-related violence that occasionally accompanies the celebrations . . . in New Mexico" (p. 194). To my knowledge, no Chiricahua Apache puberty ceremony has been held in Oklahoma since 1994.

27. Qtd. in Ove and Stockel, *Geronimo's Kids*, p. 133

Bibliography

Manuscript Collections, Unpublished Manuscripts, and Interviews

American Indian Oral History. Duke Collection, American Indian Institute, University of Oklahoma, Norman.

Apache Prisoners of War Archives. Fort Sill Museum, Fort Sill, Oklahoma.

Chiricahua Apache Collection. Frisco Native American Museum, Frisco, North Carolina.

Cleghorn, Mildred Imach. Interview by the author, August 8, 1989.

Darrow, Ruey. Conversation with the author, May 1991.

Edwards, J. D., Sr. "Waiting for the Indians." In *Indian Prisoners at Fort Marion from 1875–1877*, edited by Josephine Burgess Jacobs. Unpublished manuscript, ca. 1949, Castillo de San Marcos National Monument, St. Augustine, Florida.

Hampton Institute Archives. Hampton University, Hampton, Virginia.

Haozous, Sam. "Personal Reminiscences Concerning Geronimo, the Warm Springs Apaches, and Incidents Surrounding the Submission of the Southwestern Apaches." Unpublished manuscript, American Indian Oral History Collection, Duke Collection, American Indian Institute, University of Oklahoma, Norman.

Johnston, Ernest. "Saved by an Apache." In *Indian Prisoners at Fort Marion from 1875–1877*, edited by Josephine Burgess Jacobs. Unpublished manuscript, ca. 1949, Castillo de San Marcos National Monument, St. Augustine, Florida.

"Proceedings of Conference with the Apache Prisoners of War on Fort Sill Reservation, Fort Sill, Oklahoma." September 21, 1911, 2:00 P.M. Chiricahua Apache Collection, Frisco Native American Museum, Frisco, North Carolina.

Reed, Walter, M.D. Unpublished letters and reports. Shapard Papers, Searcy Hospital, Mount Vernon, Alabama.

Sabate, R. F. "Apaches Were Here." In *Indian Prisoners at Fort Marion from 1875–1877*, edited by Josephine Burgess Jacobs. Unpublished manuscript, ca. 1949, Castillo de San Marcos National Monument, St. Augustine, Florida.

Scott, Hugh, Papers. Frisco Native American Museum, Frisco, North Carolina.

Shapard, Bud. "Prison Life Continues in Alabama: April 1887–October 1894." Unpublished manuscript, Shapard Papers, Searcy Hospital, Mount Vernon, Alabama.

Shapard Papers, Alabama. Searcy Hospital, Mount Vernon, Alabama.

Shapard Papers, North Carolina. Frisco Native American Museum, Frisco, North Carolina.

Webb, DeWitt, M.D. "Apaches at Castillo San Marcos." Speech read before the Dutchess County New York Medical Society, September 1887. St. Augustine Historical Society, St. Augustine, Florida.

Welsh, Herbert. "The Apache Prisoners in Fort Marion." Unpublished report, Zimmerman Library, Special Collections, University of New Mexico, Albuquerque.

Western Theological Seminary of the Joint Archives of Holland. Holland, Michigan.

Books and Articles

Adams, David Wallace. *Education for Extinction: American Indians and the Boarding School Experience, 1875–1928*. Lawrence: University Press of Kansas, 1995.

Ball, Eve. *In the Days of Victorio: Recollections of a Warm Springs Apache*. Tucson: University of Arizona Press, 1970.

———. "Interpreter for the Apaches." *True West* (November–December 1971): 26–27, 36.

Ball, Eve, with Nora Henn and Lynda Sanchez. *Indeh: An Apache Odyssey*. Provo, Utah: Brigham Young University Press, 1980.

Barrett, S. M., ed. *Geronimo: His Own Story*. New York: Ballantine, 1970.

Bean, William B., M.D. *Walter Reed: A Biography*. Charlottesville: University Press of Virginia, 1982.

Bearss, Edwin C. *Historic Structure Report: Fort Pickens. Historical Data Section, 1821–1895. Gulf Islands National Seashore, Florida-Mississippi.* Washington, D.C.: U.S. Department of the Interior, Historical Preservation Division, Denver Service Center, National Park Service, n.d.

Betzinez, Jason, with Wilbur Sturtevant Nye. *I Fought with Geronimo.* Lincoln: University of Nebraska Press, 1987.

Bourke, John G. *On the Border with Crook.* Lincoln: University of Nebraska Press, 1971.

Coppersmith, Clifford Patrick. "Cultural Survival and a Native American Community: The Chiricahua and Warm Springs Apaches in Oklahoma, 1913–1996." Ph.D. diss., Oklahoma State University, 1996.

Crook, George. "Résumé of Operations Against Apache Indians, 1882 to 1886." In *Eyewitnesses to the Indian Wars 1865–1890: The Struggle for Apacheria,* vol. 1, edited by Peter Cozzens. Mechanicsburg, Pa.: Stackpole, 2001.

Davis, O. K. "Our 'Prisoners of War.'" *North American Review* (March 1912): 356–67.

Debo, Angie. *Geronimo: The Man, His Time, His Place.* Norman: University of Oklahoma Press, 1976.

Frazer, Robert W. *Forts of the West: Military Forts and Presidios and Posts Commonly Called Forts West of the Mississippi River to 1898.* Norman: University of Oklahoma Press, 1972.

Hagan, William T. *The Indian Rights Association: The Herbert Welsh Years, 1882–1904.* Tucson: University of Arizona Press, 1985.

Hutton, Paul A. *Phil Sheridan and His Army.* Lincoln: University of Nebraska Press, 1985.

Kraft, Louis. *Gatewood and Geronimo.* Albuquerque: University of New Mexico Press, 2000.

Lamar, Howard, ed. *The New Encyclopedia of the American West.* New Haven, Conn.: Yale University Press, 1998.

Landis, Barbara. "Carlisle Indian School History." Available at: http://home.epix.net/~landis/history.html.

Miles, Nelson A. *Personal Recollections and Observations of General Nelson A. Miles.* Vol. 2. Lincoln: University of Nebraska Press, 1992.

Ove, Robert S., and H. Henrietta Stockel. *Geronimo's Kids: A Teacher's Lessons on the Apache Reservation.* College Station: Texas A&M University Press, 1997.

Prucha, Francis Paul, ed. *Documents of the United States Indian Policy.* Lincoln: University of Nebraska Press, 1990.

Reed, Walter, M.D. "Geronimo and His Warriors in Captivity." *The Illustrated American* (August 16, 1890): 231–35.

Rister, Carl Coke. *Border Command: General Phil Sheridan in the West.* Norman: University of Oklahoma Press, 1944.

Roe, Walter C. "Apache Prisoners of War." *Southern Workman* (April 1912): 3–12.

Schmitt, Martin F., ed. *General George Crook: His Autobiography.* Norman: University of Oklahoma Press, 1986.

Skinner, Woodward. *The Apache Rock Crumbles: The Captivity of Geronimo's People.* Pensacola, Fla.: Skinner Publications, 1987.

Stockel, H. Henrietta. "Geronimo and the Chiricahua Apaches: The Alabama Years." *Alabama Heritage* 43 (winter 1997): 6–17.

—————. *Survival of the Spirit: Chiricahua Apaches in Captivity.* Reno: University of Nevada Press, 1993.

Swartly, Ron. *Old Forts of the Apache Wars: A Travel Guide.* Las Cruces, N.M.: Frontier Image Press, 1999.

Tatum, Lawrie. *Our Red Brothers and the Peace Policy of President Ulysses S. Grant.* Lincoln: University of Nebraska Press, 1970.

Thrapp, Dan L. *The Conquest of Apacheria.* Norman: University of Oklahoma Press, 1967.

—————. *Encyclopedia of Frontier Biography.* Lincoln: University of Nebraska Press, with the Arthur H. Clark Company, 1988.

—————, ed. *Dateline Fort Bowie: Charles Fletcher Lummis Reports on an Apache War.* Norman: University of Oklahoma Press, 1979.

Turcheneske, John, Jr. *The Chiricahua Apache Prisoners of War: Fort Sill 1894–1914.* Niwot: University Press of Colorado, 1997.

—————. "Disaster at White Tail: The Fort Sill Apaches' First Ten Years at Mescalero, 1913–1923." *New Mexico Historical Review* 53, no. 2 (April 1978): 109–32.

—————. "'It Is Right That They Should Set Us Free': The Role of the War and Interior Departments in the Release of the Apache Prisoners of War, 1909—1913." *Red River Historical Review* 4, no. 3 (summer 1979): 4–32.

—————. "The United States Congress and the Release of the Apache Prisoners of War at Fort Sill." *Chronicles of Oklahoma* 54 (summer 1976): 199–226.

"Twenty-eighth Annual Report for the Year Ending December 14, 1910." *Indian Rights Association* (1911): 27–30.

"Twenty-ninth Annual Report for the Year Ending December 14, 1911." *Indian Rights Association* (1912): 49–53.

Wratten, Albert E. "George Wratten: Friend of the Apaches." *Journal of Arizona History* 27, no. 1 (spring 1986): 91–124.

Government Documents

A Bill Authorizing the Secretary of War to Grant Freedom to Certain Apache Prisoners of War Now Being Held at Fort Sill, Oklahoma, and Giving Them Equal Status with Other Restricted Indians. 62d Cong., 2d sess., 1912, H.R. 16651 (62-2).

Conference Held March 25 and 27, 1886, at Cañon de los Embudos (Cañon of the Funnels), 20 Mile S.S.E. of San Bernardino Springs, Mexico, Between General Crook and the Hostile Chiricahua Chiefs. 51st Cong., 1st sess., 1890, U.S. Senate Exec. Doc. 88 (51-1).

Education of the Apaches in Florida. 49th Cong., 2d sess., 1890, U.S. Senate Exec. Doc. 73 (49-2).

Inquiry Concerning Apache Indians at Fort Sill, Oklahoma. 62d Cong., 2d sess. 1911–12, U.S. Senate Doc. 432 (62-2).

In Response to the Resolution of February 11, 1887, Correspondence with General Miles Relative to the Surrender of Geronimo. 49th Cong., 2d sess., 1886, U.S. Senate Exec. Doc. 117 (49-2).

Memorial from S. M. Brosius, Agent Indian Rights Association, Relating to the Apache Prisoners of War Now Confined at Fort Sill Military Reservation, Okla., Urging That Allotments of Land Be Made to the Indians and That They Be Released from Bondage. 61st Cong., 2d sess., 1911–12, U.S. Senate Doc. 366 (61-2).

Message from the President of the United States Transmitting a Letter of the Secretary of War and Reports Touching the Apache Indians at Governor's Island. 51st Cong., 1st sess., 1890, U.S. Senate Exec. Doc. 35 (51-1).

Presidential Message on Trespasses on Indian Lands. 51st Cong., 2d sess., 1891, U.S. Senate Exec. Doc. 41 (51-2).

Repair of Fort Marion, St. Augustine, Florida. 49th Cong., 2d sess., 1886, U.S. Senate Report 184 (49-2).

Repairing of Fort Marion, St. Augustine, Florida. 50th Cong., 1st sess., 1887, U.S. Senate Report 189 (50-1).

Report of Treatment of Certain Apache Indians. 51st Cong., 1st sess., 1890, U.S. Senate Exec. Doc. 83 (51-1).

Newspapers

Collinsville News, July 29, 1948, March 10, 1977.

Daily Oklahoman, July 9, 1907, October 13, 1907.

Florida Times-Union, April 15, April 19, April 21, 1887.

Frank Leslie's Illustrated Newspaper, September 25, 1886.

The Indian Helper, September 16, September 23, October 7, October 14, 1898.

Mingus Minstrel, October 3, 1894.

Mobile Register, April 23, 1887, April 19, 1894.

New York Times, May 11, 1890, February 18, 1909, February 19, 1909.

Pensacola Commercial, June 11, 1887.

Pensacola Daily News, March 4, 1905.

The Pensacolian, October 23, 1886, June 11, 1887.

Index

A

Adkisson, Maud, 119–20

Apaches, Chiricahua: children's letters from parents, 60; Congress appropriates funds for, 77; contemporary puberty ceremony in Oklahoma, 177n. 26; cultural customs about fleeing, 11; Dance of the Mountain Spirits at Ft. Pickens, 44; death toll by 1894, 101; difficulty with Alabama climate, 72, 74–75; and giving one's word, 165n. 37; imprisonment at Ft. Marion, 19; liquor and drinking, 104–105, 110, 117, 127, 175n. 42; loss of ancestral homelands, xi; men's cultural attitude toward work, 49; 1902 census, 121; pragmatism as cultural trait, 71, 114; as ranchers at Ft. Sill, 174n. 41; reasons for surrender, ix; release from Ft. Sill and controversy, 176n. 8; suicides at Mt. Vernon, 74–75; wives and children join men at Ft. Pickens and assigned living conditions, 41; youngest children's education at Ft. Marion, and plan for removal of older children, 27

B

Ballon, Lt. W.: escorts prisoners with Capron, 101; reports to Scott about general conditions, 103–104

Bergen, Rev. J.T.: impressions of Geronimo, 122; and his religious conversion, 122–24

Betzinez, Jason: biography, 167nn. 9, 10; meeting with Scott about release, 138; recollections of Carlisle, 54

Booth, Vicentine, 70

Bourke, Capt. John G.: duplicity, 90; interviews prisoners with Painter, 84–90; and potential prison sites, 82, 83–84; and Mt. Vernon, 48

J

Jacobs, Josephine Burgess (oral histories): Edwards, J. D., 23; Johnston, Ernest. 25; Sabate, R. F., 24. *See also* names of individuals

Johnston, Ernest: memories of Apache prisoners at Ft. Marion, 25

Jozhe, Benedict: biography, 176n. 2

K

Kanseah, Kathleen, 153

Kay-E-Tennay: biography, 156n. 4; interviewed by Bourke and Painter, 86

Kaywaykla, James: biography, 172n. 28; meets with Scott about release, 136, 138; recollections of Ft. Marion, 52

Kellogg, Maj. W. L., 70; praises teachers at Mt. Vernon, 71

Ketchum, William H.: as member of Board of Indian Commissioners, 145; visits Mescalero and urges appropriation, 145

Kuni (Coonie): recollections of day of removal, 16

L

Lamar, L.Q.C., Secretary of Interior: letters about children to Endicott, 53, 54; letters to Hampton Institute, 53; letters to Secretary of War about crowded conditions at Ft. Marion and proposed relief, 26

Langdon, Lt. Col. Loomis L., 12–16; allows tourists to visit Ft. Pickens, 40; biography, 158n. 23; describes Apaches as "gentle," 49; describes Chihuahua's people's condition, 12; describes work done by Apache men at Ft. Pickens, 40; invites citizens to Apache dance, 44; letters about children, 51; letters to Welsh about women who don't want to join husbands, 42–44; recommends education for Go-So, 38, 165n. 36; recommends moving prisoners to Pennsylvania, 14–15; reports about prisoners, 15, 38, 40, 45, 48–49; worried about contagion, 20. *See also* Ft. Marion; Ft. Pickens

Lawton, Capt. Henry: biography, 162n. 4; mistakenly credited by Miles, 164n. 23; surprises Geronimo in camp, 29–30

LeBaron, Charles, M.D.: reports to Scott on health at Ft. Sill, 102

Loco, Chief: interviewed by Bourke and Painter, 86

Lummis, Charles Fletcher: biography, 157n. 12; reports to *Los Angeles Times* about surrenders, 7–10. *See also* Ft. Bowie

M

Manifest Destiny, x; definition, 155n. 6

Mangus, 38; evaluated at Mt. Vernon (1894), 99; surrenders and joins Geronimo at Ft. Pickens, 38

Martine and Kayitah: talk with Geronimo about surrender to Miles, 31

Maus, Capt. Marion: biography, 158n. 15; letter to Davis about relocation from Mt. Vernon, 97–98; report to War Department about observations and Ft. Sill discussion results and recommendations, 111–14

Mescalero Apache Reservation: conditions post-release, 147; traditions observed, 147–48

Miles, Gen. Nelson: accepts Geronimo's surrender, 3; assurances made at Geronimo's surrender never followed, 36; biography, 155n. 2; describes Geronimo's surrender, 31; disobeys Sheridan, 33; ignores Gatewood and credits Lawton, 164n. 23; letter to Secretary of War about prisoners at Mt. Vernon, 91; replaces Crook, 29; telegrams about Geronimo to Headquarters, 29, 30; telegrams to Sheridan, 33

Mingus Minstral: describes health (1894), 102

Mithlo, Lawrence: biography, 176n. 1

Mobile Register: reports shooting at Mt. Vernon, 75

Mother Alypius, 161n. 54

Mt. Vernon, Alabama, 69–99; Apaches transferred to Ft. Sill, 99; children's education and described by official, 70; health problems, 74; known as Searcy Hospital, 168n. 1; train service from Mobile, 169n. 15

N

Naiche: biography, 157n. 7; escapes from Crook, 6; evaluated at Mt. Vernon (1894), 98; interviewed by Bourke and Painter, 85; meets with Scott about release, 135–36; speech to Crook at surrender, 5; surrenders to Crook, 4–5

Nana: interviewed by Bourke and Painter, 86

newspapers: *Colinsville News,* recollections of Geronimo's visits, 175n. 47; The *Daily Oklahoman,* describes Geronimo's 1907 failed escape, 130; *Florida Times Union,* chronicles prisoners' arrival in St. Augustine, 11, and general news about prisoners, 26; *Frank Leslie's*

U

U.S. House of Representatives: bill (HR 16651) authorizing freedom, 142–43

W

Webb, Dewitt, M.D.: biography, 161n. 43; report to Dutchess County (NY) Medical Society, 21–22

Welsh, Herbert: biography, 160n. 38; comments about Ft. Marion, 160; report from Ft. Marion, 18–20, 52; visits Ft. Marion and writes scathing report, 22–23. *See also* Indian Rights Association

Whitetail: Apaches move from, 147; as new homesite for former prisoners, 145–46; as part of Mescalero Apache Reservation, 145

Wood, Maj. Gen. Leonard, 139

Wotherspoon, Lt. William W.: concerned about health at Mt. Vernon, 76; contacts Secretary of Interior about congressional appropriation, 77; report about general conditions, 93–96

Wratten, George: biography, 165n. 29; gravesite, 177n. 11; influence at Ft. Pickens, 47; last days, 170n. 2; letter to Hampton School reporting child's death at Ft. Sill, 117; offers to provide guns to prisoners, 35; opposes moving prisoners, 128; poetic tribute to Geronimo, 133; requests children be returned from Carlisle, 64–65; translates and writes for Geronimo, 39

Wright, Rev. Frank Hall, 118; meets with officer in charge of Ft. Sill prisoners, 119; reports about Geronimo, 124

About the Author

H. Henrietta Stockel was educated in New Jersey's public schools and Columbia University. She moved to the Southwest in the early 1970s and began to study the history and culture of the Chiricahua Apaches. Her first article, "Lozen: Apache Warrior," was published in 1982, followed seven years later by her first book, *Medicine Women, Curanderas, and Women Doctors.* Several books followed in succession: *Women of the Apache Nation: Voices of Truth* (1991), *Survival of the Spirit: Chiricahua Apaches in Captivity* (1993), *The Lightning Stick: Arrows, Wounds, and Indian Legends* (1995), *Geronimo's Kids: A Teacher's Lessons on the Apache Reservation* (with Robert S. Ove, 1997), *Chiricahua Apache Women and Children: Safekeepers of the Heritage* (2000), and *LaDonna Harris: A Comanche Life* (2000). Her most recent book, *On the Bloody Road to Jesus: Christianity and the Chiricahua Apaches,* was published in 2004. She has published more than fifty articles about the Southwest and its cultures and has appeared in two documentary films about the Chiricahua Apaches. She is currently researching various aspects of the Chiricahua Apache presence on the Spanish colonial frontier. Stockel is affiliated with Cochise College in Sierra Vista, Arizona.